Death in Old Mexico

In a Mexico City mansion on October 23, 1789, Don Joaquín Dongo and ten of his employees were brutally murdered by three killers armed with machetes. Investigators worked tirelessly to find the perpetrators, who were publicly executed two weeks later. Labeled the "crime of the century," these events and their aftermath have intrigued writers of fiction and nonfiction for more than two centuries. Using a vast range of sources, Nicole von Germeten recreates a paper trail of Enlightenment-era greed and savagery, and highlights how the violence of the Mexican judiciary echoed the acts of the murderers. The Spanish government conducted dozens of executions in Mexico City's central square in this era, revealing how European imperialism in the Americas influenced perceptions of violence and how it was tolerated, encouraged, or suppressed. An evocative history, *Death in Old Mexico* provides a compelling new perspective on late colonial Mexico City.

Nicole von Germeten is an associate dean in the College of Liberal Arts at Oregon State University. She has written extensively on the history of crime, violence, gender, and sexuality in Latin America.

T0384603

Death in Old Mexico

*The 1789 Dongo Murders and How They Shaped
the History of a Nation*

NICOLE VON GERMETEN

Oregon State University

Shaftesbury Road, Cambridge CB2 8EA, United Kingdom

One Liberty Plaza, 20th Floor, New York, NY 10006, USA

477 Williamstown Road, Port Melbourne, VIC 3207, Australia

314–321, 3rd Floor, Plot 3, Splendor Forum, Jasola District Centre, New Delhi – 110025, India

103 Penang Road, #05–06/07, Visioncrest Commercial, Singapore 238467

Cambridge University Press is part of Cambridge University Press & Assessment, a department of the University of Cambridge.

We share the University's mission to contribute to society through the pursuit of education, learning and research at the highest international levels of excellence.

www.cambridge.org
Information on this title: www.cambridge.org/9781009261524

DOI: 10.1017/9781009261531

First published 2023

A catalogue record for this publication is available from the British Library.

A Cataloging-in-Publication data record for this book is available from the Library of Congress

ISBN 978-1-009-26152-4 Hardback
ISBN 978-1-009-26150-0 Paperback

Cambridge University Press & Assessment has no responsibility for the persistence or accuracy of URLs for external or third-party internet websites referred to in this publication and does not guarantee that any content on such websites is, or will remain, accurate or appropriate.

Contents

Figures

Tables

Preface

A rectangular wooden table measuring four feet by six feet sits in a large high-ceilinged room. The powerful midday sun slants through skylights at least thirty feet overhead, partially illuminating the table in bright blocks of light. About a hundred pieces of paper of various sizes cover the table's black surface, from ragged scraps to large files of rectangular folios sewn together in a packet. Dark slanted handwriting adorns these papers, some of which show water stains and odd-shaped holes. Some have been organized into piles and others sit on the surface.

This scene took place in Mexico City during the summer of 2013, at the Archivo General de la Nación (AGN) reading room. Archivists and historians were in the process of putting thousands of pieces of paper in chronological order. These disorganized pages comprise some of the remnants of the viceregal judicial system, which existed when Mexico was under Spanish rule from the sixteenth to the nineteenth century.[1]

This book takes inspiration from this table and its jumble of documents. It samples from the millions of pieces of paper that make up the historical record of New Spain, focusing on certain texts that were written from the mid-eighteenth century through to the twenty-first century. It gathers together some of these fragments, mingling them to offer readers a kind of historical kaleidoscope. When you look through the eyepiece down the body of this kaleidoscope/book, the multiple and shifting texts that are visible all relate to the history of death in Mexico.

---

[1] Linda Arnold guided me to this table. She generously shares her knowledge with me and many others who visit the AGN.

Inspired by the work of creative historians for the last several decades, I have written this book, to continue the kaleidoscope metaphor, with a mirror system which reflects and combines the various documents in ways that will look different than the traditional scholarship. My goal is not to confuse or distort history, but to show how texts merge and reflect upon each other to create complex patterns that change, repeat, and generate endless subtle variations.[2]

Even the largest, most complex kaleidoscope cannot contain all of the texts or reflect all of the angles on the theme of death in Mexico. Therefore I chose one compelling incident as my focus in this book – a crime that inspired a multitude of writings on the topic of violent death. The crime took place as New Spain transitioned from a European-ruled viceroyalty to a modern nation.

Court scribes, historians, and novelists have had an ongoing conversation for the last 230 years about this one horrendous event: the murder of eleven people in a large house in Mexico City, during the night of October 23, 1789. The victims included a wealthy Spanish businessman, his live-in cashier, and nine domestic servants. From the morning of October 24, when the notary viewing the bodies created his first report documenting their deaths, the massacre has held a potent yet changing symbolism. For the viceregal authorities, these killings were a call to action. They were motivated to find the murderers and wreak the state's vengeance on them. Unofficial commentators at the time wrote their impressions in shocked tones, noting the fast reactions of their leaders to solve the crime and execute the perpetrators. They pondered the cosmic order that allowed such horrors.

After independence from Spain, Mexican writers expressed more ambiguity about the crime. To them the crime and its aftermath showed both the best (strong, effective leaders) and the worst (greed and violence) of their history as part of an empire ruled from Europe. After Mexico's mid-nineteenth-century reforms, novelists felt inspired to depict the massacre according to the values that they wished to foster in their own era. They added sexual and political interpretations to the events that do not appear

---

[2] I learned a bit about kaleidoscopes from www.thekaliedoscopebook.com, accessed September 2, 2021. I was also inspired by the discussion of the messy back of a tapestry as a model for a book, as presented in Juan Carlos González Espitia, *Sifiolografía: A History of the Writerly Pox in the Eighteenth-Century Hispanic World* (Charlottesville: University of Virginia Press, 2019), 22.

in the original eighteenth-century accounts. More recently, professional historians have analyzed this case in the context of the viceregal judiciary.

This book does not take a conventional form. Instead I hope that it will allow readers to observe a variety of images in conversation with each other. Because the entire textual record consists of fragments written from individual perspectives, whether a few lines on a scrap of paper or a two-volume novel, no one source allows us to comprehend the entire story and its repercussions. I decided to surrender to the path where the texts led me, guiding readers through a fascinating journey that serves as an entry point to understanding this era.

The chapters that follow are organized into seven parts, each with a slightly different writing style and citational style. Drawing entirely from the documents that a scribe began to write on the morning of October 24, 1789, the story begins with a present-tense narration of the scene and setting of the crime and what led up to it. Part I describes what observers of this event experienced, without multiple layers of interpretation and scholarly apparatus. Part II gives a more conventional historical background of Mexico City in the 1780s and early 1790s, with an overview of the viceroys in power at this time, the justice system, and the Spanish empire. Part III returns to the style of Part I, recounting how the investigation unfolded in the 1789 case file. Part IV draws more broadly from historical scholarship to present the characters involved, including the murdered man and his killers. Part V describes the punishment of the perpetrators and places it within the context of the reforms of late eighteenth-century judicial culture.

While the first five parts of the book experiment with an unconventional writing style for an academic history book, the final two parts delve into unusual coincidences and mysterious sources. Part VI focuses on the geography of death in the late viceregal capital. It speculates on the resonance of this murder and its aftermath as it relates to the staged spectacles of death in Mexico City's central plaza and the surrounding streets.

Then the kaleidoscope twists so viewers can ponder a confusing series of events that puzzled residents in the late 1780s and early 1790s. In the same handful of years when hundreds of men and women were tortured and executed in the Plaza Mayor, laborers on public works projects unearthed Aztec artifacts only a stone's throw away from the busy gallows. The authorities reburied two of these monoliths (the Stone of Tizoc and the Statue of Coatlicue) due to their perceived association with human sacrifice. Ironies echo through the entire book as imperialism influences perceptions of violence and when it is tolerated, encouraged, or suppressed.

Another slight twist illustrates how Mexico City residents interpreted natural phenomena that occurred in the years just before and after the murders – storms, earthquakes, and celestial events – as supernatural omens. Part VII turns entirely to an analysis of the sources for information on the Dongo massacre, including two novels which add another 1,600 pages of highly personal interpretations to this story. Arguably, these texts represent early examples of True Crime in Mexico and contain many of the controversial themes that persist in this genre to the present day. Overall, this book narrates the sights, smells, and sounds of daily life in late eighteenth-century Mexico City with an effort to recreate sensory details. Most importantly, it demonstrates how one extremely violent night can shape the history of a nation.

Acknowledgments

One of the best fates that a historian could wish for is inspirational mentors who are also friends. All of the below individuals, some whom I know personally, and others whom I only admire from a distance, have paved the way for me to experiment with the unconventional structure of this book.

My dissertation mentor from the University of California at Berkeley, William B. Taylor, has inspired me since long before I met him due to his exciting books dating back to the 1970s. Their titles alone inspired me to study New Spain, and Taylor's humanity shines through in all of his descriptions, from how defendants excused their violent crimes by claiming drunkenness to how the faithful reported seeing miraculous divine signs in everyday objects.[3] More recently, Taylor has written a character-driven tale of two marginal figures whose lives were in some ways similar to the criminals who committed the Dongo murders. Taylor interweaves archival texts with works of literature, a style I attempt to emulate.[4]

Lacking the scholarship produced by Martin Nesvig and Zeb Tortorici, I would not have dared to venture into the scatological, the humorous, and the visceral aspects of viceregal history.[5] I can only aspire to Sylvia

[3] William B. Taylor, *Marvels and Miracles in Late Colonial Mexico: Three Texts in Context* (Albuquerque: University of New Mexico Press, 2019); Taylor, *Drinking, Homicide, and Rebellion in Colonial Mexican Villages* (Stanford, CA: Stanford University Press, 1979).

[4] William B. Taylor, *Fugitive Freedom: The Improbable Lives of Two Imposters in Late Colonial Mexico* (Oakland: University of California Press, 2021).

[5] Zeb Tortorici, *Sins against Nature: Sex and Archives in Colonial New Spain* (Durham, NC: Duke University Press, 2018); Martin Nesvig, *Promiscuous Power: An Unorthodox History of New Spain* (Austin: University of Texas Press, 2018).

Sellers-Garcia's model of beautiful and accessible writing and her bravery to present one strange case study as the jumping-off place for a broad study of the history of Guatemala City around 1800.[6] More than thirty years ago, Alexander Parma Cook and Noble David Cook also wrote a popular and engaging case study structured with dozens of very short chapters. Through one man's "transatlantic bigamy," they told a detailed and humanized story of sixteenth-century imperialism.[7] Of course, much of this superb scholarship on Latin America followed the classics of microhistory written by Carlo Ginzburg and Natalie Zemon Davis.[8] The memory of inspirational scholars including Paul Vanderwood, James Lockhart, and Douglas Cope also shaped this book.

This book would not exist if it weren't for the photos taken by Oregon State University (OSU) alum Ismael Pardo, during a visit to the AGN, along with Aimee Hisey, an up-and-coming historian who studies networks of knowledge created by Jewish medical practitioners in Spanish America, whom I have been fortunate to work with for more than a decade. I am very grateful to the employees of the AGN for allowing me and my students to access the precious records of the viceroyalty of New Spain.

Dean Larry Rodgers at OSU's College of Liberal Arts helped me finish this book with his unwavering support for my scholarship. He also read sections and provided his insights as an editor. The readers for Cambridge University Press encouraged me to finish the book and gave me many useful and helpful suggestions as well as a great deal of kind words. I hope that I have incorporated their very articulate and thoughtful comments well. I am very grateful for the professionalism and help generously supplied by Cecelia Cancellaro at Cambridge University Press. Kara Ritzheimer, Marisa Chappell, and Joel Zapata patiently read and commented on chapter drafts in the summer of 2021, not long after they helped me write my last book.

I am lucky to work with a team of extremely hardworking, eloquent, and kind leaders in my college, who put up with my quirks and empathize

[6] Sylvia Sellers-Garcia, *The Woman on the Windowsill: A Tale of Murder in Several Parts* (New Haven, CT: Yale University Press, 2020).
[7] Alexandra Parma Cook and Noble David Cook, *Good Faith and Truthful Ignorance: A Case of Transatlantic Bigamy* (Durham, NC: Duke University Press, 1991).
[8] Natalie Zemon Davis, *The Return of Martin Guerre* (Cambridge, MA: Harvard University Press, 1983); Zemon Davis, *Fiction in the Archives: Pardon Tales and Their Tellers in Sixteenth-Century France* (Cambridge: Polity, 1988); Carlo Ginzburg, *The Cheese and the Worms: The Cosmos of a Sixteenth-Century Miller*, trans. John Tedeschi and Anne Tedeschi (London: Routledge, 1976).

with my struggles. Among these inspirational colleagues I would especially like to thank Katie Bolzendahl, Susan Bernardin, and Kathy Becker-Blease. David Bishop and Suzanne Giftai probably spent the most time dealing with my need for solitude to write while they helped lead my school. Chris Lindberg and Meghan Naxer, course designers at OSU's E-Campus program, had the amazing idea to turn this book into an experimental video game as part of an online course called Crime in History. With the support of Naomi Aguilar, we will try to bring these events to life for students. I am also grateful for the inspirational work and friendship of Nicholas Jones.

My family patiently puts up with my early dawn writing time and so many other things. Michael Lopez listened to many of my diatribes about work and boring historical topics. My sisters and my parents, Joan and James von Germeten, set my path in life with their constant reading throughout my childhood. They've encouraged me in my writing since I wrote my first twenty-page paper for my Wellesley Senior High School English class. Inez Ayrey, who promised she would read this book, is already my role model with her energy, creativity, and kindness. I am so fortunate to have the chance to see how her future unfolds. Any errors remain my own.

Introduction

Please note: This Introduction frames the crime at the heart of the book with vignettes of historical and textual background, adding a few additional fragments to the kaleidoscope of murder and its aftermath in late eighteenth-century Mexico City. It proposes the 1789 murders, which are the topic of this book, as early examples of Mexican True Crime. The Introduction also includes select critiques regarding this genre and other comments on the different genres of literature depicting murder in Mexico. Along the way, a few spoilers are revealed. Some readers might prefer to skip directly to Chapter 1.

This book recreates a paper trail of Enlightenment-era greed and savagery that began with a brutal massacre. The events that took place on the night of October 23, 1789, led to a vast array of politicized depictions in a variety of fiction and nonfiction writings for the next century. The action in this book takes place in a city square called the Zócalo. Before 1521, this plaza represented the sacred center of the Aztec city. From 1521 to 1524, the Spanish tore down the Zócalo's pyramids and other structures, rebuilding it as the epicenter for both church and state.[1] The plaza became the site for hundreds of officially sanctioned executions and spectacles of torture. When Mexico City/Tenochtitlán is envisioned as a quincunx, the Zócalo represents the center point. The Zócalo is also adjacent to the location where the three killers carried out

---

[1] José Álvaro Barrera Rivera and Alicia Islas Domínguez, *Arqueología Urbana en la Reconstrucción Arquitectónica del Recinto Sagrado de Tenochtitlan* (Mexico City: Secretario de Cultura, INAH, 2018), 33–34.

their massacres.[2] The victims and their killers were buried with suitable Baroque pomp. Then they were symbolically covered with thousands of handwritten and typed pages discussing their deaths. Unlike these bodies, the priceless stone treasures discussed in later chapters of this book refused to remain buried.

WRITING THE MURDERS

Mexico City, October 24, 1789 dawned with the most noteworthy misfortune it has ever seen: in his own house, in the course of a robbery, Don Joaquin Dongo was killed, along with his brother-in-law, and nine of his servants, five men and four women, eleven people in all. These deaths were a greater spectacle than has ever been seen before or read about in stories.[3]

So begins a short narration of the crime, a small section of a memoir known as the *Diary of the Events of Mexico by the Halberdier José Gómez*. This memoir chronicles the month-by-month happenings in the viceregal court from 1776 to 1798. Gómez, a Spaniard born in Granada in 1732, maintained this handwritten journal until a year before he died.[4] Although his topics range from current fashions to earthquakes, most of his entries focus on the latest news relating to his fellow halberdiers, public judicial punishments, and the movements of the viceroys, under whom Gómez served as an armed guard during the decades that he wrote his journal.

Gómez witnessed close to 250 executions in the twenty-two years covered by his journal, but his account of the 1789 massacre stands out for its superlatives. In the few lines quoted above, he repeats the phrase "no se ha visto," conveying his shock with this "never seen before" violence. From his self-described uneducated point of view, even fiction

[2] Barbara E. Mundy, *The Death of Aztec Tenochtitlán, the Life of Mexico City* (Austin: University of Texas Press, 2015), 107. Mundy also discusses the Christian and Indigenous geographic and sacred axes of Tenochtitlán, 94–98, 169–189. For the layers of sacrifice in Mexico City that especially interested mid-twentieth-century authors after the 1968 Tlatelolco Massacre, see Octavio Paz, *Posdata* (Mexico City: Siglo XXI, 1970), 114–149; David Carrasco, *City of Sacrifice: The Aztec Empire and the Role of Violence in Civilization* (Boston, MA: Beacon Press, 1999). Sacrifice continues to define some genres of Mexican literature. See Persephone Braham, *Crimes against the State, Crimes against Persons: Detective Fiction in Cuba and Mexico* (Minneapolis: University of Minnesota Press, 2004), 82.
[3] Ignacio González-Polo y Acosta, ed., *Diario de sucesos de México del alabardero José Gómez (1776–1798)* (Mexico City: UNAM, Instituto de Investigaciones Bibliográficas, 2008), 208.
[4] González-Polo y Acosta, "Introduction," *Diario*, 18–19.

had never depicted anything of this kind.[5] Interspersed with the events of the new viceroy's first few weeks in New Spain, Gómez's memoir narrates the investigation of the crime and its rapid and gruesome resolution. Little did he know that his *Diario* would be the first of at least a dozen commentaries that would be written about the massacre for more than two centuries, and arguably an early contribution to Mexico's version of the True Crime genre.

THE DONGO STORY AS TRUE CRIME

> ... *true crime has become a multifaceted, multigenre aesthetic formulation, a poetics of murder narration. True crime is a way of making sense of the senseless .... But true crime always fictionalizes, emphasizes, exaggerates, interprets, constructs and creates "truth," and any relationship to the facts is mediated and compromised.*[6]

The massacre of 1789 led to numerous published and unpublished accounts, which all contain the essential elements of the familiar True Crime narration. One of the defining characteristics of the genre is the presentation of conventional ways to think about and discuss evil, which change over time and across societies, while making a confident but dubious claim to accuracy, truth, and fact. Scholars of True Crime trace its origins back to sermons and broadsheets that were printed in the context of the executions of notorious killers. These focused on sin and the ways that church and state successfully reincorporated even executed killers back into the fold. The mid-eighteenth-century development of Gothic horror popularized adding graphic descriptions, gore, and inscrutable or supernatural elements to accounts of murder. Killers became beasts or monsters, inhuman interlopers in civil society. Later in the nineteenth century, a social science-influenced approach developed, which included psychological analysis and forensically detailed descriptions of the crime scene, narrated with a tone of objectivity and lacking the previous eerie mystery.[7]

---

[5] Gomez's words echo Bernal Díaz del Castillo's famous reaction as he crested the mountains surrounding Tenochtitlán: "And the reader must not feel surprised at the manner in which I have expressed myself, for it is impossible to speak coolly of things which we had never seen nor heard of, nor even could have dreamt of, beforehand." *The Memoirs of the Conquistador Bernal Diaz del Castillo*, trans. John Ingram Lockhart (London: J. Hatchard and Son, 1844), 218–219.

[6] Jean Murley, *The Rise of True Crime: Twentieth-Century Murder and American Popular Culture* (Westport, CA: Praeger, 2008), 2, 13.

[7] Murley, *The Rise of True Crime*, 2–13.

With the growth of podcasts and streaming, True Crime has experienced such a boom that scholars can barely keep up with the constant international developments.[8] As the True Crime genre becomes more popular in different media, it has inspired more criticism. As it is a repetitive and formulaic genre, the biases inherent in contemporary True Crime existed even in the eighteenth and nineteenth centuries, and proliferate in the texts examined in this book. First, the prevalence of psychological analysis has detached most True Crime from any historical contextualization, instead situating perpetrators on their own isolated and deranged psychic islands. Murderers seem to emerge sui generis out of troubled families, influenced only by their immediate circle and their disordered psyches.[9] Secondly, from time immemorial, crime and its public punishment has brought communities together, under the illusion that "most victims are ordinary people."[10] Even in the Dongo case, with a victim born to an elite social sphere, all observers and commentators assume that Mexico City residents, rich and poor, vulnerable and powerful, European, Black, and Indigenous, celebrated the "solving" of the murders.

Lastly, modern True Crime entertains consumers with stories that juxtapose a belief in the effectiveness of authority figures, law enforcement, and technology with the spectacle of tortured and dehumanized bodies. With the development of law codes and courts and later professional law enforcement, the emphasis in True Crime moved from divine to human order. The rapid "solving" of murders by professional or amateur detectives argues for following the rules. It reaffirms social, governmental, and judicial structures. Chaos becomes order. Danger transforms into safety and trust that authorities are doing their jobs. The Dongo massacre also offered commentators the opportunity to narrate their political opinions. These range from the comforting medieval vision of God quickly resolving all crimes to blaming only the killers' self-contained and isolated evil.

[8] Ian Case Punnett, *Toward a Theory of True Crime Narratives: A Textual Analysis* (New York: Routledge, 2018), 11, 100, speaks of a dearth of Asian True Crime series – by late 2021, these can be found easily. Punnett also highlights that True Crime has embraced various media for a century.
[9] Murley, *The Rise of True Crime*, 152–154.
[10] Robert Buffington and Pablo Piccato, *True Stories of Crime in Modern Mexico* (Albuquerque: University of New Mexico Press, 2009), 3.

TRUE CRIME AS HISTORY

True crime reports on past newsworthy murder narratives, with an emotional component intended to prioritize such sensations as horror, fear, pain, and frustration, which is either to its shame, or its credit, depending on the disposition of the observer.[11]

Some crimes, such as the Manson Family killings or the murders attributed to Jack the Ripper, change the course of history and as such constitute a useful field of study for academic historians. Historians can narrate and analyze accounts of crime to investigate how the authorities in any given society manipulate emotions to effect policy – most notably the "politicalization of fear."[12] Crime narrations, including the Dongo case, allow historians to engage their readers by presenting detailed accounts of mundane life interspersed with bizarre and sensational events. Most accounts of crimes by necessity dwell on a certain geographic locale, allowing historians to recreate some aspects of this space for their readers.[13]

The most terrifying crimes inspire political action. Twenty years after the Dongo killings, London also experienced shocking news: the nighttime homicide of two families in buildings where they both lived and carried out their businesses – the infamous Ratcliffe Highway murders.[14] Similar to Mexico City in the late eighteenth century, these deaths prompted major reforms in law enforcement, and eventually the creation of the so-called bobbies or peelers in 1830, instigated by Robert Peel.[15] Newspaper accounts of the Ratcliffe Highway murders continued a popular tradition of True Crime writing in English that had already existed for at least two centuries, a genre which grew and arguably reached its peak over the course of the nineteenth century.[16]

Genres of crime narrations, whether fiction or nonfiction, have certain binding conventions, including a suspenseful tone, an easy-to-read style, familiar and stereotypical characters, and an ending that proves that

---

[11] Punnett, *Toward a Theory of True Crime Narratives*, 12.

[12] Buffington and Piccato, *True Stories of Crime in Modern Mexico*, 4.

[13] Anita Biressi, *Crime, Fear, and the Law in True Crime Stories* (Basingstoke, UK: Palgrave, 2001), x–xi, 2, 8–9, 16–37.

[14] P. D. James and T. A. Critchley, *The Maul and the Pear Tree: The Ratcliffe Highway Murders, 1811* (London: Constable, 1971).

[15] Wilbur R. Miller, *Cops and Bobbies: Police Authority in New York and London, 1830–1870* (Chicago: University of Chicago Press, 1977), 2.

[16] Biressi, *Crime, Fear*, 44–55, 112–115.

"reason always triumphs over irrationality and order over disorder."[17] In their introduction to an edited volume on Modern Mexican crime stories, Robert Buffington and Pablo Piccato draw from the work of Émile Durkheim, Carlo Ginzburg, and others to summarize a number of important theoretical perspectives on crime as history: In late eighteenth-century New Spain and today, most societies, and especially those in power, eagerly exploit evidence of growing crimes to criticize the degradation of some of their subjects. However, the perpetrators of what are perceived as criminal activities can actually show us the problematic aspects of any given society and the areas where change must or will occur. Narrations that seem focused on rational crime-solving based on evidence and so-called common-sense analysis actually reveal how the judiciary or amateur investigators perceive and assess subtle social behaviors as clues. Lastly, critiquing presentations of the rational crime-solving mindset of judges or other law enforcement can remind us as historians to question our confidence in our own methods.[18]

CRIME GENRES IN MEXICO

[James] Bond could never exist in a country like Mexico, where the organs of modern security, the police and the bureaucrats, are assassins whose xenophobia is directed internally, at the Mexican people.[19]

The problems with the True Crime genre and other crime-related forms of writing, either fictional or nonfiction, multiply when applied to Mexico. From Gómez's memoirs to the most recently published scholarship, all accounts of the Dongo massacre and its aftermath absorb the Enlightenment vision of a tidy ending effected by decisive, rational, European men.[20] The story of the Dongo massacre repeats the common tropes of the genre: a setting in a major urban metropolis; hardworking and intelligent sleuths who succeed in uncovering the identity of those who disrupt order; and criminals who appear to be respectable

---

[17] Ilan Stavens, *Antiheroes: Mexico and Its Detective Novel*, trans. Jesse H. Lytle and Jennifer A. Mattson (Madison, WI: Associated University Presses, 1997), 43–45, quote on 45.

[18] Buffington and Piccato, *True Stories of Crime in Modern Mexico*, 5–14. The authors lay out how their contributors present their case studies, which resembles this book: starting with documents and reports that sum up the crime; relating the crime, investigation, and punishment to values and culture of the setting; and finally commenting on its significance.

[19] Braham, *Crimes against the State*, 79.

[20] See Part VII of this book for an analysis of these texts.

contributors to society, but who actually only foment disorder. Early crime writers Thomas De Quincey and Edgar Allan Poe proposed the idea of murder as a fine art or as an opportunity to create intellectual heroes out of those who solve crimes, whether professional law enforcement or amateur sleuths.[21]

As a man influenced by the Enlightenment culture of his time, Gómez follows the classic crime-writing style of tying up loose ends. This approach contradicts how crime writing functions in modern Mexico, where authors reject what they view as an "Anglo-Saxon, middle-class" genre that has "little applicability ... in the Mexican context." From this perspective, retellings of the Dongo story to the present day endorse the "colonial paternalism" of those viceregal officials who brought the perpetrators to their interpretation of justice. Each textual reiteration of these murders and their resolution reinforces two of the essential aspects of Western modernity: "government monopoly on violence" and a celebration of increasing surveillance.[22] Overall, the most acclaimed Mexican crime writing takes an anti-establishment tone critical of globalization and the failures of revolutionary ideologies, along the way, "subvert[ing] the hegemonic narratives of modernity."[23]

However, writings about the Dongo events first appeared during the viceregal era and continued throughout the nineteenth century, long before Mexican authors embraced this anti-colonial, anti-capitalist stance. As such, these accounts imitated European models, even to the point of including elements of eighteenth-century Gothic literature. This imitation of European styles of narrating crimes began with the first handwritten document describing the massacre. Within a few days of the murders, all accounts focus on how the state reinstated order and safety, protecting the populace from danger. Dongo stories repeatedly reinforce European ideas of governments controlling the darkness and madness of Mexican subjects. Even in the twenty-first century, academic

---

[21] Fernando Fabio Sánchez, *Artful Assassins: Murder As Art in Modern Mexico* (Nashville, TN: Vanderbilt University Press, 2010), 2, 9–10, 37.

[22] Braham, *Crimes against the State*, 28, 65–66, 87.

[23] For a concise overview of literary critiques of crime writing in Spanish, see William J. Nichols, *Transatlantic Mysteries: Crime, Culture, and Capital in the "Noir Novels" of Paco Ignacio Taibo II and Manuel Vázquez Montalbán* (Lewisburg, PA: Bucknell University Press, 2011), 11–21, quote on 18. Stavans proposes that Mexican detective fiction, as of the mid-1990s, "favors ... dirty realism and espionage novels." Stavans, *Antiheroes*, 51.

historians have not yet rejected this rationalist approach born out of viceregal worldviews.[24]

As opposed to the Enlightenment-influenced crime-solving narrations so common in True Crime and fictional detective stories, Fernando Fabio Sánchez suggests that death, not law and order, functions as the central national symbol influencing Mexican crime writing. Sánchez argues that in a nation born via assassinations dating back to the 1810s, murderers are suitable national heroes, in contrast to the Enlightened authorities who resolved this crime.[25]

This book's retelling of the 1789 case takes advantage of the popularity of the True Crime genre while also attempting to complicate it by contextualizing its horrific violence, challenging the narrative which presents participants, commentators, and scholars repeatedly congratulating the viceregal authorities for rapidly resolving the Dongo murders. This book also questions the highly conventional political goals of True Crime as seen in the dozens of retellings of the Dongo story throughout the last two centuries. Most importantly, the goal of revisiting this multiple homicide is to engage readers with Mexico City's viceregal history, even if we must enter this Baroque urban space through the doorway of True Crime.

[24] Stavans, *Antiheroes*, 48, 55–56, 60–61. Without access to a nuanced history of Mexican policing, Stavans misses the subtleties of law enforcement during the Revillagigedo era, shaped by the viceroys who came just before. An erudite historical account of a murder which strongly contextualizes the lack of easy solutions is Mark W. Lentz, *Murder in Mérida, 1792: Violence, Factions, and the Law* (Albuquerque: University of New Mexico Press, 2018). The Dongo case and the murder examined by Lentz offer opposing scenarios of how Novohispanic justice worked: In one the solution seemed rapid, focused, and brutal, in the other, prolonged, diffuse, and weak.
[25] Sánchez, *Artful Assassins*, 9, 13–14.

PART I

MURDER

I

The Scene of the Crime

OCTOBER 24, 1789

3:00 a.m.

After several hours of quiet rest, a few light sleepers in the northern blocks of central Mexico City toss and turn in their beds. Rumbling noises coming from the street disturb their slumber. A Dominican friar pacing his cell hears a rapidly moving carriage, traveling toward the north. A Spaniard who runs a nearby tavern starts awake, jarred by a sound.[1]

6:00 a.m.

Melchor de León always wakes up before the first weak rays of sunlight pass above the horizon. He's a busy man who must start his day early. He leads a squadron of dragoons in Mexico City and must look the part. Sitting up in bed, he pulls on his coat, breeches, and boots, in the dark barracks, before opening the door onto the street. Today, blinking his eyes in surprise, León notices something strange. An expensive-looking coach stands empty in the middle of the street. Still attached, well-fed mules shift their legs and stare at him, confusion evident in their brown eyes. León walks up to the coach, calms the mules, and then looks up and down the street. No one is around. He calls out loudly for the driver or any passengers, but the street remains quiet. He reenters the barracks and addresses the sleepy soldiers who are

---

[1] AGN, Mexico, Criminal Vol. 337, Exp. 2, 22–23.

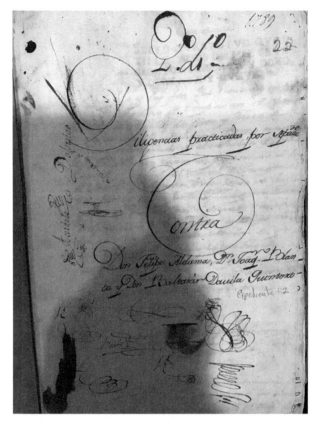

FIGURE 1.1 Title page of the Dongo murders case file. Retrieved from the Archivo General de la Nación, Mexico City. Photo by Ismael Pardo.

starting to wake up, "Do you know who this coach belongs to?" None of them have any idea. León walks to the rooms where his colonel sleeps, and finds the coachman already at work. They decide to store the mysterious vehicle in the colonel's coach house until they figure out who owns it.[2]

6:30 a.m.

José Laurcano Rosas steps out of his father's room on a higher floor of the palace occupied by Don José Fernández Córdova. Rosas fumbles for his broom in the dim corridor. Every morning, he cleans the street outside the

---

[2] AGN, Mexico, Criminal Vol. 337, Exp. 2, 22.

prosecutor's home and attends to any tasks that the higher-ranking servants need done. Just before he starts sweeping, he notices something on the ground: three keys, one large and two small, bound together with a piece of Cordovan leather. He picks them up and tucks them inside his clothes. A few hours later, he hands them over to his boss, Don José, who stares at them blankly and replies, "*gracias, mozo* [thank you, boy]."[3]

7:00 a.m.

When he was a young boy, José Antonio Arrieta's parents worried about supporting another child. They worked hard in Cholula as domestic servants, grateful that they were not stuck laboring as hacienda slaves like their parents. When his mother's sister María said that she could raise José in the capital city, they took advantage of her offer. María knew how to find powerful patrons.[4] She had worked her way up to a prestigious position as a servant to the head inquisitor, Don Juan Mier y Villar, and lived comfortably in his home in the *Calle de la Perpetua*.[5] Inquisitor Mier listened to her when she spoke of her poor family in Cholula. Eventually, he agreed to her nephew coming to live with her, as long as the boy worked hard and served with pious devotion as page and lackey. As he grew up under his aunt's harsh discipline, José became one of the inquisitor's favorites. Step by step, he rose through the ranks of the inquisitor's staff. In time, he earned a good living as a coachman to Don Juan, who even supported and helped fund his marriage. His family could rest easy in the thought of him as a respected urban resident, a quiet observer of the movements of the rich and powerful viceregal leaders who interacted with the inquisitor.

Now an adult, Arrieta's routine requires him to mirror the inquisitor's schedule. They return to their home each evening by 9:00 p.m. Arrieta wakes up early to ready the coach by no later than 7:00 a.m. each day. Walking south a few blocks from his workplace to the street then known

---

[3] AGN, Mexico, Criminal Vol. 337, Exp. 2, 11, 15.

[4] See Douglas Cope, *The Limits of Racial Domination: Plebeian Society in Colonial Mexico City, 1660–1720* (Madison: University of Wisconsin Press, 1987).

[5] Felipe de Zúñiga y Ontiveros, *Calendario manual y guía de forasteros de México para el año de 1790* (Mexico City: Zúñiga y Ontiveros, 1790), 47; Sharon Bailey Glasco, *Constructing Mexico City: Colonial Conflicts over Culture, Space, and Authority* (Basingstoke, UK: Palgrave Macmillan, 2010), 135–136; Pilar Gonzalbo and Pablo Escalante, *Historia de La Vida Cotidiana en México* (Mexico City: Fondo de Cultura Económica, 2004).

as the Calle de Cordobanes early on October 24, Arrieta sees a man riding a mule.[6] He does not know the man but recognizes his insignia as that of a coachman to a military officer. The man introduces himself as Dragoon Corporal Melchor de León and asks if Arrieta has heard of anyone losing a coach. Arrieta says that he has not, but he follows the man to take a look at it. They proceed north for four blocks and enter the colonel's coach house at the dragoon barracks. Arrieta recognizes the coach as belonging to Don Joaquín Dongo, a wealthy man who lives in a large house on the Calle de Cordobanes. With this information, Arrieta and Corporal León quickly walk to Dongo's house, eight blocks to the south. Arrieta knows the coachman who works for Dongo would want to know the location of his employer's expensive vehicle. Along the way, he separates from Corporal León, who enters a tavern to share the strange happenings with some of the neighborhood men.[7]

Arrieta reacts with surprise when he sees that Dongo's main entrance remains shut at this hour. He calls out to the occupants but to no avail. The noise catches the attention of some of the workers employed in the houses, convent, church, and businesses located on the same block as Dongo's establishment. The annoyed servants ask why Arrieta insists on waking everyone up at this hour. When he tells them that Dongo's coach was found abandoned an hour ago, they panic and start shoving at the wealthy man's main door. They cannot open it. In frustration, a young lackey moves over to the coach-house door and begins kicking it. Set in motion by his kick, the latches release and the large double door slowly sways open.

Arrieta and the rest of the curious group walk in. They pause in the empty coach house, held back by an ominous silence emanating from the usually bustling establishment. Shouldn't at least some of Dongo's nine resident employees be working by now? Why don't they smell the cooking fire in the kitchen? With dawn approaching, Arrieta begins to see several disturbing and immobile shadows on the patio floor. He takes a step into the house, squints, and observes a silver candlestick that has fallen on the tiles. What he sees next stops him short as bile rises into his mouth. He quickly holds out his arms, blocking the group of people behind him from entering the house. Arrieta then backs out slowly, mumbling under his breath and shaking his head. Terrified, one of Dongo's neighbors runs out to the street, calling for neighborhood law enforcement.[8]

[6] Bailey Glasco, *Constructing Mexico City*, 145–146.
[7] AGN, Mexico, Criminal Vol. 337, Exp. 2, 21–22.
[8] AGN, Mexico, Criminal Vol. 337, Exp. 2, 21.

7:30 a.m.

On this early Saturday morning, Don Ramón Lazcano (also spelled Lascano) chats with some of the local men gathered in a store. For the last few years, he has volunteered in the honorary but sometimes burdensome position of *alcalde del cuartel* (a neighborhood-level judicial official). This appointment, a new level of neighborhood judicial oversight created in 1782, means that he patrols the dark streets near his home at night. He also responds to any conflicts that arise among the residents of the *barrio*. His superior is Don Agustín de Emparan, the *alcalde mayor* (judicial official) for the larger jurisdiction known as the fourth *cuartel*, which comprises about forty square blocks to the north of the cathedral.[9] The busy Emparan also works as a judge in the royal criminal court.

This morning, the friendly banter stops when a man races into the store, breathlessly shouting, "have you heard what happened to Don Joaquín Dongo? There is a crowd gathered outside his house!" Gathering up a couple of homeowners from the neighborhood who had been conversing with him at the store, Lazcano walks the short distance to Dongo's doors. The main door remains locked, but they push open the coach-house door and cautiously enter into the patio. They are greeted by a scene of unbelievable horror.[10]

7:40 a.m.

A young Spanish man named Don Miguel de Lanuza y Dongo drags himself along the short walk to his uncle's warehouse this morning. His work routine starts each day with opening Don Joaquín's warehouse door promptly at 8:00 a.m. He slept terribly, grotesque nightmares haunting him and waking him with a feeling of dread. As he turns onto his uncle's block trying to prepare himself for the workday, he is surprised to see a small crowd gathered outside the building. Some of them turn to stare at him. Their eyes are wide and their faces are pale. The barber from across the street grabs his arm, "Don Miguel, your uncle ... and his whole household ... have been killed ... the *alcalde* is inside already," he exclaims. Don Miguel pushes his way through the people gathered in the coach house and steps into the patio.[11]

[9] Zúñiga y Ontiveros, *Calendario manual*, 89.
[10] AGN, Mexico, Criminal Vol. 337, Exp. 2, 17.
[11] AGN, Mexico, Criminal Vol. 337, Exp. 2, 24–25.

THE INVESTIGATION BEGINS

I, Don Agustín de Emparan, representing His Majesty and the royal audi-
ence of New Spain, provincial judge in this city, do record that at around
7:45 in the morning, I was informed by the alcalde del cuartel, *Don Ramón*
de Lazcano, that in the Calle de los Cordobanes at the house of Don Joaquín
Dongo, he and all of his dependents were found dead from injuries, [their
bodies] *scattered around the patio, and other rooms in the house. In due*
administration of justice, I order this investigation to begin. The notary
currently [writing this document will] *assist me. We will proceed to the*
aforementioned house to investigate the position in which the corpses are
found, who they are, what wounds each one has, where on the body, and the
condition of the locks on the doors, the chests, the drawers, and the location
of all of the relevant keys. . . . Master surgeons will examine the bodies, their
wounds, and what weapons they were made with, and if by themselves they
were enough to deprive [the victims] *of life. . . . We will discover and find out*
the truth. The offenders, whose apprehension is entrusted to the captains
and commissioners of this royal court, will act quickly, carefully, and
efficiently . . . and report back to me immediately so I can bring justice
upon these criminals.

Signed by Agustín de Emparan and Rafael Luzero

7:45 a.m.

Accompanied by one of Dongo's relatives and another court official,
Emparan enters Dongo's house to begin investigating the crime scene.[12]
Emparan has ordered a complete and detailed report of what they find in
the home on the Calle de Cordobanes. To perform this task, he has
brought along a court scribe named Rafael Luzero (also spelled Lucero).[13]

Now part of Donceles Street, in 1789 this prestigious street comprised
a single block located in the most central section of the viceregal capital.
The house sat one city block to the north of the cathedral, which, as the
crow flies from its lavish Baroque spires, was just four hundred feet away.
Dongo's block also hosted the convent known as *La Enseñanza*, where
nuns instructed young girls. Construction on the adjacent elaborate
church, decorated in the Churrigueresque style, had finished just ten
years before this awful morning.

The two men examining the scene of the crime are doing the work of
what would now be four different people. Emparan and Luzero have no

---

[12] AGN, Mexico, Criminal Vol. 337, Exp. 2, 1–2.
[13] See AGN, Mexico, Criminal Vol. 337, Exp. 2, 2–6, for all of the details regarding this
initial investigation.

obvious modern counterparts. In 1789, Mexico City did not have a salaried professional police force who patrolled the urban streets, guarded crime scenes, interviewed witnesses to determine the perpetrators, or interrogated suspects. Emergency medical responders and detectives also did not exist. In the Dongo case, Emparan functions both as the leading investigator of the massacre and later as the judge who questions witnesses and draws out confessions from the perpetrators. His tasks combine those of today's detectives, crime scene investigators, and district attorneys. As the official notary for this investigation, Luzero takes all of the notes at the scene, transcribes them into a narrative, and handles evidence.

Starting outside of the building, Emparan and Luzero immediately observe clues hinting at the events that had taken place the night before. First, they notice that the large main door to the house, which opens up to a vestibule or short corridor leading to the internal patio, remains bolted shut. In contrast, the coach house, where Dongo's carriage normally waited for his outings, stands empty and lacks a bolt on its door.

Guided by the nephew of the victim, Don Manuel Lanuza, who served as his uncle's cashier, Emparan and Luzero enter the edifice where Dongo lived and worked. They see that a staircase climbs up to a mezzanine which contains Dongo's warehouse. Under the staircase, they observe a crate full of candles, with a silver candlestick above it. Passing the staircase, the horror begins. On their right side, they see the body of a young man wearing livery on the floor. They guess, by looking at his boots, that he was Dongo's coachman. The youth's blood spreads across the floor and there are spatters on a door leading to a storage room.

Looking toward the wall that faces the central staircase of the house, they see the body of Don Joaquín Dongo, lying face up, with his head propped up against a pillar. Dongo, like all but one of the victims, was dressed in his normal daily attire, minus his expensive gold accessories. His killers had stolen his shoe buckles, watch, and rosary. A few feet away, the officials observe another deceased male servant in livery, whom they guess was Dongo's page, lying on his right side.

In a room beneath the mezzanine, Emparan and Luzero find two dead men on the ground lying on their sides. One had worked as Dongo's doorman, and the other was an Indigenous man visiting from the wealthy family's rural properties. Not far away, in an alcove beneath the staircase, lies another servant, named Juan Francisco, face up in a pool of blood. Both the doorman and Juan Francisco died with their hands tied behind their backs with cords. Due to the horrific wounds suffered by these six men, blood soaks the floor of this entire section of the house.

Emparan and Luzero now climb the stairs to the mezzanine, where they notice an unlocked and empty trunk on the floor. As they continue to ascend to the warehouse, they see the body of Don Nicolás Lanuza, another one of Dongo's relatives and employees, face up on the floor. From the report, it is unclear whether Lanuza was murdered in the nude or in his nightshirt. However, it is clear that the murderers had roused him from his sleep. Proceeding toward the warehouse, the investigators notice a destroyed door. The killers must have smashed the lock that held it shut, breaking through a bar that fortified it. Behind the door remains an empty cash box. Don Manuel Lanuza estimates for Emparan and Luzero that this box had contained fourteen thousand pesos the night before. A few pieces of burned white paper litter the floor.

The investigators now proceed up a final staircase, to the main floor of the house, which served as living quarters for Dongo and Don Nicolás Lanuza. On the patio outside the kitchen, they observe a dead maidservant on the ground. Entering the kitchen through another broken door, Emparan and Luzero find Ignacia, the cook, murdered in front of the metal pan where she would have maintained her cooking fire. Leaving the kitchen and crossing a hallway into a room, they encounter another woman, identified as the servant who did the laundry, struck down. Up one more flight of stairs, the officials see a final body, that of the scullery maid, Clara.

The investigators make note of several scattered clues that suggest how the massacre played out. In a cupboard, they find an empty box, which usually contained the keys to Dongo's warehouse. On one of the patios, they find carriage pillows thrown about and an empty packet that had previously contained silk stockings. As of the morning of October 24, all of these small items enter into the possession of the court, as does Dongo's elegant carriage found abandoned near the dragoon barracks. The perpetrators had torn apart some of its interior upholstery and benches.[14]

Luzero writes up his superficial observations of the gruesome wounds that he and Emparan saw during their initial tour of the building. Next they call on two master surgeons, Manuel José Ruillas and José Miguel de Vera, to officially describe the carnage in medical terms.[15] Vera and

---

[14] AGN, Mexico, Criminal Vol. 337, Exp. 2, 3–6.

[15] Luz María Hernández Saenz, *Learning to Heal: The Medical Profession in Colonial Mexico, 1767–1831* (New York: Peter Lang, 1997); according to Hernández Sáenz, *Carving a Niche: The Medical Profession in Mexico, 1800–1870* (Chicago: McGill-Queen's University Press, 2018), 311n197, "The law required an autopsy on anybody who died from wounds or under suspicious circumstances. The *Escuela de Medicina* was limited to bodies that were not autopsied or claimed by relatives."

Ruillas measure close to fifty brutal cuts on the eleven corpses, using the units of measurement of "dedos [fingers, roughly equivalent to two-thirds of an inch]" and "varas [rods, approximately thirty-two or thirty-three inches]."[16]

The surgeons first examine the entire body of Don Joaquín Dongo. The head of the household suffered two massive head wounds, each over three *dedos* in width, completely fracturing his skull. He also had deep wounds on his forehead and neck. The latter wound reached a depth of five *dedos*. His attacker had sliced through Dongo's muscle tissue and his carotid artery, and had penetrated his chest wall. Dongo must have reached up his right hand defensively as he was attacked, resulting in a cut to his right elbow. He also had a three-inch slice through his entire right hand, separating his metacarpal bones and severing three of his fingers. He possibly held up his hand against another blow, because he had another huge wound in his right arm.

Dongo's relative Don Nicolás also seems to have defended himself, resulting in the severing of his hand from his right wrist. A cutting weapon split the crown of his head at three places. In anatomical terms, the surgeons described this wound as completely fracturing the parietal and coronal bones of his skull. Don Nicolás's three head wounds measured between four and almost ten inches. In plain language, his killers had nearly sliced off the entire top of his skull.

Moving on to the five murdered male servants, Revillas and Vera next examine the page named José, who had died, like his master, from two enormous wounds measuring five- and seven-inches deep. In José's case, the weapon virtually cut his head in half. The coachman Juan must have struggled as his killers gave him four brutal cuts that opened up his head with a five-inch wound. His left elbow bone had been broken and his chest also cut. José and Juan's wounds all appeared on their left sides.

The doorman suffered three deep wounds on the left side of his head. His attacker also cut into his cheek almost three inches to the buccinator muscle. The Indigenous man visiting from Dongo's hacienda had suffered a massive head wound (in his case, almost seven inches long). He also had two cuts in his neck, one penetrating deeply, estimated a quarter of a *vara*, or approximately eight inches, through to his scalene muscles. The servant, identified as Juan Francisco, who hid himself in a storage space under the stairs, received two cuts measuring around two inches each to

---

[16] The medical reports summarized here come from AGN, Mexico, Criminal Vol. 337, Exp. 2, 7–9.

his left shoulder extending down to his humerus bone. He also suffered a devastating fracture of the bones at the base of his skull.

The killers did not offer the four female servants any mercy. The first woman whom the two surgeons examined had suffered two skull fractures, similar in brutality to those inflicted on the men. The murderers had nearly cut her head into three parts. One of these cuts measured over eight inches in length. She also had wounds on her shoulders and upper back, penetrating to her chest. Ignacia the cook died from wounds grotesquely concentrated on her face. One of these cuts was over eight inches long and completely fractured her cheek bone. She also suffered a total fracture of her petrous bone, located at the base of her skull, due to a cut measuring almost nine inches.

The washerwoman and the scullery maid fought their attackers, resulting in gruesome defensive wounds similar to those seen on the men's bodies downstairs. The washerwoman's body shows evidence of at least seven blows on both her left and right sides, including three to her right hand, arm, and wrist. Her killer initially approached her from behind, as the surgeons find evidence of three wounds on her back, although not as deep as those seen on the rest of her body. Her forearm had a five-inch cut penetrating down to her muscle. Her hand was split between the pinky and ring fingers, and her wrist was severed. Even as she ineffectively raised her right hand to defend herself from her killer or killers, she suffered two deep cuts measuring around six inches each on the right side of her head.

The scullery maid Clara also endured an attack resulting in seven wounds. Again, her assailants may have come up behind her, as the left side of her back shows a weapon had penetrated through her body. The killer cut her head three times, completely fracturing her skull and cutting through her ear in the process. Clara raised both of her hands to defend herself, resulting in a wound on her right arm and the severance of her right thumb and index finger. Her attacker also cut off her left thumb. As possibly the last person killed due to her location on the higher level of the house, maybe the killers had worn themselves out by this moment of their massacre. Clara's wounds were slightly smaller than those of the other servants.

All four of the investigators, including the court officials and the anatomical experts, emphasize that the killers focused on slicing open the heads of all of their victims. After detailing all of the damage done to the bodies of the eleven residents and employees of the Dongo house and business, the medical examiners Revillas and Vera conclude their report with the obvious observation that every wound was mortal and made with a sharp instrument.[17] Luzero provides a more detailed speculation about the weapons:

they had to be of sufficient weight . . . not only to wound, but to destroy everything, even an object harder than human bones. [It seems that] one person used the same weapon on all [of the victims], with others holding them, or that willing accomplices did it [the killings] with similar weapons. [The victims'] hair is cut so accurately that it could not be done better and more intentionally with scissors.[18]

Emparan and Luzero complete these initial reports before noon on October 24, approximately sixteen hours after the massacre occurred. They then leave Dongo's house to continue their investigations in the nearby streets and to send out word across the viceroyalty about this unusual crime.

---

[17] AGN, Mexico, Criminal Vol. 337, Exp. 2, 9. See William B. Taylor, *Drinking*, 80–81, for details on murder weapons in eighteenth-century New Spain.
[18] AGN, Mexico, Criminal Vol. 337, Exp. 2, 5.

2

The Dongo House

The viceregal home, warehouse, and shop where the murders took place on October 23, 1789, 13 Calle de Cordobanes, have not existed for at least 120 years. This location currently has the address 88 Calle de Donceles. In place of Dongo's house, there is a three-story building constructed around 1900 in the Eclectic style.[1] It now features a restaurant, small stores, and a nightclub on the top floor.

In the mid-nineteenth century, True Crime aficionados could probably still enter and look around the edifice once occupied by Dongo and his dependents. From the detailed description published in the first volume of his 1873 novel *Los Asesinos de Dongo: Novela Histórica*, it seems that Manuel Filomeno Rodríguez knew this house well enough to give a sense of the layout of the rooms, staircases, and corridors. While some of the largest pieces of eighteenth-century furniture may have still sat in the house, it is likely that most of the specific details about the decor are a product of the novelist's imagination. However, the following tour of Dongo's residence from this novel still helps readers picture the scene of the crime.

Both its entryway and its coach house (situated at the far right of the first floor), lack a sense of architectural regularity. The width and height of these spaces are not proportional.

Once you enter the house, to the left of the entrance you can see a large door that accesses the coach house. Two other doors open to two additional rooms that comprise the main front section of the ground floor. There is also a storage room and a staircase up to the next level. Another door opens to a corridor that leads to the second patio. This patio contains

---

[1] Christopher Garnica, "Donceles 88: a Sangre Fría en el México del Siglo XVIII," https://mxcity.mx/2018/10/donceles-88-a-sangre-fria-en-el-mexico-del-siglo-xviii/, accessed June 23, 2021.

FIGURE 2.1 Modern building that occupies the space where the Dongo murders took place. Photo by Inez Ayrey.

a sink attached to a well. Crossing the patio, we come up to the doors to the stables and a barn, which contains a large quantity of straw, filling an extensive loft. Two huge boxes overflow with barley for the team of mules that pull the carriage. These are all of the features of the lower part of the house. We will continue by ascending the seventeen steps of the first flight of the stairs to the landing, where a window opens up to a mezzanine. We now proceed to the interior rooms.

The first room functions as a passage to the following ones. This function is apparent due to the small quantity of objects that the room contains: only a dozen chairs of coarse wood with straw seats; a trunk placed on benches; and a few other small items. Next is an entirely vacant room with two doors set into wood paneling. One of these leads to the warehouse and office used by the master of the house. The third room is larger than those that precede it. Within it are two beds in their respective corners, a two-shot harquebusier at the head of one of the beds. There is an enormous wardrobe. The paintings are Chinese landscapes in the style of the [late eighteenth century]. The washstand is made of white pine with an elaborate porcelain basin and pitcher. This room also contains some chairs with straw seats, a large, square, coarse wooden table in the center. There are a few religious paintings and images hanging from the wall.

As we enter the warehouse, we find a desk with a writing set, an armchair with a black horsehair seat and a pewter spittoon at its foot, and a thick wool rug. These high-quality furnishings placed together characterize this space as the workplace for the boss or the head of the household. In front of this desk sit two tables covered in files where two clerks work. There is a raised platform for receiving clients equipped with a large sofa with a decorated wood back. A counter divides the room in halves. Several bags of pesos pile up under it. On the back wall, a door leads to another room. This is the entrance to the holy shrine, the vivifying soul of the world. The boxes enclosed within this small space contain a great fortune, locked up within heavy iron and wooden chests. At the opposite end of the room, we find a mahogany cupboard placed underneath shelves full of books, documents, and other papers. Lastly, this mezzanine room contains an empty table of ancient construction but capable of supporting the entire weight of the house, occupying the center of the room.

We leave by the same path from which we came, to find ourselves again at the staircase landing. Ascending one by one the nineteen steps above the landing, we encounter a corridor. At its end is a window opening up to an anteroom which leads to the servants' quarters. Another corridor accesses the roof terrace, from which one can see the second patio below. Another room serves for washing clothes. Next to this is the staircase up to the roof. On the other side is the entrance to the kitchen and the maid's room. There are also a dining room and two connected bedrooms. The first contains a screen to separate off the flow of traffic. The second has a bed, two large cedar wardrobes, a washstand, and chairs.

From here, a stained-glass window looks out to the main room, with its floor painted in a harmonious checkered pattern. A gold chandelier with six arms, each holding two candles, hangs from the ceiling. On the main wall we see a large and magnificent painting of the mystery of the Holy Trinity, in a solid silver frame, flanked by two gold sconces holding three candles each. These heavy objects have considerable value. Underneath the painting, on a dais, sits a black horsehair sofa, decorated in gold studs, two matching stools upholstered in tapestry, and two brass spittoons. This room has three stained-glass windows, two of which open out to balconies over the Calle de Cordobanes. The other looks into a nicely decorated anteroom. This room takes us back to the top of the staircase.[2]

---

[2] Manuel Filomeno Rodríguez, *Los Asesinos de Dongo: Novela Histórica* (Mexico City: Barbedillo, 1873), vol. 1, 309–314; for more on housing for wealthy people in viceregal Latin America, see Ann Jefferson and Paul Lokken, *Daily Life in Colonial Latin America* (Santa Barbara, CA: Greenwood Press, 2011), 66–71.

3

October 23, 1789

The day after the massacre, Emparan and Luzero canvas Dongo's neighbors, seeking information about any strange sounds or other unusual events that they observed the day before. Although Dongo paid a hefty sum to rent his spacious home and warehouse, he shared the neighborhood with a diverse group of small businessmen and their families. Some rent rooms, and others maintain large households in two-story buildings. The local residents have a good reputation. All are known as honorable men, however humble. By all reports, Dongo shared his street with "hombres de bien."[1]

Presumably, on a normal night on the Calle de Cordobanes, these hard-working residents enjoy the quiet. A sudden noise surprises them, so everyone takes notice of the sound of a coach at such an odd time of night. Some of Dongo's neighbors have the good fortune to sleep soundly on this Friday night. A twenty-five-year-old unmarried barber tells investigators that he heard absolutely nothing. The barber explains that he lives directly across from Dongo's house, but in a building set far back from the street. A forty-seven-year-old hatmaker who also resides across the street went to bed at 10:00 p.m. and slept soundly through the night. One of the more prominent residents, Don José Fernández de Córdova, a wealthy lawyer employed by the viceregal high court and the royal criminal court, spends most of his time at work on Friday and neither hears nor sees anything unusual during the night. The prosecutor's free Black coachman passes the evening caring for his sick wife and paid no attention to anything going on outside.[2]

---

[1] AGN, Mexico, Criminal Vol. 337, Exp. 2, 19.
[2] AGN, Mexico, Criminal Vol. 337, Exp. 2, 10–11, 14.

These witnesses were lucky to have one last quiet night before awakening to the shocking massacre that took place just steps from their doorways. But others experience strange sightings and sounds that disrupt their rest and foreshadow the terrible discovery made the following morning.[3] Perhaps even Dongo himself might have had a premonition of the danger that he would soon face.

7:00 P.M.

Don Joaquín Dongo pulls his large silver watch out of his pocket, notices the time, and signals to Juan, his coachman, who waits for his orders in the patio. Dongo has felt anxious all day but does not want to miss his visit to the nightly *tertulia* (salon) organized by his friend Doña María Josefa. Tonight, he feels a strange impulse to strap on his sword as he dresses for the event.

Despite not sleeping well the previous night, Don Joaquín follows his normal routine throughout the day. He leaves his bed just after 5:00 a.m., quickly dresses, and goes out to hear mass from the Dominicans, as he did every day. As always when he leaves the house, he carries with him his precious gold rosary from Jerusalem.[4] At the church, he makes his confession with his close friend Fray Manuel Fernández before returning home. After eating his breakfast around 7:00 a.m., he retires to his private rooms to pray and quietly gather his thoughts for a few hours, before heading out to take care of his daily business. Then he comes home and eats an early, large meal around 1:00 p.m. He takes a few moments' rest before spending a couple of hours in his warehouse, checking the accounts prepared by his twenty-three-year-old nephew Miguel, who helps him maintain the business and support the Dongo and Lanuza family who remain in Spain.[5]

After sitting still at work until 4:30 p.m., Dongo stretches his stiff legs with a stroll around the Plaza Mayor in the late afternoon. He then returns home to quietly pray at 6:00 p.m. After evening prayers, he dismisses his

---

[3] This chapter sums up a few of the testimonies made regarding noises in the streets close to Dongo's house. The investigation also took down accounts from residents in other parts of the city, who either slept through the night peacefully or heard the carriage. See AGN, Mexico, Criminal Vol. 337, Exp. 2, 23, 30, 39–42.

[4] See AGN, Mexico, Criminal Vol. 337, Exp. 2, Part 2, 40–41, for a description of Dongo's accessories.

[5] John E. Kicza, "The Great Families of Mexico: Elite Maintenance and Business Practices in Late Colonial Mexico City," *Hispanic American Historical Review*, vol. 63: 3 (1982), 429–457.

nephew Don Miguel for the night. As a newlywed, Dongo's young
nephew is always eager to race home to his wife as soon as he finishes
his work. In the evening, Dongo gathers the energy he requires for the
salon, where he typically socializes with his friends while listening to the
music provided by the cultured and intelligent Doña María Josefa. He
sighs with fatigue as he steps up into his carriage but reminds himself of his
enviable good health. Not many men can keep such a busy schedule at the
age of seventy-four.[6]

7:30 P.M.

Doña María Josefa Fernández Córdova y Jáuregui scans the refreshments
set out on delicate tables in her parlor. Thankfully, the servants already
know from experience that Doña María Josefa's beloved and distinguished guests expect the finest delicacies presented on the finest Chinese
porcelain. Doña María Josefa hosts a lively *tertulia* most nights.[7] She has
the privilege of providing the attendees with music played by her own
small orchestra.[8] As she almost always does, she hears Don Joaquín
Dongo's carriage stop outside her house precisely at the expected hour.

Yet something about her elderly friend's appearance strikes her as different tonight. He seems anxious and he carries a sword. She has never seen
him do this before. Doña María Josefa asks him why he felt the need to arm
himself tonight. Don Joaquín passes his hand over his white head and closes
his eyes briefly, looking tired. He admits that he feels worried and relates
a strange anecdote. Recently, he sensed someone's eyes on him while he
worked. Looking around his warehouse, he observed his cashiers bent over
their files, his lackeys sweeping the floors. All as it should be. Still feeling

---

[6] AGN, Mexico, Criminal Vol. 337, Exp. 2, 18, 24–26. Dongo's twenty-three-year-old
nephew Don Miguel Lanuza y Dongo provided the court with his uncle's daily schedule.
[7] A *tertulia* is "a social gathering in which the participants met regularly to discuss various
topics, usually with some intellectual pretensions." This kind of event functioned to
demarcate the elite Mexico City residents from what they viewed as the barbaric masses.
See Juan Pedro Viqueira Albán, *Propriety and Permissiveness in Bourbon Mexico*, trans.
Sonya Lipsett-Rivera and Sergio Rivera Ayala (Wilmington, DE: Scholarly Resources,
1999), xv–xx, 125, 205, quote on 255.
[8] For information of her noble family, see Yohana Yessica Flores Hernández and José María
de Francisco Olmos, "La certificación de Armas de la Familia Fernández de Jáuregui en
México. Un análisis Documental y Ligatorio," *Estudios de Historia Novohispana*, no. 61
(December 2019), 75–110. The Mexican nobility enjoyed musical evenings in *tertulias* in
the 1780s. See Javier Marín López, "Música, nobleza y vida cotidiana en la
Hispanoamérica del siglo XVIII: Hacia un replanteamiento," *Acta Musicológica*, 89: 2
(2017), 123–144.

watched, he turned around rapidly. To his shock, he saw a man, who appeared to be a respectable Spaniard, staring at him through a window. Dongo shouted out, "Who are you? What do you want?" The man quickly disappeared, leaving the merchant shaking with fear.

Doña María Josefa listens in amazement to this story from her normally calm and reserved friend. Even odder, immediately after he finishes his story, Don Joaquín stands up suddenly. He tells her that he has to check on something at home and cannot linger with her any longer. He rushes out the door to his waiting coach. Although she does not know it, Doña María Josefa will never see her friend alive again.[9]

9:30 P.M.

Ildefonso Gil Guerrero worries about the robberies he had heard about in his city. With many debts to pay, he just manages to make a living as a master shoemaker. He does not want his wife and children to always live in a ground-floor rented room, so he takes extra care to protect his tools and the small amount of money that he keeps in his lodgings. Every night he walks out onto the Calle de Cordobanes before locking up. On October 23, doing his standard reconnaissance, Guerrero feels a prickling at the back of his neck. A figure approaches him, striding rapidly through the dark night. Guerrero has made a habit of noticing people's appearance. Every day he deals with picky customers who make demands of him and his employees. In the dim light of his small handheld lantern, the shoemaker sees that this unknown man is thin but with regular proportions. He wears black breeches, white stockings, and a white vest, but no coat or cap. He wears neither a hat nor a wig. As the strange man passes by, he clutches something to the side of his body. Was it a weapon? The shoemaker loses sight of the stranger as the man picks up his pace and weaves his way through the propped-up wood of the construction project at the end of the block.[10] Feeling unsettled, Guerrero checks his door locks three times tonight.

11:30 P.M.

After a long day's work in his carpentry workshop on the Calle de Cordobanes, twenty-eight-year-old José Mariano Luna sleeps heavily beside his wife in their rented rooms. As an illiterate man from Pachuca

---

[9] AGN, Mexico, Criminal Vol. 337, Exp. 2, 26–27.
[10] AGN, Mexico, Criminal Vol. 337, Exp. 2, 13.

known as a *mestizo* (a race label which often suggests indigenous and European ancestry), Luna takes pride in the fact that he has created a life in the teeming capital city, staying busy with different jobs and living near the cathedral and the viceroy's palace. On this night, despite his fatigue, he sits up in bed, shocked out of sleep by the noise of a carriage outside his building. As the rumbling fades away, Luna drowsily wonders where it is going and why someone would drive out in this dark night. All of his neighbors work hard and keep regular hours. He does not worry too much about it and fades back into unconsciousness.[11]

11:45 P.M.

Like his neighbor José Mariano Luna, José Ignacio Ioano enjoys his quiet street and the steady income that he earns as a small shopkeeper. A literate man of Spanish descent, born and raised in the viceregal capital, Ioano makes a steady living selling all of the fripperies that everyone currently wears on their clothes – lace, bric-a-brac, and twisted decorative cords.[12] Although the countryside has suffered a terrible few years of hunger and disease, there are signs of new wealth in Mexico City. Rich people in the court city want to dress up and follow the styles coming in from Madrid and Paris. They also dream up some exotic local trends. Ioano works hard each day to stay up to date with each new sartorial whim imagined by the fashionable men and women who come to his shop.

Before retiring to bed, Ioano steps out on his balcony and looks up and down the empty street. As usual, he sees no movement whatsoever at the impressive establishment just across the street – the home and business of the highly respected Don Joaquín Dongo, staffed by a businesslike and discreet corps of maids, porters, and clerks. Relaxed by another calm night in his prosperous neighborhood, Ioano goes back inside and dozes off. After a few hours of heavy rest, he awakes and hears a carriage arrive at Dongo's house. Surprised by this activity, Ioano cannot fall back to sleep. Fifteen minutes later, his house shakes with the sound of the

---

[11] AGN, Mexico, Criminal Vol. 337, Exp. 2, 9–10.

[12] For the love of luxurious clothes and accessories, see Rebecca Earle, "'Two Pairs of Pink Satin Shoes!!' Race, Clothing and Identity in the Americas (17th–19th Centuries)," *History Workshop Journal*, vol. 52 (2001), 175–195; I also discuss this in Nicole von Germeten, *Violent Delights, Violent Ends* (Albuquerque: University of New Mexico Press, 2013), 146–152, 220–223.

carriage leaving at a "violent" speed.[13] In response to this bizarre occurrence, Ioano forces himself out of bed and peers out the window. He observes the carriage return again after another fifteen minutes, and then it races away to the west. He loses sight of it and cannot sleep for the rest of the night. These strange comings and goings seem ominous.

1:00 A.M.

Only blocks away from the quiet and peaceful buildings that sit solidly on the Calle de Cordobanes, drinkers carouse and fight each other every night. Throughout the day, they wander in and out of stalls and tents selling the Indigenous fermented cactus juice known as *pulque*. The violence always picks up after 8:00 p.m. This does not happen on the Calle de Cordobanes because there are no *pulquerías* (taverns selling the popular Indigenous drink known as pulque) on the street or in the surrounding neighborhood.[14]

In the early hours of October 24, three surgeons find themselves dealing with the injuries that commonly occur after people pass several hours drinking *pulque*. Don José Medina, a master surgeon, stiches up minor wounds on the bodies of two Indigenous men incarcerated in the public jail. Fortunately, while on his rounds, the *alcalde* managed to arrest their attackers. Medina feels grateful that tonight he did not have to attend to any serious wounds or run to assist men or women bleeding out in the street. Working in the jail is a slight improvement. His Spanish colleague, Don José Suveldía, also has a relatively quiet night, with only one patron, a man on a volunteer patrol beat who incurred a leg wound in the line of duty.

The master surgeon based in the royal hospital *de naturales* (Indigenous people) meanwhile handles only one case – an intoxicated man with wounds in his forehead and nose.[15] No one with any injuries comes to the three other hospitals in the city that deal with these kinds of

---

[13] AGN, Mexico, Criminal Vol. 337, Exp. 2, 12. Three bricklayers working on the street's construction project also heard the 11:30 p.m. carriage. It is unclear where they slept. AGN, Mexico, Criminal Vol. 337, Exp. 2, 15–16.

[14] For Mexico City nightlife and drinking see, Nicole von Germeten, *The Enlightened Patrolman* (Lincoln: University of Nebraska Press, 2022), Chapter Four. For drinking in general, see Taylor, *Drinking*, 66, 90–91; Deborah Toner, *Alcohol and Nationhood in Nineteenth-Century Mexico* (Lincoln: University of Nebraska Press, 2015), 11–13.

[15] AGN, Mexico, Criminal Vol. 337, Exp. 2, 31–32, 40; I describe the numerous deaths and injuries that occurred regularly after drinking bouts in late eighteenth-century Mexico City in Germeten, *Enlightened Patrolman*.

emergencies: San Andrés, San Juan de Dios, and Espíritu Santo.[16] Mexico City surgeons know that it is not unusual for drinkers to die due to excessive intoxication or to attack and maim others while in a drunken rage. Homicides are not uncommon in and around taverns but are usually unintentional and the result of drunken brawls. Across all groups in the Mexico City population, young men of Indigenous ancestry were the most common victims of deadly disputes of this kind.[17] Lacking any fatal fights, October 23 feels like a relatively peaceful night to the surgeons on duty.

---

[16] AGN, Mexico, Criminal Vol. 338, Exp. 1, 23; for more on these hospitals, see Guenter B. Risse, "Medicine in New Spain," in *Medicine in the New World: New Spain, New France, New England*, ed. Ronald L. Numbers (Knoxville: University of Tennessee Press, 1987), 12–63.

[17] Teresa Lozano Armendares, *La Criminalidad en la ciudad de México, 1800–1821* (Mexico City: UNAM, 1987), 65–73, 126–127, indicates that in the early nineteenth century, Indigenous men between the ages of twenty-one and thirty most often came up for prosecution for homicide.

PART II

CONTEXT

4

The Setting

Nine servants were murdered on the night of October 23, 1789: five men and four women. In contrast to Dongo, his uncle, and the killers, every detail of the biographies of these working people has disappeared. This chapter attempts to restore their place in history by imagining what three of these humble employees did on the day of the crime, a recreation of the typical experiences of plebeian daily life in late eighteenth-century Mexico City.[1] Four of the nine working-class victims, including two discussed in this chapter, remain anonymous due to their lack of identification in the original documents.

THE MESSENGER

On the morning of October 23, a young Indigenous man was finishing up a two-day walk. He had left his rural home to bring messages to an important merchant based in Mexico City. He started out at the Hacienda de San Antonio de Padua, commonly known as "Doña Rosa," owned by Don Joaquín Dongo. This property was located between Toluca and the village of Lerma, thirty-three miles southwest of Dongo's urban mansion on the Calle de Cordobanes.

Coming down from an arduous climb in the freezing mountain air, the messenger passed through the villages of Mixcoac and Tacubaya as he approached the viceregal court city. With only an hour or so left in his trek, he began walking along the Calzada de Chapultepec, which dated back to the

---

[1] For the concept of plebeians making up a multiracial population in Mexico City, see the classic source for this topic: Cope, *The Limits of Racial Domination*, 6, 15, 22–23.

time before the Spanish arrived in Mexico.[2] As this causeway crossed the Paseo de Azanza, large stone buildings loomed just a short distance away. He walked past an empty guard station at the edge of the city, noticing a tiny group of houses just to the south, the small *barrio* known as Romita.

As he finished the last few miles of his trek, the messenger started up conversations with other Indigenous men and women who were entering the city. A group of them encouraged him to share a drink with them as they passed a stand selling *pulque*. Although his throat was parched, he knew that Dongo's upstanding servants would not approve if he stopped for a drink, delaying his arrival with important communications regarding his master's property, so he shook his head at the invitations. As he walked across the busy San Juan de la Penitencia plaza on the southwest edge of the city, he also ignored the inviting laughs and loud talking that he heard drifting out of the *pulquería de los Camarones*. Instead, he took a sharp left to move north toward the large complex of the San Francisco friary.

Turning right, he continued walking along three more city blocks, pausing to take off his ragged hat when an elderly, brown-robed friar, clasping his rosary, stepped in front of him. The messenger again took a ninety-degree turn to the north onto the Calle del Empadrillo. Tired and hungry, striding quickly up this busy street, he held his breath against the stench of the cesspool in the middle of the Plaza Mayor, full of the waste left behind by humans and cows, as well as the debris from the nearby market stalls. A tempting smell of food drifted from cooking fires, but the messenger reminded himself that he would enjoy a delicious hot meal prepared by Dongo's cook on the upper floor of the mansion within moments of his arrival. Just after passing the immense Baroque cathedral, he took a final right turn onto Dongo's street, without realizing that he had just walked the last few steps of his life.[3]

The Population

Dongo's messenger was one of up to two thousand Indigenous plebeians who traveled in and out of Mexico City on any given day in order to sell their goods or deal with other business matters or court cases.[4] The number of permanent residents in the viceregal capital had recently

---

[2] Lozano Armendares, *La Criminalidad*, 15.

[3] James Manfred Manfredini, "The Political Role of the Count of Revillagigedo Viceroy of New Spain 1789–1794" (Ph.D. diss., Rutgers University, 1949), 23–27.

[4] Taylor, *Drinking*, 37.

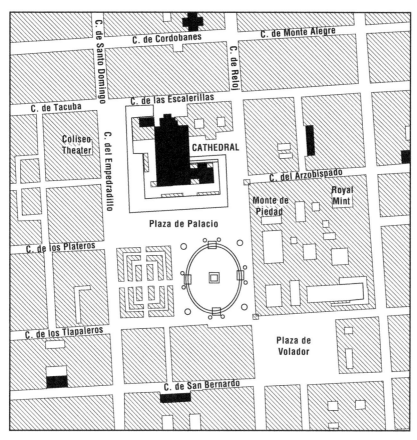

FIGURE 4.1 Map of central Mexico City. Map by Erin Greb.

grown very quickly, especially in 1786, known as the "Year of Hunger."[5] According to the 1790 census decreed by Viceroy Revillagigedo (who will be discussed in Chapter 5), 113,240 individuals lived in the court city, a 14 percent jump from midcentury, with 43 percent of inhabitants claiming a different place of birth.[6] The methods of counting based on occupation and head-of-households suggest that the total number might be over 120,000 or even approaching 200,000. The census data indicates that the population was close to 60 percent women, which seems unlikely

---

[5] Silvia Marina Arrom, *Containing the Poor: The Mexico City Poorhouse, 1774–1871* (Durham, NC: Duke University Press, 2000), 7, 25.
[6] Lozano Armendares, *La Criminalidad*, 43.

and also suggests undercounting.[7] Residents labeled *indio* comprised 28 percent of the population. Another 19 percent were designated *casta*, or racially mixed. Those maintaining the label *español* did not become the majority of the population until the nineteenth century.[8]

In total, Dongo employed eleven people: nine servants and two clerks. Four out of these eleven employees were women, which reflected the fact that women made up approximately one-third of the workers in Mexico City in the late viceregal era. Among women labeled *indias*, closer to half worked performing plebian tasks such as domestic service or food sales.[9]

THE GALOPINA

Clara, aged sixteen, found out in early October of 1789 that her grandmother had organized a job for her at the sprawling premises of the elderly Don Joaquín Dongo. Her grandmother knew Dongo's cook Ignacia. This trusted servant sent for Clara, ordering her to make the one-day journey to Mexico City from her small outlying village of San Joaquín, known for its old, red-walled Carmelite friary. Clara was instructed to make her way to the mansion in the center of the viceregal court city to start working immediately as a *galopina* (scullery maid). With a good reputation as a shy and devout girl, Clara could consider herself very lucky to have this opportunity to work and live in a fine establishment. She could hope for a secure job and an even better position soon if she obeyed Ignacia.[10]

At dawn one morning in late October, Clara joined a group of women from her village who were walking a few hours to the southeast into the city to sell their produce. In just over an hour's easy walk, they had reached the empty guard shack across from the parish church of Saints Cosme and Damian. They stopped for a moment to bend over the ornate Tlaxpana fountain, built fifty years before, to quench their thirst with the

---

[7] Manuel Miño Grijalva, ed., *La Población de la Ciudad de México hacia 1790: Estructura Social, Alimentación, y Vivienda* (Mexico City: Colegio de México, 2002), 25, 31–37.

[8] Michael Scardaville, "Crime and the Urban Poor," 1; Richard A. Warren, *Vagrants and Citizens: Politics and the Masses in Mexico City from Colony to Republic* (Wilmington, DE: Scholarly Resources, 2001), 9–10.

[9] Silvia Marina Arrom, *The Women of Mexico City, 1790–1857* (Stanford, CA: Stanford University Press, 1985), 157–164.

[10] For the widespread immigration of young rural women to Mexico City, see Arrom, *Women of Mexico City*, 105–111.

water that came down from an ancient aqueduct.[11] As they came closer to the city, they crossed the Alvarado Bridge. Clara started to see more plazas and churches. The other women planned to sell their food in and around the Alameda Park, so Clara followed them there.[12]

Although she had never seen anything like this huge meadow full of trees and fountains dating back two hundred years, she walked as quickly as possible to leave the park.[13] Clara's eyes widened at the sight of groups of men and women embracing drunkenly, daring to act this way in public in the bright morning sun. She only knew of this behavior during her village's annual raucous *fiestas*, and, even then, she avoided going to close to the drinking, as did most of the other women and girls.[14] She also saw unconscious people prone on the ground near piles of animal and food waste.[15] Clara shuddered when she saw a rather sad looking young man staring into space, his face dirty and his clothes in rags.[16] All one could do was to pray for such a person, she thought. With that thought in mind, she crossed herself and kept her eyes on the three religious buildings on the edges of the park: the large Santa Isabel convent, the San Francisco friary, and the new Corpus Christi convent designated for *indias*.[17]

Poverty

Perhaps up to 80 percent of Mexico City's late eighteenth-century residents worked as low-paid laborers or servants. Common employment options for the poor included working as domestics, street peddlers, artisans, small shopkeepers, porters, builders, coachmen, water carriers, and cigarette rollers in a huge new factory, established in 1769, that employed up to seven thousand men and women. Others had other proto-industrial jobs in essential crafts, including metal workers, textile workers, or the producers of leather goods. Those descended from the

---

[11] See Vera Candiani, *Dreaming of Dry Land: Environmental Transformation in Colonial Mexico City* (Stanford, CA: Stanford University Press, 2014) for the history of water, canals, and the drainage project in and around Mexico City.

[12] Amy C. Hamman, "Eyeing Alameda Park: Topographies of Culture, Class, and Cleanliness in Bourbon Mexico City, 1700–1800," Ph.D. dissertation, University of Arizona, Tucson, 2015, 33–35.

[13] Hamman, "Eyeing Alameda Park," 12, 198.

[14] Sonya Lipsett-Rivera, *The Origins of Macho: Men and Masculinity in Colonial Mexico* (Albuquerque: University of New Mexico Press, 2019), 67, 127–128; Taylor, *Drinking*.

[15] AGN, Mexico, *Libros de Reos*, Caja 73, Exp. 50, November 19 and December 1, 1798.

[16] AGN, Mexico, *Libro de Reos*, Caja 73, Exp. 50, July 10 and October 10, 1798.

[17] Lozano Armendares, *La Criminalidad*, 16; Hamman, "Eyeing Alameda Park," 73, 107–108.

Indigenous peoples of the region most often worked in occupations that depended on strength, including hauling, bricklaying, or masonry.[18]

From the mid-eighteenth century to the 1810s, poverty grew due to extreme fluctuations in the cost of corn, the basic staple, bad harvests, and three major smallpox outbreaks between 1761 and 1798.[19] Inflation soared after 1770. The most destitute might only earn sixty pesos a year and spend three-quarters of that amount on food for themselves and their families.[20] While day laborers earned only two reales, adding up to a total of five or six pesos monthly, master craftsmen might earn a peso a day. Small families could not survive on the income of one worker, which led to children working in domestic service or selling goods on the street. These people bought tiny quantities of bread, chocolate, beans, coal, butter, and candle ends each day or two from neighborhood stores, unable to gather enough cash to buy anything more than a few ounces of food at a time.[21]

THE LAUNDRESS

In the early morning hours of October 23, a woman employed as a laundress slowly walked away from her sister's *jacal* (hut), carrying a large basket of fruit and vegetables that her family grew in their plot just south of Mexico City. She approached the canal and watched the brown water, observing some filth drift by, and even what looked like a dog's carcass. Covering her mouth and nose, she waved down a passing canoe, recognizing the boatman as an acquaintance from her childhood. His craft was already loaded with vegetables, but she stepped in the remaining space, and they gradually moved to the north along the waterway, passing other familiar men and women going in the same direction. Their destination was the Plaza del Volador, just south of the viceregal palace, where she would disembark.[22]

After stepping out of the canoe, the washerwoman dropped off her bundle of fruit with her aunt, who had constructed a pile of fruit on a blanket to tempt passing shoppers in the Plaza del Volador. Keeping her shawl pulled over her mouth to block the stench emanating from trash piles,

[18] Scardaville, *Crime and the Urban Poor* (Gainesville, FL: University of Florida), 4, 21, 49–53; John Tutino, *Mexico City, 1808: Power, Sovereignty, and Silver in an Age of War and Revolution* (Albuquerque: University of New Mexico Press, 2018), 41–43, 75–94.
[19] Lozano Armendares, *La Criminalidad*, 35.
[20] Lozano Armendares, *La Criminalidad*, 121–123.
[21] AGN, Mexico, Ayuntamiento Vol. 107, Exp. 1, 1777, 29; Gabriel Haslip-Viera, *Crime and Punishment in Late Colonial Mexico City* (Albuquerque: University of New Mexico Press, 1999), 30–32.
[22] Haslip-Viera, *Crime and Punishment*, 15.

the laundress carefully weaved passed several other blankets displaying produce, dodging stray dogs and trying to keep her shoes and skirt hem clean from the mud as she walked toward the cathedral. A crowd of people stood in and around the plaza's fountain, washing their bodies and collecting murky water in gourds. Others laughed loudly, leaning against makeshift stalls that sold *pulque*.[23] Quickly leaving all of this behind her, she crossed herself as she saw the stone monolith of the cathedral on her right side. She nodded as she passed a few groups of women exiting the church with their veiled heads tilted toward the ground, their long skirts trailing in the muddy puddles of the plaza. Only a few steps later, she turned right into the Calle de Cordobanes. A few doors past the corner, she greeted the porter and walked up the stairs to pick up the dirty linens that had accumulated in the last few days while she had been visiting her family.

Living Conditions

Visitors and Spanish functionaries commented on the extremes of wealth and poverty in New Spain's capital. Although Revillagigedo and others decried the city's filth and disorder, the late eighteenth century represented a time of prosperity for many. Mexico City did not maintain geographic segregation in terms of economic class or racial designations, so plebeians lived alongside the richest landowners, merchants, and mine owners in the hemisphere. Wealthier residents tended to congregate in large stone establishments, either rented or owned, in the streets surrounding the Plaza Mayor. The very rich lived with a dozen or so servants, and several dependent relatives, ensconced in palaces worth hundreds of thousands of pesos. If at all possible, married couples of middling status and above tried to establish their own households.[24] In contrast to the large elite establishments, the poor who did not live in their places of work tended to occupy unimposing structures in areas that had a much more rural appearance several blocks away from the city center. Some of these buildings offered an income to their rich owners, who might rent out up to fifty buildings in the capital city. Even with a monthly cost of only four reales, renters frequently fell behind in their payments.[25]

Half of all working-class families in the city occupied only a single rented room, which was also a popular option for the 60 percent of workers who

---

[23] Hamman, "Eyeing Alameda Park," 71, 178, 186–187.
[24] Hamman, "Eyeing the Alameda," 79; Lozano Armendares, *La Criminalidad*, 140–141.
[25] Lozano Armendares, *La Criminalidad*, 14, 27–29; Haslip-Viera, *Crime and Punishment*, 12–13; Hamman, "Eyeing the Alameda," 82.

lived alone.[26] The next most common form of housing (occupied by 20 percent of solo workers, 25 percent of working families) was the ubiquitous *acesoría*. Described as "de taza y plato [cup and saucer]," this kind of rental, located in a substantial building or even just a small, rundown one, opened directly to the street. The entryway was the "saucer [plato]" and steps climbed to a tiny room above, the "cup [taza]." Oftentimes, the lower level might contain a small business. For two-and-a-half pesos a month (perhaps close to half of a worker's income), an individual could rent an *acesoría* with whitewashed walls, wooden ceiling beams and staircase, and an area for cooking.[27] The remaining plebeian population lived in *jacales* or, in rare cases, houses, which were, of course, almost impossible for a single laborer to afford. Although these ramshackle shanties only represented a small fraction of abodes, the authorities, detesting their lack of permanency and design, perceived them as ubiquitous and ruining the appearance of the city.[28]

Just under nine thousand people lived in the central neighborhood officially designated as *cuartel menor* (urban region) one, occupying 2,413 residences, which included seventy-six *acesorías* and forty-six single rooms. One of the densest streets in this part of town was known as the *Alcaicería* (Arabic for market), where over two thousand people occupied *manzanas*, the term used for a square of city blocks enclosed by residences. Hundreds of people occupied any given manzana in this crowed neighborhood. The large buildings that formed the manzanas contained up to thirty rental rooms and *acesorías*. True to its name, which derives from the Arabic *al-qaysariya* and originally referred to a market district in Granada, Spain, a packed concentration of small businesses also crowded Mexico's *Alcaicería*.[29] Unfortunately for Dongo and his ten servants, in 1789, one particular Spaniard had set up residence in this busy, densely populated neighborhood. Despite an ominous reputation of alleged past misdeeds and even an accusation of murder, he succeeded in disappearing among the thousands of hard-working plebeians living and working in the *Alcaicería*.

[26] Miño Grijalva, *La Población*, xix–xx; Michael Scardaville, "Trabajadores, Grupo Domestico y Supervivencia durante el Periodo Colonial Tardío en la Ciudad de México," in *La Población de la Ciudad de México hacia 1790: Estructura Social, Alimentación, y Vivienda*, ed. Miño Grijalva (Mexico City: Colegio de México, 2002), 244.
[27] Gabriela Sánchez Reyes, "La accesoria: una tipología de la arquitectura virreinal en la ciudad de México," *Boletín de Monumentos Históricos*, vol. 35 (2015), 135–148.
[28] Manfredini, "The Political Role," 23–24.
[29] Diana Birrichaga Guardida, "Distribución de Espacio Urbana en la Ciudad de México en 1790," in *La Población de la Ciudad de México hacia 1790: Estructura Social, Alimentación, y Vivienda*, ed. Miño Grijalva (Mexico City: Colegio de México, 2002), 292–318.

5

The Viceroys

The viceroy was, generally, a powerful figure whose competence, methods, attitudes, and character were of vital importance to millions of people, as well as to the status and progress of the Spanish empire.

Bernard E. Bobb, *The Viceregency of Antonio María Bucareli*

Some of the key themes in this book – reforms of the judiciary, the planned and gruesome spectacles of late eighteenth-century justice in the viceregal capital, and the monopoly that the government asserted over violence – rest upon the decisions made by the viceroys who ruled New Spain in the 1770s and 1780s.[1] These men combined a huge number of tasks in their daily routine, including holding ceremonies honoring the king and the Catholic Church, commanding the military, collecting taxes, supervising crown monopolies, ensuring an adequate food supply, managing the budget, overseeing mining, and increasing the revenues sent back to Spain. In this era, public health and urban beautification rose to the top of their lists of responsibilities.[2] The late eighteenth-century viceroys' actions resonate throughout Mexican history. They offered an example of strong, centralized leadership to Mexican intellectuals reacting to the French invasion and the wars of the *Reforma* in the mid-nineteenth century. This chapter very briefly introduces the six viceroys who are featured in this book, either as main characters or minor characters.

[1] The quote above is Bernard E. Bobb, *The Viceregency of Antonio María Bucareli in New Spain, 1771–1779* (Austin: University of Texas Press, 1962), ix.
[2] Manfredini, "The Political Role," 30–31.

For over a century, most writers who told the story of the Dongo massacre dedicated more words to the aristocratic viceroy who had just disembarked in Veracruz than to describing the crime itself. The newly arriving Novohispanic head of state at the time of the murders was Juan Vicente de Güemes Pacheco de Padilla y Horcasitas, the Count of Revillagigedo. Although Revillagigedo (as he is commonly referred to) did not play an active role in the investigation, many authors who discuss the Dongo case depict him as the most effective viceroy in all of New Spain's history and the reason why the judiciary could so effectively resolve the crime. However, the rapid actions taken after the murder were more likely a result of reforms instituted by the previous five viceroys in the two decades before October 23, 1789, than from a leader who had been in office for just a week when the events took place. All of the viceroys carried out mandates emanating from Spain, as well as negotiating their positions in Mexico City. However festive and positive their terms in office might seem, they all supported an active calendar of harsh and cruel justice administered in a public setting, as well as other violent performances that featured death as entertainment.

BUCARELI

Antonio María de Bucareli y Ursúa has a special connection to the Dongo case. The victim served as an executor of the viceroy's last will and testament when Bucareli died on April 9, 1779. Scholars since the nineteenth century have recognized Bucareli as one of the most active and energetic viceroys in Novohispanic history.[3] This distinguished military man left his position as the governor of Cuba to come to Veracruz in August 1771 when he was fifty-four years old.[4] He arrived in the midst of the fourth Mexican Provincial Council, the first gathering of this kind

---

[3] Bucareli has been of interest in the United States due to his actions relating to what is now the US state of California. See Hubert Howe Bancroft, *History of Mexico*, vol. 11 (San Francisco: A. L. Bancroft and Company, 1883), 370–373; Herbert Ingram Priestly, *The Mexican Nation: A History* (New York: Macmillan, 1923), 186; Manuel P. Servin, "The Instructions of Viceroy Bucareli to Ensign Juan Perez," *California Historical Society Quarterly*, vol. 40: 3 (1961), 237–248.

[4] Bobb, *Viceregency*, 19–27, 38–59. He had been frustrated by his limited powers in Cuba, wished to return to Spain, and did not wish to serve for long in New Spain. He had also served as inspector of fortifications in the New Kingdom of Granada. Bucareli had financial issues and received special royal dispensations so that he could afford to move to New Spain. One major controversy based in the Church was imposing communal life in convents. See Bobb, *Viceregency*, 63–84.

since the sixteenth century. Bucareli tried to carry out the council's proposed religious reforms without escalating internal tensions within the church in the classic style of "Enlightened" viceroys: "burnish[ing] a mystique of absolutist order without banishing the divine from human affairs."[5] He avoided further conflicts with the few remaining Jesuits in New Spain and with the Tribunal of the Inquisition.

During his eight years in office, Bucareli performed as an active, meticulous, and efficient viceroy.[6] He claimed to work ten hours every day, only taking a break to chat with a military companion, or go to the theater on Sundays as a gesture to fit into the local culture.[7] Bucareli succeeded in building up the Novohispanic fortifications in the north and on the coasts. He attempted to improve the colonial militia in the face of war between Spain and England. He encouraged further colonization of California. Overall, he did his best to support the royal reforms of this era, which extended to the judiciary, free trade, and church involvement in marriage. His urban beautification projects included commissioning a new broad avenue later named after him but known as the Paseo Nuevo in this era.[8] Due to a variety of factors, royal revenues increased during Bucareli's time in power, but he also considered those who did not benefit from the massive silver exports. He helped create the Mexico City Poor House and the Monte de Piedad, a government-sponsored pawnshop.[9]

Bucareli felt a strong connection with local religious beliefs and institutions in New Spain. He died in 1779 after a short illness interpreted as an attack of pleurisy. He had asked that his body be buried in the threshold of the Guadalupe shrine. Carefully following Bucareli's devout last wishes, Dongo made sure that the viceroy's heart went to the convent of Capuchin nuns, who had received his ardent support during his lifetime.[10] This was an unusual gesture that only an elite and powerful

---

[5] William Taylor, *Theater of a Thousand Wonders: A History of Miraculous Images and Shrines in New Spain* (Cambridge: Cambridge University Press, 2016), 95.

[6] Mónica Abigail Morales Ramírez, "'El nivel más popular de la legislación': Los bandos del virrey Antonio María de Bucareli y Ursúa, Ciudad de México, 1771–1779," *Legajos: Boletín del Archivo General de la Nación*, vol. 8: 14 (2018), 71–92.

[7] Bobb, *Viceregency*, 28.

[8] Bobb, *Viceregency*, 94–100, 227, 269–270. Bucareli received instructions and reports from the powerful royal visitor José de Gálvez upon his arrival and organized inspections of the militia while in power. Niceto de Zamacois, *Historia de Méjico, desde sus tiempos mas remotos hasta nuestros días, Tomo V* (Barcelona: Parres, 1878), 617–618.

[9] Arrom, *Containing the Poor*, 14, 54–55.

[10] Bancroft, *History of Mexico*, 370–373; Bobb, *Viceregency*, 37.

man could request. For the next four months, until the arrival of the next viceroy, the high court based in Mexico City (the Audiencia) served as the interim government of New Spain. Bucareli's death began a decade of rapid changes in administration – a total of eight governments in ten years if one counts the interim phases – which only added to the disruptions generated by the many other crises experienced in New Spain leading up to the Dongo massacre.[11]

MAYORGA

Don Martín de Mayorga had just ended his term as the Captain General of Guatemala when he was called to serve as an interim viceroy of New Spain in August of 1779. This appointment was the result of a mix-up; the successor to Bucareli was supposed to be Matías de Gálvez, the incoming Captain General of Guatemala. Gálvez was the brother of the very powerful royal inspector José de Gálvez, who had left instructions on this matter in a sealed letter to be opened upon Bucareli's death. Matías de Gálvez had not yet arrived to assume his appointment in Guatemala, so Mayorga traveled to Mexico City to take on a temporary viceregency. While in office under these confusing circumstances, he frequently attempted to resign.

Along with his contentious assumption of the viceregency, Mayorga also dealt with epidemics and disasters, as well as the war that Carlos III had just declared against England.[12] Due to these crises, Mexico City residents did not enjoy the typical festivities that welcomed a new viceroy upon his arrival. The continuing military and public health emergencies even prompted the cancellation of the routine fall season of bullfighting. Finally, in early 1780, Mayorga began to attend the theater and participate in Holy Week processions.[13]

Mayorga's first year in power was consumed with military concerns. He also decreed a provocative increase in taxes on *pulque* and tobacco, leading to a riot among the workers who rolled cigarettes in the new factory. Mayorga attempted to regulate the working hours at the tobacco factory and dealt with the workers' demands throughout his time in

---

[11] Manfredini, "The Political Role," 34.   [12] Bancroft, *History of Mexico*, 282–283.
[13] Gómez, "Diario curioso de México de D. José Gómez, cabo de alabarderos," in *Documentos para la historia de México, Tomo VII* (Mexico City: Antigua Imprenta de la Voz de la Religión, 1854), 69, 74–76, 86. When the bullfights returned in 1780, Mayorga personally gave the *toreros* thousands of pesos.

power.[14] He made important reforms in low-level judicial surveillance and issued a law limiting the conditions under which Indigenous people could sell their land.[15] While dealing with a need to improve Veracruz's fortifications, Mayorga faced a devastating outbreak of smallpox. In response, he organized inoculations for the few people who dared to try this new advance in medicine.[16]

Meanwhile, this physically and mentally active viceroy still found time for less political activities. He sponsored and wrote presentations that were staged at the Coliseo theater at the end of plays. Mayorga often sat in the audience at the theater accompanied by his personal guards.[17] With a tendency to change his day-to-day undertakings unpredictably, the viceroy wandered around the city unaccompanied, a shocking activity for a man in his position. His habit of walking the urban streets made more sense when it was connected to rituals, such as processions held during Corpus Christi. Unlike some later viceroys, Mayorga seemed happy to take part in the frequent masses and religious ceremonies staged to honor events in the lives of the royal family in Spain.[18]

After serving four years, Mayorga finally received royal permission to step down from his office. He left New Spain in 1783 but died just before arriving in Cádiz, possibly due to poisoning by one of his powerful enemies connected to the Gálvez brothers. Perhaps it was not an accident that only a week after his successor took office, a painting of Mayorga shattered in a fall down the palace staircase.[19]

MATÍAS DE GÁLVEZ

In March of 1783, Matías de Gálvez left Guatemala to finally take up his role as viceroy of New Spain. Although he had a successful military career, he maintained the public persona of a simple hardworking farmer.[20] Gálvez and his wife Ana de Sayas immediately became active in the requisite ceremonies, which included attending masses. Another early activity was judging works of art at the Royal Academy. In an interesting

[14] Gómez, "Diario," 74, 109.
[15] For the land issues, see Frederic Hall, *Laws of Mexico* (San Francisco: Bancroft, 1885), 63.
[16] Zamacois, *Historia de Méjico*, 628–629.
[17] Gómez, "Diario," 77–78, 81, 82, 86. A few months later, Mayorga banished his co-author, who worked with him on the speeches.
[18] Gómez, "Diario," 86, 96–99, 102.
[19] Bancroft, *History of Mexico*, 385; Gómez, "Diario," 113–114.
[20] Bancroft, *History of Mexico*, 385–386. This author exaggerates Galvez's affability – justice was very harsh under this viceroy.

twist, he awarded a prize to a woman artist. Although this institution was founded under the viceregency of Mayorga, Gálvez supported the academy as a way to address his perception of his subjects' pernicious idleness. Gálvez helped the new school gain more financial support from Carlos III, who sent money and works of art. He took an active interest in projects to beautify the city, going out on the streets to examine the recently installed paving stones. He supported the publication of the *Gazeta de México* under the editorship of Manuel Valdés y Munguía.[21] He even inspected every corner of the secret jails of the Holy Office tribunal.[22]

Upon taking this appointment, Gálvez was sixty-six years old and sickly. He survived only nineteen months as viceroy. His gradual decline began in April of 1784, while the city made processions to appeal for divine mercy during an outbreak of an illness known as "dolores de costado [side pains]," possibly related to the lung ailment that killed Bucareli.[23] By September, Gálvez could no longer sign his name. He died in early November.[24] The Audiencia again stepped in as an interim government until the arrival of Gálvez's son as the new viceroy.

BERNARDO DE GÁLVEZ

Before taking on the leadership of New Spain, the younger Gálvez already had an illustrious military career in Texas (resulting in the name Galveston for a port city), later fighting against England in Mississippi and Florida as governor of Louisiana.[25] Only thirty-eight years old when he entered Mexico City in June of 1785, Gálvez enjoyed almost as much popularity as his French-descended wife Felícitas de Saint Maxent, known as *La Francesita*. This well-connected daughter of the merchant founder of St. Louis, aged twenty-eight upon her arrival in Mexico City, became beloved by the locals, who wrote humorous poems in her favor. Gálvez immediately assumed a very public persona, attending mass in the cathedral with his wife.

[21] Susan Deans Smith, "'A Natural and Voluntary Dependence': The Royal Academy of San Carlos and the Cultural Politics of Art Education in Mexico City, 1786–1797," *Bulletin of Latin American Research*, vol. 29: 3 (2010), 281–284; Zamacois, *Historia de Méjico*, 635, 639–642.
[22] Gómez, "Diario," 115.
[23] Oziel Ulises Talayera Ibarra, "La crisis de los años 1785–1786 en Michoacán: ¿el 'Gran Hambre' o las grandes epidemias?" *Tzintzun: Revista de estudios históricos*, vol. 61 (2015), 83–128.
[24] Gómez, "Diario," 184, 193.   [25] Priestly, *The Mexican Nation*, 187–188.

Overall, Gálvez's very short viceregency had a martial, festive, and innovative tone.[26] He opened the palace to a ceremony known as *besamanos* (hands-kissing) in August. The lavish chamber impressed visitors with its decor:

A magnificent salon draped in crimson damask with gold braid, fringes and tassels; a very special portrait of the king; ten dozen fine wooden chairs, 24 lined in velvet with gold braid and the rest in crimson damask; fourteen unique mirrors; sixteen [decorative] screens; four stained-glass windows; three crystal lamps and a luxurious carpet.[27]

After this ostentatious welcome ceremony, Gálvez walked around the city and toured the royal mint with his family. He staged ceremonies involving his young children and attended the theater, dances, and bullfights, transported in a stylish carriage while handing out money. A heady combination of celebration, violent diversions, and love for the young viceroy is depicted in an observation by one of his personal guards:

In June of 1786, there was more confusion than diversion: two days of bullfights, cockfights, fandangos, dogfights and gambling in all of the houses, plazas, and streets with everyone taking part. Since the conquest of this kingdom, there has not been anything like this, nor a viceroy [who received so much] applause and cheers.[28]

All of these entertainments took place amid frequent earthquakes and less festive violent spectacles, including public executions and lashings.

Amid all of this energetic activity, most *novohispanos* suffered a great deal in 1785 and 1786, which came to be known as the Hunger Year. The corn harvest had failed due to unpredictable precipitation, both too much and too little, combined with unusually cold weather. In response to the crisis, Gálvez organized relief in the form of food distribution and shelter for women, children, and others in need. He also hired men to labor on public works projects, which continued to beautify the city, and supported agriculture. He donated his own inheritance to this cause.[29] His dashing public persona and his efforts to help the victims of the famine made him extremely popular and provoked jealous rumors that he had renovated the

---

[26] González-Polo y Acosta, *Diario*, 211–252, covers the era of the younger Gálvez; Zamacois, *Historia de Méjico*, 647–649.

[27] González-Polo y Acosta, *Diario*, 214–215. [28] González-Polo y Acosta, *Diario*, 240.

[29] Luz María Espinosa Cortés, "El año del hambre" en Nueva España, 1785–1786: escasez de maíz, epidemias y 'cocinas públicas' para los pobres," *Diálogos: Revista Electrónica de Historia*, vol. 17: 1 (2016), 89–110; Zamacois, *Historia de Méjico*, 650–652; Bancroft, *History of Mexico*, 394.

Chapultepec castle to fortify the city without Spain's intervention. This gossip proved ridiculous given the trusting relationship between Gálvez and Carlos III.[30] Sadly, the young viceroy passed away in late November of 1786, leaving his wife with three young children and a new baby born less than two weeks later. In honor of her Mexican birthplace, the infant was named Guadalupe. The family returned to Spain, as dictated in Gálvez's will.[31]

FLÓREZ

After Gálvez's sudden death, first the Audiencia and then the archbishop stepped in to govern New Spain. Finally in August of 1787, Manuel Antonio de Flórez arrived. In his midsixties, he was an experienced leader who had spent eleven years presiding over the New Kingdom of Granada (a region which now comprises Colombia, Venezuela, and Ecuador). During Flórez's viceregency, the powers of viceroys both contracted and expanded. First the intendant system introduced a new level of regional bureaucrat. Then royal inspector José de Gálvez died, leading to an increase in Flórez's authority over finances. The shifting parameters of his powers allowed him to create three new regiments and focused on expeditions to northern New Spain. Flórez did have an affinity for the military, but he preferred to spend his time and energy on cultural and scientific projects instead of attending bullfights. Several Mexico City savants became well known in this era, contributing to discussions about astronomy and the nascent field of archeology. Under Flórez's rule, Mexico City gained a new botanical garden, and he invited Spanish and German experts on mining to improve New Spain's silver production.[32] Despite these developments, the late 1780s were violent years, complete with frequent bullfights and other cruel spectacles involving animals, a spate of murders, and many brutal executions in the plazas of the city.[33]

   Some historians describe Flórez as a hypochondriac. After a year in the viceregency, he begged the king to send him back to Spain due to his poor health. While posted in Mexico City, he escaped to the countryside for

---

[30] Priestly, *The Mexican Nation*, 188; Bancroft, *History of Mexico*, 395–397.

[31] Felícitas de Saint Maxent became known as an intelligent and cultured hostess in Spain, where she lived until her death, in 1799. See Eric Beerman, *España y la Independencia de los Estados Unidos (1776–1783)* (Madrid: Colección MAPFRE, 1992).

[32] Zamacois, *Historia de Méjico*, 665–670; Gómez, "Diario," 295–296.

[33] See Gómez, "Diario," 280–291 and Chapter 16 for a summary of these events.

months at a time to attend to his maladies, which were perceived by his personal guards as minor. Perhaps his attitude toward his health affected the opinion of the general population. In contrast to the popular Gálvez, some locals rated Flórez's government as, literally, "shit." Criticism stooped as low as remarking that the balls that he threw for his sons allegedly only drew unattractive and low-ranking attendees.[34] The last several months that Flórez spent in New Spain focused on ceremonies relating to the death of Carlos III and the accession of Carlos IV. After he left Mexico in the fall of 1789, the allegedly sickly Flórez lived another ten years, well into his late seventies, quite a long life for the eighteenth century.[35]

REVILLAGIGEDO

Residents of Mexico City first learned about their new viceroy in mail that arrived from Spain on May 2, 1789. Five months later, the Count of Revillagigedo received the staff of office from his predecessor in the Villa of Guadalupe and arrived in Mexico City on October 17, 1789. The son of a viceroy of New Spain in power from 1746 to 1755, the younger Revillagigedo amazed the populace with his entrance in an ostentatious English-style coach pulled by six horses, bedecked with lavish plumes on their heads.[36] Two highly decorated open carriages called *volantes* proceeded the viceroy's conveyance.[37]

Only a week after Revillagigedo's arrival, the city heard about the massacre on the Calle de Cordobanes. As a result, the viceroy did not attend a mass organized for him, nor did he receive a formal procession by the judges of the Audiencia. All of his personal guards were too busy to guard him as they went out to patrol the city streets. Revillagigedo began his formal public appearances in early November, attending a procession of three hundred convicts sentenced to forced labor in presidios and finally attending his first official mass. It is not clear if he watched the execution of the Dongo killers.[38]

---

[34] Gómez, "Diario," 293, 298, a trip to Coyocan from March until June, and 299 on the criticisms.

[35] Bancroft, *History of Mexico*, 407.

[36] The younger Revillagigedo lived in Mexico from age six until fifteen during his father's viceregency. Manfredini, "The Political Role," 2.

[37] González-Polo y Acosta, *Diario*, 203. Starting from this impressive entry and to the present day, Revillagigedo has fascinated many historians both in Mexico and the English-speaking world. It would require another book to detail all of his actions while in New Spain. This brief summary just touches on some highlights that relate to the Dongo story.

[38] González-Polo y Acosta, *Diario*, 208–209.

At the end of the month, Revillagigedo began to celebrate by occasionally attending the several weeks of bullfights organized in his honor, taking part in ceremonial events at the cathedral, and ordering artillery salutes for the queen's birthday. Continuing to show his devotion to the Spanish monarchs, Revillagigedo ordered the closure of all business in his capital city at the end of December when Carlos IV was sworn in as the new king. The city enjoyed three days of celebrations, including multiple fireworks displays and images of the king and queen placed in all offices where royal business took place, respectfully covered by canopies. The city government organized a dance, and the viceroy attended until one in the morning, leaving three hours before the party finally ended. (He reputedly survived on only four to five hours of sleep.)[39] Shortly after these welcoming festivals, Revillagigedo supported the erection of a statue of the king on his horse (not the famous bronze *Caballito* statue, which was erected in 1803), formally inspecting it and the brightly illuminated streets around it, upon its completion.[40]

Even during the round of celebrations welcoming him, Revillagigedo carried out a huge workload, which is represented in the hundreds of pages of documents that he created (with the help of his secretary, who allegedly died of exhaustion), read, or signed in the first two months of his reign. His predecessor, Flórez, warned him that since the death of Bucareli, the viceregency had functioned chaotically, due to the rapid turnover of the appointees. This proved to be true.[41] Revillagigedo traveled around the city early in his reign, showing his interest in the drainage project and the royal mint. One of his other tasks during these early months was further implementation of the king's orders regarding free trade in the port of Acapulco.[42] Military strategy of course also demanded his attention when Spain declared war on France, and Revillagigedo corresponded with the Veracruz intendant and also examined the costs of presidios around the Caribbean.[43] A three hundred-page file attests to complex interactions regarding the tobacco monopoly just as the new

---

[39] Manfredini, "The Political Role," 4.

[40] González-Polo y Acosta, *Diario*, 211–213. This image remained on display until February of 1792. See González-Polo y Acosta, *Diario*, 240.

[41] Manfredini, "The Political Role," 8, 34.

[42] AGN, Reales Órdenes Caja 475, Exp. 1, 1789; Correspondencia de Virreyes Caja 2417, Exp. 5, 1789.

[43] AGN, Cárceles y Presidios Caja 1953, Exp. 19, 1789; Correspondencia de Diversas Autoridades Caja 2245, Exp. 7, 1789; Correspondencia de Diversas Autoridades Caja 6610, Exp. 28, 1789.

viceroy assumed his office.[44] There were ongoing worries about tribute payments, collecting taxes and issues among customs officials.[45] Revillagigedo also had to concern himself with papal bulls, tithes, and numerous other church-related issues.[46]

On one occasion, Revillagigedo surprised his guards by respectfully walking with the Eucharist when he encountered a procession of priests transporting it to administer the sacrament of last rites.[47] Despite this display of piety, viceroys in this era had to balance their European-influenced skepticism with the strong Baroque Mexican traditions they encountered in New Spain. Carrying out reforms that would not win him broad popular support, Revillagigedo tried to regulate religious alms, lay brotherhoods, and other practical matters involving miraculous images and shrines.[48] Oftentimes Revillagigedo chose not to attend formal masses, even on important days such as the festival in honor of the Virgin of Guadalupe. He ordered the removal of religious images from the viceregal palace.[49] In 1792, Revillagigedo chose to take a walk to the theater instead of attending a mass in honor of the king on the day that honored San Carlos Borromeo, his namesake. A week later, he also skipped all ceremonies in honor of the king's third anniversary as monarch.[50] In terms of religious rituals, it seems that every detail of his actions fascinated observers. For example, Revillagigedo made a point to dress all in black, including his stockings, when he attended a formal mass, matching the formally draped seat set up for him in the cathedral.[51]

Historians have rated Revillagigedo as the single most successful viceroy of the eighteenth century, if not the entirety of Novohispanic history.[52] Nineteenth-century commentators even interpret him as open to complaints from the general populace about Spanish rule and individual bureaucrats.[53] Revillagigedo receives most of the credit for improving the sanitation and general order in the court city, although reforms such as lighting and night patrols had concerned viceroys for decades and lingered on as contentious problems for Mexicans well into the nineteenth

[44] AGN, Renta del Tabaco Caja 3322, Exp. 1, 1789.
[45] AGN, Correspondencia de Virreyes Caja 5666, Exp. 36, 1789; Real Hacienda Caja 6508, Exp. 9, 1789; Alcabalas Caja 2634, Exp. 15, 1789.
[46] AGN, Reales Órdenes Caja 4792, Exp. 1, 1789; Diezmos Caja 4565, Exp. 16, 1789.
[47] González-Polo y Acosta, *Diario*, 215–216, 220.
[48] Taylor, *Theater*, 96–99, 105, 113–115, 145.
[49] González-Polo y Acosta, *Diario*, 238; Taylor, *Theater*, 117.
[50] González-Polo y Acosta, *Diario*, 252.   [51] González-Polo y Acosta, *Diario*, 227.
[52] Priestly, *The Mexican Nation*, 188–189.
[53] Bancroft, *History of Mexico*, 480–481; Zamacois, *Historia de Méjico*, 676–677.

century.[54] Ultimately local leaders looked critically at his spending for all of these achievements, and he was sent back to Spain in 1794. He was investigated under the viceregency of his successor Branciforte, but acquitted, leaving another bill for his previous subjects in Mexico.[55]

From Bucareli to Revillagigedo, the viceroys set the tone for life in Mexico City before and after the Dongo massacre. They inherited a justice system but made significant changes to it in the 1780s. Because of this, all of these men played important roles in the Dongo drama.

[54] Germeten, *Enlightened Patrolman.*   [55] Zamacois, *Historia de Méjico*, 687–690.

6

The Judiciary

Justice in the ancien régime combined legal and theological principles.
Society was conceived of as a body in which the criminal was the "rotten
member" that had to be removed to avoid corrupting the healthy parts. The
main function of the prince was to maintain order. When human transgres-
sions (such as crimes) violated order, the prince had to punish [criminals] to
restore it. The prince was not a legislator. He embodied justice.

Odette María Rojas Sosa, "Cada uno viva a su ley"

That the judiciary should assume a political role in the New World was
hardly surprising ... Hernán Cortés rightly feared the crown's lawyers.

Colin MacLachlan, *Criminal Justice in Eighteenth-Century Mexico*

The Spanish judiciary thrived on complexity. Judges in the Americas
worked within multiple court systems with interwoven jurisdictions and
could consult seven different overlapping law codes when considering
their decisions.[1] This system developed as monarchs in different regions
of the Iberian Peninsula consolidated their rule by codifying laws and
courts from the thirteenth century onwards. Influenced by both Roman
and Islamic conquest, judicial codes derived from a centuries' long process

---

[1] Haslip-Viera, *Crime and Punishment*, 37. Haslip-Viera and other scholars have deeply
analyzed race and class within the judicial system, the general incidence of various crimes,
jail conditions, and the judicial process, none of which will be discussed in this book. For
these topics, see also Scardaville, *Crime and Urban Poor* and Lozano Armendares, *La
Criminalidad*. For the quotes, see Odette María Rojas Sosa, "'Cada uno viva a su ley'; Las
controversias entre el Tribunal de la Acordada y la Real Sala del Crimen, 1785–1793,"
Estudios de Historia Novohispana, vol. 47 (July–December 2012), quote on 129; and
Colin MacLachlan, *Spain's Empire in the New World: The Role of Ideas in Institutional
and Social Change* (Berkeley: University of California Press, 1988), 140 n13.

of negotiation as the crown clashed with the wide-ranging powers of the church and powerful warrior and landed aristocrats. By the sixteenth century, the Spanish vision of global imperialism derived in part from an understanding of the king as the source of justice, a role which challenged the ambitions of another set of violent men – the conquistadors in the Americas.[2]

Dating back to the 1512 Laws of Burgos, the crown created additional laws applicable to their empire haphazardly. This never amounted up to a comprehensive criminal law code. Not without controversy, the Spanish king, Carlos IV, approved a new compilation of the laws relating to his empire in 1791. While these and other law codes set out different types of punishments for viceregal subjects depending on their lineage, in practice it is not clear that sentencing judges carried penalties out as the written sources intended.[3]

Although localized and paternalistic, with deliberately overlapping jurisdictions, the Novohispanic judiciary still had a fearful strength, which it exercised in response to any threat of civil unrest, such as when rumors of conspiracies circulated in the early seventeenth century.[4] Another harsh reaction occurred after the 1692 uprising in Mexico City. These riots and the burning of a section of the viceregal palace led to brutal punishments for the perpetrators, which were meant to terrify the populace into quiescence.[5] Eighteenth-century reforms and consolidations strengthened the vindictive might of the courts and especially sought to control banditry in the countryside.[6]

Whether sentencing an individual to death or just humiliating them with a public feathering applied on top of sticky syrup, Spanish justice followed typical European standards of the day in its violence and severity. Over the course of centuries, capital punishment demonstrated that monarchs executed divine justice within their Christian-centered world view. As nation states, including Spain, solidified around the judiciary, the power of rulers to execute some of their subjects reaffirmed that

[2] Joseph F. O'Callaghan, *A History of Medieval Spain* (Ithaca, NY: Cornell University Press, 2013), 57–67.
[3] Colin MacLachlan, *Criminal Justice in Eighteenth-Century Mexico* (Berkeley and Oakland: University of California Press, 1974), 2–7, 38–39, opening quote on pages 13–14. See Part V for more on this topic.
[4] Pablo Miguel Sierra Silva, *Urban Slavery in Colonial Mexico: Puebla de Los Ángeles, 1531–1706* (New York: Cambridge University Press, 2018), 158–162.
[5] Cope, *The Limits of Racial Domination*, 154–160.
[6] Adriana Terán Enríquez, *Justicia y Crimen en la Nueva España Siglo XVIII* (Mexico City: Porrua, 2017), 64.

vindicating royal honor required carrying out a terrifying display of the king's rage.[7] Hangings, beheadings, and torture functioned as educational spectacles for the masses, demonstrating that the ruler had the right to exercise public vengeance for publicly known crimes against him and his laws. In 1734, King Felipe V confirmed that robbers and thieves should be executed by garroting, even if no injuries or deaths occurred. Even after the writings of the most celebrated eighteenth-century jurist, Cesare Beccaria, which philosophized on reforming the criminal justice system, appeared in Spanish in 1774, Benito Feijoo defended the death penalty, arguing that it offered the only way to prevent the "multiplying bad deeds of evildoers." However, Feijoo and other Spanish Enlightenment figures argued that torture did not have the same efficacy.[8] In the same era, Catholic religious organizations reminded spectators that even men climbing the gallows had souls and deserved compassion.[9]

The judicial institutions that had the most influence on Mexico City during the years before and after the Dongo massacre were the *audiencia* and its affiliated *Real Sala del Crimen*, as well as the tribunal called the Acordada. Through the actions of these courts, the Novohispanic viceroys asserted their control over acceptable forms of violence in New Spain.

THE AUDIENCIA AND REAL SALA DEL CRIMEN

Founded in 1527 and presided over by the viceroy in the role of its president as of 1536, the Audiencia, in a sense the supreme court of New Spain, coexisted with a variety of competing municipal and royal structures that originated out of fourteenth- and fifteenth-century Spanish institutions.[10] These other sources of authority and justice included a town council (*cabildo* or *ayuntamiento*) led by the *alcalde de primer voto* (official of the first vote), who was a type of city mayor. A second office with judicial powers was the *corregidor*, another leading royal institution with jurisdiction over Mexico City. The viceregal office

---

[7] Alejandro Cañeque, "The Emotions of Power: Love, Anger, and Fear, or How to Rule the Spanish Empire," in *Emotions and Daily Life in Colonial Mexico*, eds. Javier Villa-Flores and Sonya Lipsett-Rivera (Albuquerque: University of New Mexico Press, 2014), 89–121; Haslip-Viera, *Crime and Punishment*, 101–102.

[8] Terán Enríquez, *Justicia y Crimen*, 13, 124–127, quote on 124. Some Spaniards supported Beccaria, see Haslip-Viera, *Crime and Punishment*, 43.

[9] Adriano Prosperi, *Crime and Forgiveness: Christianizing Execution in Medieval Europe*, trans. Jeremy Carden (Cambridge, MA : Belknap, 2020), 15–23, 45–51.

[10] MacLachlan, *Criminal Justice*, 9–10; Haslip-Viera, *Crime and Punishment*, 43–44; Lozano Armendares, *La Criminalidad*, 155–158.

overlapped with that of the Mexico City *corregidor*.[11] Additional governmental structures ranged from the *Juzgado General de Indios* (the General Indian Court), presided over by the viceroy, to the 1771 addition of intermediary regional bureaucrats, known as intendants, between the *corregidor* and the viceroy. Lower-level courts (*alcaldías ordinarias* and *mayores*) provided the first point of contact for litigants who wished to settle their disputes in cases when verbal negotiation had not succeeded or if the seriousness of the offense demanded prosecution. Lastly, the Audiencia had a *sala de crimen* (criminal court) starting in 1568, which functioned as a court of appeals with oversight over other judicial officials throughout the viceroyalty.[12] Its four or five members were called *oidores* ("one who listened").[13] The cabildo, *corregidor*, and the civil branch of the Audiencia all had political duties that took time away from enforcing criminal law. For example, the cabildo, manned by American-born creoles and European-born Spaniards, funded the efforts to increase the orderliness and general upkeep of the city, financed by taxes and income from city-owned properties.[14]

The Audiencia often stepped in to rule the viceroyalty in transition periods between viceroys. Its *sala de crimen* handled prolonged criminal investigations and trials for the most serious offenses, including murder.[15] Although the Audiencia official jurisdiction only comprised a fifteen-mile radius around the capital, this court signed off on all death sentences throughout New Spain. The Audiencia also prosecuted offenders brought in by volunteer night patrols. In the late eighteenth century, the Audiencia maintained one of the three jails in Mexico City. Known as the *cárcel del corte* (court jail), it imprisoned approximately 218 men and women in 1790. The other two jails were affiliated with the Acordada and the town council. The *cárcel del corte* and the court itself sat within the viceregal

---

[11] Carlos E. Castañeda, "The Corregidor in Spanish Colonial Administration," *The Hispanic American Historical Review*, vol. 9: 4 (1929), 446–470; Manfredini, "The Political Role," 31; Alejandro Cañeque, *The King's Living Image: The Culture and Politics of Viceregal Power in Colonial Mexico* (New York: Routledge, 2004), 70–75.

[12] Patricio Hidalgo Nuchera, *Antes de la Acordada: La Represión de la Criminalidad Rural en el México Colonial (1550–1750)* (Sevilla: University of Sevilla, 2013), 24–25.

[13] For the makeup of the Audiencia, see Lozano Armendares, *La Criminalidad*, 162–165.

[14] The crown of Castile appointed *corregidores* with oversight over specific towns in the early fourteenth century. The first *audiencias*, with civil and criminal jurisdiction in different *salas*, began in the late fourteenth century and began its criminal prosecutions in Mexico City in 1554. There was also a "separate Indian judicial structure." See MacLachlan, *Criminal Justice*, 9–12, 21–24, quote on 25; Lozano Armendares, *La Criminalidad*, 155–158; Haslip-Viera, *Crime and Punishment* 44–45.

[15] Terán Enríquez, *Justicia y Crimen*, 57.

palace until 1831, although the viceroy's control over the Audiencia waned by the eighteenth century. Its physical position underscored the Audiencia's status as the highest court of appeal in New Spain and the Spanish focus on justice as a central facet of their rule. If a litigant did not achieve their desired results in a case before the Audiencia, they could only appeal to the Council of the Indies in Spain or the king himself.[16]

THE ACORDADA

In the last several decades of Spanish rule in Mexico, the Acordada functioned to cut through the confusing and sometimes corrupt courts and offices described above. This branch of the judiciary derived from the *Santa Hermandad*, the "Holy Brotherhood" of late medieval Spain. In the last few decades of the fifteenth century, Queen Isabel reformed an already ancient semi-vigilante volunteer municipal and rural police force. Her successors continued to reform this organization into the seventeenth century.[17]

The creation of the Mexican Acordada represented one of the strongest judicial reforms of the eighteenth century and it became the most powerful court of the era.[18] The process began with the rebirth of the *Santa Hermandad* in New Spain in 1710 after several false starts during the first two centuries of Spanish rule.[19] The Acordada initially focused on roaming bandits in rural areas, a problem that escalated in the late seventeenth century.[20] It had jurisdiction extending far into the northern and southern regions of New Spain. All but 5 percent of the patrolmen employed by the Acordada were voluntary and unpaid.[21] The viceroy separated out the *Santa Hermandad* from the Audiencia in 1719, founding the *Tribunal de la Real Acordada*. It existed for the next ninety-three years, acting as a strong and violent arm to impose viceregal law and

---

[16] The Audiencia received criticism for not controlling bandits on the rural roads, as well as in the capital city itself. Valeria Sánchez Michel, *Usos y Funcionamiento de la Cárcel novohispana: El Caso de la Real Cárcel de Corte a finales del siglo XVIII* (Mexico City: Colegio de México, 2008), 9, 33–54, 83; Hidalgo Nuchera, *Antes de la Acordada*, 26; Manfredini, "The Political Role," 35–37; Terán Enríquez, *Justicia y Crimen* 60–61.

[17] Terán Enríquez, *Justicia y Crimen*, 67–73.   [18] MacLachlan, *Criminal Justice*, 36.

[19] Hidalgo Nuchera, *Antes de la Acordada*, 31–84, sums up the early history of law enforcement *hermandades* (brotherhoods) in Spain and New Spain. A briefer survey can be found in Terán Enríquez, *Justicia y Crimen* 73–79.

[20] Hidalgo Nuchera, *Antes de la Acordada*, 27, 107–143.

[21] MacLachlan, *Criminal Justice*, 58–60. In the 1790s, salaries for around 110 agents come from a liquor tax.

order. At its beginning, after more than a dozen years of disputes and negotiations, this court gained jurisdiction over urban areas in 1756 and had its own patrols and jail in Mexico City. As in Queen Isabel's day, a key reason for establishing the Acordada in New Spain was to remind subjects of the crown's authority, but in practice it seemed to operate with almost no oversight from the viceroy or the Audiencia. Even Viceroy Revillagigedo himself underestimated its fearful might – his attempts to limit its powers were reversed after he left New Spain.[22]

The Acordada cultivated a fearful reputation and focused all of its energy into suppressing property and violent crimes, as well as illegal *pulque* sales and theft of livestock. Its name comes from the "agreement" or *acuerdo* by which the viceroy and the Audiencia decided that this court could issue its own death sentences without informing the *Real Sala del Crimen*. As such, this court answered only to the viceroy, although the viceroys often complained about its overextended powers. The Audiencia immediately regretted this agreement. From its first revitalized years and well into the 1790s, the Acordada captured and executed bandits with brutal speed.[23] Over the course of the century, the tribunal imprisoned just under 63,000 individuals, sentenced 30 percent of them to forced labor in presidios, and executed approximately 1 percent or 888 people. Roughly 35,000 of those arrested by the Acordada spent short periods of time incarcerated or suffered public lashings. Even with this intimidating record, provincial authorities at times roused the courage to oppose the Acordada. This court also handled disputes with the Audiencia over jurisdiction and death sentences.[24]

REFORMS BEFORE THE DONGO MASSACRE

The institution of the Acordada, with its autonomous and centralized authority, initiated the judicial reforms which took place in the second half of the eighteenth century, eventually leading toward new law enforcement institutions in the 1790s. In 1776, during the era of the first Viceroy

---

[22] Paul J. Vanderwood, *Disorder and Progress: Bandits, Police, and Mexican Development* (Wilmington, DE: Scholarly Resources, 1992), 18–19; Hidalgo Nuchera, *Antes de la Acordada*, 158–160; Manfredini, "The Political Role," 37; Terán Enríquez, *Justicia y Crimen*, 118, 137.

[23] Terán Enríquez, *Justicia y Crimen*, xxv, 84.

[24] MacLachlan, *Criminal Justice*, 10–11, 26–27, 32–36, 53–57, 69–70, 79, 95–97, 114; Lozano Armendares, *La Criminalidad*, 160–162; Hidalgo Nuchera, *Antes de la Acordada*, 145–158.

Revillagigedo, the Acordada attempted to formalize its ad hoc procedures with regulations for imprisonment, trials, and executions. The Acordada had more resources to pay for its jail and officers in the 1770s due to oversight over "prohibited drinks" and an increase in the tax on *pulque*. Later in the decade, the Acordada discontinued the practice of selling its prisoners off to work in businesses such as bakeries, butchers, and sugar mills.[25] Penalties shifted to working on construction projects, street cleaning, or the ancient sentence of rowing for the king. In 1782, a year after rebuilding its jail after the devastating earthquakes of the mid-1770s, Manuel Antonio de Santa María started his twenty-six-year term as the judge of the Acordada. Under his leadership, the agents of the Acordada arrested close to 43,000 individuals, sending almost 25 percent of them to forced labor in presidios and carrying out 246 death sentences.[26]

Also in 1782, the Mexico City council divided the city into thirty-two *cuarteles*, each with an unpaid, unarmed, honorary *alcalde del barrio* to patrol his own neighborhood. Within this new system, there were eight major districts called *cuarteles mayores*, with leading judicial officials in each one (*alcaldes ordinarios*), and a corps of armed guards who also did rounds.[27] Along with the *corregidor*, the magistrates of the *cuarteles mayores* ran tribunals that issued rapid verbal judgments on nightly disputes – that is, the thousands of cases listed in an important documentary source known as the *Libros de Reos*. In reaction to the Dongo murders, Viceroy Revillagigedo added a ninth municipal court and a new force of paid nightwatchmen in 1790.[28]

However intimidating these courts were in their era, their reach was extremely limited in contrast to more recent judicial systems. Historians have shown that, in general, many Novohispanic subjects of all ranks and

[25] For a summary of this abusive and money-making practice, see Haslip-Viera, *Crime and Punishment*, 106–112.

[26] MacLachlan, *Criminal Justice*, 71–76; Lozano Armendares, *La Criminalidad*, 161. Perhaps his teenage son gleaned some sense of these efforts and continued to carry them out in his viceregency. See also Terán Enríquez, *Justicia y Crimen*, 79–82, 92, 96–97, 111, 117–118. For work and living conditions as a convict laborer, see Haslip-Viera, *Crime and Punishment*, 116–125.

[27] Lozano Armendares, *La Criminalidad*, 18–26; Haslip-Viera, *Crime and Punishment*, 47.

[28] Germeten, *Enlightened Patrolman*, covers the three decades of the history of the Novohispanic "lantern guards." See also Michael Scardaville, "(Hapsburg) Law and (Bourbon) Order: State Authority, Popular Unrest, and the Criminal Justice System in Bourbon Mexico City," *The Americas*, vol. 4 (April 1994); and MacLachlan, *Criminal Justice*, 114.

backgrounds knew how to negotiate the judicial system effectively to achieve their own goals.[29] But the opportunities to evade justice should not be exaggerated. Personalized negotiation in court did not flourish when the Audiencia and the Acordada combined in the late eighteenth century to crack down harshly on banditry and urban crimes such as family-based killings and robbery. The Dongo killers must have had some sense that their society did not tolerate homicide, theft, and the disruption of social hierarchies, but perhaps hoped that they could slip through the cracks and disappear. Unless they had not noticed the decades-long judicial offensive taken against banditry and other property crimes, they should have realized that, if they were arrested, they would suffer horrific consequences. With an energetic judge in charge of the investigation, the perpetrators could not hide from their fate.

[29] MacLachlan, *Criminal Justice*, 43, 51–52.

PART III

JUSTICE

7

Investigations

Only hours after discovering the victims' bodies, Emparan initiates investigations in the neighborhood around Dongo's house and other sections of the central city. He also sends out an alert to New Spain's local leaders, calling on judicial officials across the viceroyalty to participate in the search for the perpetrators. Their initial goal is to find witnesses who observed any suspicious activities in the area. Secondly, the judge sought to determine the provenance of the still-unknown murderers' weapons. Emparan's interrogations allow him to create a timeline of events leading up to the Dongo massacre. These initial efforts do not provide the clues necessary to solve the case. However, as gossip spreads throughout the city and the court works hard to find the perpetrators, Emparan's rapid actions encourage Mexico City residents to think carefully about anything unusual that they might witness in the days after the crime. As a result, Emparan identifies and arrests the perpetrators within a few days. The entire process proves the effectiveness of the Novohispanic judiciary.

Immediately after the surgeons finish examining the bodies, Emparan and Luzero gather statements from Dongo's immediate neighbors, ranging from a shoemaker to a wealthy lawyer. No one observed anything particularly revealing, other than a few light sleepers who heard the noises of the coach passing through the Calle de Cordobanes. These initial statements suggest that internal domestic conflicts did not cause the crime. Witnesses assure Emparan that Dongo ran a "harmonious" establishment staffed by quiet and peaceful servants.[1]

Having done their best to gather more information from the residents of the immediate area surrounding Dongo's house, Emparan has Luzero

---

[1] AGN, Mexico, Criminal Vol. 337, Exp. 2, 18–24.

draw up a decree asking for other inhabitants of the city to report any activity that might help solve the crime. The decree demands that the captains of the Acordada question any suspicious individuals, whether they appear to be traveling on foot, by carriage, or on horseback. The loosely organized nightwatchmen corps known as "whistle guards" should also report anything unusual that they saw on the night of the murders. The decree points out the various places people might notice the consequences of the crime: silversmiths might receive stolen goods; carriages might be rented by questionable people; gamblers might have an unusually large amount of money to bet; wounded men might ask for treatment by surgeons; and inns could have suspicious guests.[2]

After questioning some of Mexico City's surgeons, Emparan and Luzero turn to the local knife sharpeners to determine whether they unknowingly prepared the murderers' weapons for their brutal task. The first "master knife grinder" who they question, a twenty-seven-year-old Spanish man from Toluca, reports that in mid-October he had a job request to sharpen three machetes for a butcher. This puts the judge on the alert, so he calls in the butcher, a fifty-nine-year-old Spaniard, who provides the court with the receipt for the transaction. The court also tracks down the young knife grinder who actually did the work. After wasting time on this dead end, Emparan and Luzero question seven other knife grinders and two blacksmiths. All of them report very little activity other than trivial domestic jobs sharpening scissors, razors, pocketknives and the like.[3] After spending the weekend losing precious hours listening to these unhelpful statements, the judge must have felt very discouraged. Emparan could only hope for witnesses to come to the court with more clues.

By 1:00 p.m. on October 24, Emparan and Luzero compose another document with the goal of starting a *cordillera* in the towns surrounding the capital. The term *cordillera* refers to an information-spreading process put into effect in emergencies – most notably during large-scale rebellions.[4] Each government official outside Mexico City who receives this written command from the judge has to create another document confirming that he has read the missive and will carry out its mandates to the best of his ability. Then he must document that he has passed the

---

[2] AGN, Mexico, Criminal Vol. 337, Exp. 2, 27–29.

[3] AGN, Mexico, Criminal Vol. 337, Exp. 2, 33–42.

[4] For analysis of another *cordillera*, see Elizabeth Penry, "Letters of Insurrection: The Rebellion of the Communities (Charcas, 1781)," in *Colonial Lives: Documents on Latin American History, 1550–1850*, eds. Richard Boyer and Geoffrey Spurling (Oxford: Oxford University Press, 1999), 201–215.

decree on to the next settlement. Ultimately, the collection of documents created by each of these local administrators returns to the capital. This paper trail proves that provincial officials take their positions seriously and obey Spanish leaders.

Emparan's order emanates out of Mexico City, initiating multiple chains of information across the viceroyalty, resembling a web as the communication stretches out in four directions.[5] The missive moves through different population centers, carried by different types of couriers: "extraordinary mail," regular mail, or messengers who just happen to be on hand. Many of the locations do not even have a judge or scribe in residence. Even so, someone in an official capacity still manages to respond and continue the *cordillera*. In these understaffed towns and villages, an all-purpose Spanish functionary carries out the command. Dozens of pages in the Dongo file testify to this cascading display of obedience to the judicial authorities in the viceregal capital. Through the *cordillera* process, over a period of six weeks, knowledge of the massacre extends across the landscape of New Spain.

In the document that starts the *cordillera*, Emparan calls on all of the Novohispanic judiciary to act quickly, cooperatively, and obediently in order to solve the murders. He describes the killings as "inhumane and cruel deaths," and presents Dongo as "a distinguished republican and merchant resident in this city," who was killed alongside his entire family. Emparan orders the provincial officials to arrest "anyone whosoever presents the most minimal suspicion of being a fugitive." If they encounter such a person, they must take a statement asking where they come from, making an efficient, accurate, and punctual report back to the royal criminal court. Emparan urges his colleagues to help him punish this "horrible and heinous crime, and prevent and teach a lesson" to other potential wrongdoers. To encourage a speedy response, he asks that the recipient in each locale note when they receive his letter, and when they pass it on to the next settlement. He orders them to continue the *cordillera* as rapidly as possible.[6]

Emparan simultaneously sends out four exact copies of this mandate to three different towns outside of Mexico City. Once received in the initial stop, the document moves on to the next town as the team of messengers

[5] For distance and communications in the Spanish viceroyalties, see Sylvia Sellers-Garcia, *Distance and Documents at the Spanish Empire's Periphery* (Stanford, CA: Stanford University Press, 2013).
[6] AGN, Criminal Vol. 338, Exp. 1, 78.

slowly fan outward to the outlying regions of the viceroyalty.[7] Only three hours after Emparan signs his decree, two of the four couriers make their first stop in Tacuba, just over four miles west of the center of Mexico City. Today, a metro rider can make this journey in less than a half an hour, riding ten stops on the metro's blue line.[8] Around 4:30 p.m. on October 24, 1789, the Tacuba official confirms that he has received two copies of Emparan's message.[9] Back in the central city, a third messenger heads north, walking roughly nineteen miles. He arrives at Cuautitlán at noon on Sunday, October 25. The fourth and final courier proceeds to the northeast. He does not pass on the document until four days later, after arriving in Otumba, which is only ten miles away from Mexico City's Plaza Mayor.[10]

Returning to October 24: after two of Emparan's letters reach Tacuba, this branch of the *cordillera* separates into two separate arms. One messenger carries the document in northwesterly direction. Several different couriers pass on the document until eventually it reaches its final destination of Pénjamo in early November of 1789. On modern roads, 220 miles separate Tacuba and Pénjamo, located in the modern state of Guanajuato. However, because Emparan's document stops in towns along the way, the journey becomes 150 miles longer. The various messengers on this particular leg of the *cordillera* must journey up and down mountains for more than ten thousand feet of altitude gain and loss. During this arduous trip, the letter passes through the indigenous towns of Tlalnepantla, Tepotzlán, and Huehuetoca, before proceeding further west to regional agricultural settlements and important administrative centers including Querétaro, San Miguel, León, and Celaya. Toward the end of the journey, officials in the booming mining town of Guanajuato receive the information about the Dongo massacre.[11]

The second copy that Emparan initially sends to Tacuba also proceeds further west. It eventually ends up in Valladolid, now Morelia, the seat of the massive viceregal diocese of Michoacán. This journey (only 167 miles on modern highways – about four hours on a luxury bus today), in 1789, requires seventeen grueling days on foot or mule through very mountainous

[7] Sellers-Garcia, *Distance*, 81–86.
[8] See https://mexicometro.org/metro/metro-line-2/ accessed September 14, 2021.
[9] AGN, Criminal Vol. 338, Exp. 1, 79, 94.   [10] AGN, Criminal Vol. 338, Exp. 1, 84, 105.
[11] Several different officials confirm receipt of the message in AGN, Criminal Vol. 338, Exp. 1, 79–84.

terrain.[12] The couriers first travel west to the breathlessly high-altitude city of Toluca (over 8,700 feet above sea level), in the general direction of Valladolid. The letter then dips far to the south, passing through Malinalco and Sultepec. The final exhausting leg from Huétamo to Valladolid requires five-days trekking through regions that even today shelter no major towns. The message does not make it to the seat of the diocese of Michoacán until November 10. By then, the case is closed.[13]

The third *cordillera* branch grows out of Cuautitlán on October 25 with an ultimate destination of the northern silver-mining town of San Luis Potosí. On modern toll roads, one could drive between these two towns in approximately five hours. In 1789, the message does not arrive in San Luis Potosí for sixteen days. In order to spread the news to several different towns in the modern states of Mexico, Hidalgo, Querétaro, and Guanajuato, the messengers working this branch of the *cordillera* zig zag across the mountainous landscape north of the viceregal capital. This adds at least an extra two hundred miles to the journey. Instead of heading in a general northwest direction toward San Luis Potosí, the message detours dramatically south from Zumpango back to Tula. Then it doglegs through higher altitude terrain to Zimapán after stopping in Ixmiquilpan. Another swerve happens when the courier climbs into the Sierra Gorda and the town of Cadarete (now Cadereyta de Montes), before finally embarking on the more direct road from San Luis de la Paz to San Luis Potosí. This last leg demands a full week's journey. Once the officials confirm receipt of the message at its final destination on November 9, all of the documents return to Mexico City, without stopping for any further check-ins at any other towns. Emparan receives the confirmations from this branch of the *cordillera* at the capital on November 16.[14]

The fourth and final *cordillera* goes incredibly slowly to reach its end point in the city of Zacatlán, in the modern state of Puebla. Although this town, as the crow flies, is only about one hundred miles northeast of the capital, the message does not arrive there until five weeks after the murder. During the entire month of November, this fourth copy of Emparan's mandate journeys well over eight hundred miles, making a huge circle to the northeast of Mexico City, and almost reaching the Gulf. Couriers

---

[12] For a detailed account of roads and travel conditions, see Rachel A. Moore, *Forty Miles from the Sea: Xalapa, the Public Sphere, and the Atlantic World in Nineteenth-Century Mexico* (Tucson: University of Arizona Press, 2011).

[13] AGN, Criminal Vol. 338, Exp. 1, 96–103.

[14] AGN, Criminal Vol. 338, Exp. 1, 88–93.

carry the paper from the judge through the damp, hot lowlands in the modern state of Veracruz to the breathless chilly mountains of the Sierra Gorda.[15] Finally, this effort becomes pointless. On December 1, the official in Zacatlán observes: "From the *Gazeta* [a periodical published in Mexico City], it is publicly known and notorious that the aggressors who killed Don Joaquín Dongo have been apprehended, so this message should be returned to the *señor* Judge."[16]

This complex web of communication demonstrates that provincial authorities respected and perhaps even feared the Mexico City-based viceregal judiciary. Roughly eighty different officials and notaries process the four copies of the mandate that move along these four *cordilleras* during the five weeks after Emparan sends them from his office in the central city. Each official takes the judge's commands very seriously and strives to prove his efficiency. As directed, almost all of them record when they receive the message and when they send it on to the next town or village.

Responding rapidly to the emergency orders from the capital, local authorities seem to enthusiastically work odd hours. For example, the messenger working the first branch of the *cordillera* arrives at Tlanepantla, just to the north of the capital, at 10:45 p.m. on October 24. By 9:30 the next morning, a Sunday, the command has already traveled another fourteen miles to the north to Cuautitlán. Other timestamps suggest that some of the messengers traveled through the night. The official in Aculco confirms that he received Emparan's message at 8:00 p.m. on Monday, October 26. By 8:15 p.m. that same night, he sends another courier on to San Juan del Rio. Starting his journey in complete darkness, this messenger arrives at his destination, which is almost thirty miles away, at 8:30 a.m. on October 27. Either he had a fast horse, or he walked a steady two to three miles an hour all night long.[17]

By recording when they receive Emparan's command and when they sent it on, the local authorities prove their obedience to the viceroy. Some pass it on within fifteen minutes, and others delay no more than two hours, perhaps searching for a trustworthy messenger. Only rarely does the message stay overnight without moving on to the next town.[18] Whoever writes the confirmation of receipt, a judge, a scribe, or any other available official, typically includes a statement pledging how seriously they take this task:

---

[15] AGN, Criminal Vol. 338, Exp. 1, 105–111.   [16] AGN, Criminal Vol. 338, Exp. 1, 112.
[17] AGN, Criminal Vol. 338, Exp. 1, 79–81.   [18] AGN, Criminal Vol. 338, Exp. 1, 100.

With extreme enthusiasm, zeal, and efficiency we will question all travelers who present even the slightest suspicion, arresting them, taking their statements, and asking them their destinations . . .. Each official dedicates himself to carrying out the most effective procedures in order to apprehend the aggressors who perpetrated the homicides.[19]

According to the documents sent back to Emparan, only one snafu took place in the entire six-week-long *cordillera* process. On the morning of October 30, an "indio correo [indigenous messenger]" sets off from Cadereyta traveling to San Luis de la Paz. A few hours later, he returns, not knowing the correct path. The Cadereyta-based official tracks down a soldier to do the job instead. This second messenger arrives at San Luis de la Paz, about one hundred miles away, three days later, on November 2, 1789.[20]

Emparan and Luzero initiate all of this activity across the viceroyalty only sixteen hours after the crime occurred. They also work hard throughout the weekend of October 24 and 25 questioning witnesses. Perhaps due to their persistence and diligence, or perhaps just by luck, the famous clue that quickly solves the case falls into their hands on Monday, October 26, just three days after the massacre. This minuscule piece of evidence has obsessed writers for almost two hundred years – even more than the bloody scene of the crime, the piles of stolen pesos, and the many other fascinating and ridiculous clues uncovered during these investigations. All of these details pale in comparison to the compulsion to interpret this "crime of the century" as revolving around *one drop of blood*.

---

[19] AGN, Criminal Vol. 338, Exp. 1, 83, 85.   [20] AGN, Criminal Vol. 338, Exp. 1, 91–92.

8

The Drop of Blood

For many writers, one singular clue symbolizes the Dongo massacre and its rapid resolution by the Novohispanic judiciary. One tiny bloodstain played a critical role in the events that took place from October 23 to November 7.[1] Why the enduring fixation on this drop of blood instead of the many other pieces of evidence compiled during the investigation?

This famous red mark first appears in the written record at 5:30 p.m. on October 26, 1789. A man named Don Gerónimo Covarrubias comes to Emparan's chambers to report a strange observation that he made on the afternoon of October 24. On this fateful Saturday, Covarrubias strolled on the Calle de Santa Clara with a friend, Don Antonio Medina, to another friend's house for a meal. They approached a group of three men having a conversation about the Dongo massacre. Covarrubias recognized one of them as a watchmaker from Madrid who owned a shop on the Calle de San Francisco. He knew the second man slightly. It was the third man who caused Covarrubias the most distress. This unknown person was wearing a hair tie around his ponytail that was stained with a drop of fresh blood, slightly larger than a lentil. Covarrubias connected this mark with the recent homicides, already the subject of gossip. Before coming to Emparan, he sought advice from a trusted friend, who advised him to report the observation.[2]

After hearing Covarrubias's report, the judge immediately calls the watchmaker, Don Ramón Blasio, in for questioning. Blasio, who also volunteers as a neighborhood *alcalde*, identifies the man with the

---

[1] This clue may have influenced the title of Enrique Flores Esquivel and Adriana Sandoval, eds., *Un Sombrero Negro Salpicado de Sangre: Narrativa criminal del siglo XIX* (Mexico City: Universidad Nacional Autónoma de México, 2008).

[2] AGN, Mexico, Criminal Vol. 337, Exp. 2, Part 2, 1–2.

bloodstain as Don Felipe Aldama, who lives on the crowded street known as the *Alcaicería*. Blasio knows that Aldama recently spent time in the Acordada jail for another homicide. Ultimately, the court had absolved him of the crime. When Emparan orders Blasio to find Aldama and escort him to Emparan's chambers, the prime suspect is nowhere to be found. Emparan sends out Don Vicente Elizalde, a captain employed by the royal criminal court (in a role similar to a sheriff's deputy today), to bring back the hair tie. Elizalde finds two hair ties in Aldama's lodgings. Luzero examines them and documents his observations in his case notes. The notary agrees that the thicker tie has a stain on it that looks like blood. He comes to this conclusion even though the stain has a dusting of hair powder over it.[3]

Covarrubias's statement leads to Aldama's first interrogation by Emparan, after a group of soldiers track down the suspect.[4] Aldama's testimony opens with a brief biography. After learning about his background, the judge asks Aldama to describe his activities on the afternoon of October 24. Aldama says that he went to the cockfights and spent time with Don Joaquín Blanco. Luzero makes a careful note of this associate. Emparan then prompts Aldama to detail when he learned about the Dongo homicides and from whom. Aldama replies that at 8:30 a.m. on Saturday he had a conversation with Don Ramón Blasio. As they stood outside on the Calle de Refugio, a "galleguito [small Gallegan man]" approached them. The *Galleguito* said, "Man, they say that Dongo and his whole family were killed!" The three men then decided to ask about the murders at the Acordada court. The judge there confirmed the news. Considering Aldama's dealings with this court since the mid-1780s, related to the accusation of murder, it seems odd that he would want to return to a building where he endured imprisonment and was made to defend himself from serious accusations. But True Crime fans will remember the modern theory that killers enjoy involving themselves in law enforcement activities. And perhaps Aldama views his last trial as proof that he could work the judiciary to his advantage.

Returning to the interrogation, Emparan probes Aldama for more information about his Saturday activities. Aldama responds that he talked about the Dongo case with Blasio and another acquaintance in the cemetery of the Santa Clara convent. Aldama also mentions stopping by the

[3] AGN, Mexico, Criminal Vol. 337, Exp. 2, Part 2, 2–4.
[4] Pablo Rodríguez, "Crímenes coloniales: codicia y crueldad en el asesinato del señor Dongo y sus dependientes (Ciudad de México, 1789)," *Historia y Sociedad*, vol. 40 (2021), 50.

lodgings of Don Baltasar Dávila Quintero, a lieutenant in the Canary Islands militia, before continuing on to the cockfights. Once again, the court pays very close attention to this mention of another associate.[5]

Emparan now begins to interrogate Aldama more aggressively, pushing for an emotional reaction through a rapid series of confusing questions:

On Saturday afternoon, were you wearing the same clothes that you have on now? Do you recognize this hair tie? Why did it have a fresh blood stain on it at 3 p.m.? Why do you look so upset? Why is your hair so messy?

Aldama responds evasively:

Yes, I am in the same clothes, although I changed my vest. I am not sure if that is blood. I do not know if this alleged blood causes me any agitation. But yes, this is an atrocious case.

Given his prior acquittal on another homicide charge, Aldama possesses a certain confidence when answering these questions, at least for the moment. He knows that, so far, a single bloodstain is not enough evidence for Emparan to accuse him of eleven murders. He doesn't even admit that he recognizes the hair ribbon yet.

In a classic move for a Novohispanic judge, Emparan decides to call Don Gerónimo Covarrubias back in for a *careo*, a judicial interrogation process which involved Aldama and Covarrubias making their statements face-to-face. As judges tried to resolve any discrepancies in the testimonies of witnesses and defendants, *careos* often produced more truthful statements because men of honor in this time and place felt very offended if they acquired a reputation for lying. Calling an honorable man a liar ranked among the worst possible insults and could provoke violent reactions.[6]

After swearing to tell the truth, Don Gerónimo confirms his previous statement about seeing the drop of blood. The judge then asks Aldama to take another look at the hair tie. Finally, Aldama admits that he recognizes it. Emparan points out the red stain and asks why it is covered in hair powder, which Aldama does not use. Aldama explains that he found the tie a few weeks back while he was at the theater. He picked it up because it

[5] AGN, Mexico, Criminal Vol. 337, Exp. 2, Part 2, 6.
[6] See Zeb Tortorici, "Heran Todos Putos: Sodomitical Subcultures and Disordered Desire in Early Colonial Mexico," *Ethnohistory*, vol. 54: 1 (2007), 35–67, especially 38, 60 n12; Lee M. Penyak, "Midwives and Legal Medicine in México, 1740–1846," *Journal of Hispanic Higher Education*, vol. 1: 3 (2002), 254; and Germeten, *Violent Delights, Violent Ends*, 54–102.

looked better than the one he wore at that moment, despite the dusting of powder left by a previous owner. Emparan presses him for more information about the bloodstain. Aldama replies:

I went to the cockfights that morning. Blood might have dripped on me because the owners of the dead cocks lift them over the heads of the spectators sitting on the benches.[7]

The judge mentally files away this unconvincing excuse, choosing to reveal his knowledge of blood spatter patterns a bit later, at a more strategic moment for solving the case.

Instead, Emparan shifts the line of questioning, asking Aldama about other items that Captain Elizalde found in his lodgings when he went to retrieve the hair tie. The judge asks: Why did you have several empty money bags in your lodgings? Why were there ropes and cords found with the bags? Why did these objects have blood on them? Aldama explains that all of these objects were related to his previous work as a mine administrator for the wealthy mine owner José Samper in Cuautla de Amilpas (an important sugar-producing region now in the state of Morelos where the defendant actually first made the acquaintance of his victim).[8] He argues that a mule might have bled on the ropes and that the stain looks very old.

Changing the subject again, Emparan continues the interrogation. He mixes questions about Aldama's clothes with aggressive grilling about his source of income, another common line of inquiry in viceregal court cases. If a judge could figure out where a suspicious person's money came from, usually they could make a convincing argument for criminal behavior. The viceregal judiciary knows that a craving for material goods in order to present oneself well in public often motivates lawbreaking or defying the era's moral codes.[9] So Emparan asks:

How do you manage to support yourself so that you look so respectable? Where are your white linens? Where are your outer colored clothes? Where is the vest that you were wearing on Saturday?

---

[7] Quotes on AGN, Mexico, Criminal Vol. 337, Exp. 2, Part 2, 6–7.

[8] For the economic importance of this region for the powerful Mexican *consulado*, of which Dongo was a member, see Ernesto Sánchez Santiró, "Comerciantes, Mineros, y Hacendados: La Integración de los Mercaderes del Consulado de México en la Propiedad Minera y Azucarera de Cuernavaca y Cuautla de Amilpas (1750–1821)," in *Mercaderes, Comercio y Consulados de Nueva España en el Siglo XVIII*, ed. Guillermina de Valle Pavón (Mexico City: Instituto Mora, 2003), 150–190. This essay also details Samper's production in the years that he employed Aldama.

[9] Robert Buffington, *Criminal and Citizen in Modern Mexico* (Lincoln: University of Nebraska Press, 2000), Chapter One.

Aldama explains that he takes his clothes to a family of sisters on the Calle de Tacuba who do his laundry. He also lists the recent gifts of money that he has received from his friends, and his cousin, the Marquis of Villar de la Águila.[10]

Emparan continues to push Aldama about his lack of employment. He also reveals that Dongo's surviving nephew, Don Miguel Lanuza, has testified that Aldama came to their warehouse to negotiate what Dongo might pay for some beans for sale. Don Miguel claims that he saw Aldama walking down the Calle de Cordobanes on the same day that the suspect allegedly spoke to Lanuza's deceased uncle. Aldama vehemently denies this testimony. After this statement, Emparan calls for a break from the interrogations.[11]

Returning later the same day, the judge calls in Don Ramón Blasio again, who he suspects may have some involvement in the massacre. After his last session with Emparan, Don Ramón had been incarcerated in the royal jail. The judge suspected him of some involvement in the murders. However, the watchmaker has a very solid alibi involving several other trustworthy people who also work in law enforcement. In response to a question about his Friday night, Blasio narrates a typical evening in the life of a volunteer *alcalde* (a kind of proto-police officer):

I sat in my watchmaking shop with the notaries Moctezuma and Camargo, gossiping and discussing the latest scandals. Then I did my rounds with the notaries and six *alguaciles* [lower-ranking judicial functionaries]. We had to deal with a complaint until 11 p.m. I dropped off eight women and three men at the public jail, and then went home with the *alguaciles*.[12]

Don Ramón provides more information about his encounter with Aldama in this second interrogation. He says that he came upon Aldama alone in the cemetery on October 24. When Don Ramón approached him, Aldama said, "What does Your Grace have to say about this outrage?" Once again, in hindsight Aldama sounds suspiciously interested in the massacre, questioning this *alcalde* for details. Don Ramón has one more rumor to pass on – he also heard from a silversmith that Aldama pawned six hundred pesos worth of rings and then lost all the money in a popular card game called *monte*.[13] After listening to this information, Emparan

[10] AGN, Mexico, Criminal Vol. 337, Exp. 2, Part 2, 8.
[11] AGN, Mexico, Criminal Vol. 337, Exp. 2, Part 2, 9.
[12] AGN, Mexico, Criminal Vol. 337, Exp. 2, Part 2, 11–12.
[13] Marie Eileen Francois, *A Culture of Everyday Credit: Housekeeping, Pawnbroking, and Governance in Mexico City, 1750–1920* (Lincoln: University of Nebraska Press, 2006).

dismisses this witness with a promise from Don Ramón that he will not leave the city and will respond to any further summons to testify.[14]

For the next two days, Luzero makes note of statements made by a continuous parade of witnesses filing through Emparan's court. These include Aldama and the two men he mentioned as his companions on October 23 and October 24, Blanco and Quintero. Aldama's two servants also testify to his movements during those days. He has the wherewithal to employ two widows, aged 65 and 74, who work as his cook and maid.[15] They both claim that Aldama came home early on Friday night and spent his time playing the flute at their request. By giving their statements, these mature and respectable women help bolster Aldama's reputation as an honorable, blameless man. Emparan also speaks with Blanco's aunt as well as various men who had recent dealings with Aldama. All of the judge's questions seek to ascertain precisely who was where and when, as well as how the prime suspect made his income.

Ultimately, the court returns to the physical evidence, including more bloodstains. Luzero shows Aldama a white cape decorated with gold braid around the neckline and velvet fasteners, along with an old black hat encircled with a black ribbon. Aldama acknowledges that he bought both of these items in 1783. Now Emparan questions him about the wax and bloodstains on the hat and cape. Once again, Aldama's response suggests a fascination with law enforcement. He explains that the last time the Acordada court executed a criminal, he prayed to and lighted candles for the "Lord of Mercy [*Señor de la Misericordia*]." Wax from the candles must have dropped on his hat. He does not own an iron, so he tried to use a heated spoon to remove them. He says that his maids could confirm all of these details.[16]

Emparan presses Aldama regarding the blood. First, the prime suspect says that he suffers from continuous nose bleeds. He holds up his handkerchief to prove this fact. The judge disagrees, pointing out that the nosebleed stains look very different from the splattered stains on the hat. So Aldama's mind naturally returns to his obsession with the judiciary. He changes his approach and declares that he followed the procession of prisoners that took place the previous week. Men sentenced to corporal punishment often received hundreds of lashes, which were administered as they paraded through specific city streets. Aldama

---

[14] AGN, Mexico, Criminal Vol. 337, Exp. 2, Part 2, 12–13.
[15] AGN, Mexico, Criminal Vol. 337, Exp. 2, Part 2, 17–18.
[16] AGN, Mexico, Criminal Vol. 337, Exp. 2, Part 2, 34–35.

explains that he felt two drops of blood land on his face while he observed this public ceremony. Others may have fallen on his hat. Regarding the bloodstained cape, he declares that he had a terrible nosebleed on the night of Tuesday, October 27. The judge could look at his mattress for further proof.[17] Deciding to go no further with this line of questioning, Emparan dismisses Aldama for the moment.

After this interrogation, Emparan finds several other important clues, which solve the case definitively. Bloodstains continue to play a role, but other objects become much more significant. Emparan wants to learn more about Aldama's associates, so he interrogates Quintero, an experienced and worldly man in his fifties, and Blanco, a youth barely out of his teens. What Emparan discovers about Blanco's recent behavior from a variety of trustworthy witnesses suggests that the young man had a tendency to resort to violence. And it appears that Blanco and Aldama have a very close relationship. They spent a series of nights sleeping together around the time of the Dongo massacre. This fact strongly implicates the men in the murders. Blanco admits that he feels very scared throughout his interrogation. Perhaps this was meant as an excuse to explain his false and confused statements, or perhaps it was a ploy to inspire Emparan to pity him as a young, ignorant man.[18]

As the investigation continues, Emparan calls in various witnesses and tries to piece together a timeline. He also closely observes his suspects, homing in on their facial movements, their dress, and other indicators of their current states of mind. The experienced judge does not seem affected by Blanco's dissimulations. He also finds Quintero's testimony highly suspicious. While narrating his biography and giving details of his recent interactions with Aldama, Quintero contradicts himself and his face changes expression rapidly. This alerts the judge to his discomfort under interrogation and inspires Emparan to look further into the older man's recent activities.

Emparan learns that Aldama and Quintero did business as a team with a few different shopkeepers. When brought to the court, the small businessmen testify that the pair pawned and redeemed several items of clothing in the days before and after the massacre. While extremely common among gamblers and other desperate residents of the city, these actions appear suspicious in the context of the timing of the Dongo home invasion.[19]

---

[17] AGN, Mexico, Criminal Vol. 337, Exp. 2, Part 2, 34–35.
[18] AGN, Mexico, Criminal Vol. 337, Exp. 2, Part 2, 14–23.
[19] Lozano Armendares, *La Criminalidad*, 146–149.

Emparan asks one of these pawnbrokers if Aldama appeared disheveled during their interactions, but the witness could only say that he wore shoes without buckles and clean white linen. When interrogated about his financial dealings, Aldama could recite some of the information with confidence, but at other times, he made mistakes.[20]

Motivated by this growing mountain of clues and the revealing emotional behavior on the part of the suspects, Emparan, Luzero, and other judicial officials decide to search Quintero's rented room. When they ask for the key from his landlady, she explains that Quintero just moved all of his belongings to another room located deeper in the interior of the building. Adding a touch of irony to the proceedings, the landlady explains that her tenant told her that he wanted to change rooms because he feared robbers.[21]

When Emparan and his men enter Quintero's previous rented room, they find it emptied of all furnishings and decorations. However, when they lift up some floorboards, they find twenty-three bags of money. Under heavy guard, the money travels by carriage to the viceregal palace where it is counted. It adds up to 21,634 pesos and one real. At this time, a working man might only earn ten or fifteen pesos a month, so this sum represents several lifetimes' worth of income for the average person. In this secret cache, the officials also find gold shoe buckles, a large silver watch, two rosaries, and several pairs of new stockings. Dongo's nephew confirms that all of these items come from Dongo's house or warehouse. In Quintero's new room, they find a bloodstained vest and hat. Lastly, the room contains a thick wooden plank or bar, marked with deep cuts. The court interprets this item as evidence that the suspects practiced their strength and agility in wielding the murder weapons before they raided Dongo's establishment.[22]

Emparan probes Quintero for more information about the clothes and the apparently stolen objects found in his rooms. Quintero first claims that he has never seen the expensive accessories or the stockings before and that he knows nothing about them. He does admit that the vest and hat belong to him.

The judge then asks him about the bloodstains on these objects. Quintero again resorts to denial, effectively insulting Emparan's intelligence with an implausible excuse. He asserts that the marks come from his habit of taking snuff, which causes his nose to expel the dark material seen on his

[20] AGN, Mexico, Criminal Vol. 337, Exp. 2, Part 2, 27–33.
[21] AGN, Mexico, Criminal Vol. 337, Exp. 2, Part 2, 35–36.
[22] AGN, Mexico, Criminal Vol. 337, Exp. 2, Part 2, 35–36.

belongings. The judge now has heard enough nonsensical explanations from these two men. Emparan outright rejects Quintero's ridiculous account: "How can you say this is not blood when the evidence is so clear that there cannot be even the slightest doubt? Also – there are bloodstains all over the door of your room."[23] This direct verbal challenge represents a turning point in the investigations.

This last question and the bloodstains in Quintero's lodgings, *not* the famous *single drop of blood* on Aldama's ribbon, result in the beginning of the murderers' confessions. At this point in the case file, Luzero notes that Quintero has requested Emparan's full attention. This purposeful shift in focus signifies that he now wants to tell the truth. Quintero goes on to provide a detailed confession, implicating Aldama and Blanco.

In response to Quintero's confession, the judge again calls in Aldama. The suspect enters the court, and sees the gold shoe buckles, the silver watch, a snuff box, two rosaries, and other objects on display. At this moment, Aldama utters these fateful words:

The hour for telling the truth has arrived. All of these objects come from Don Joaquín Dongo's house. I killed him and his entire family, with the help of Don Baltazar Dávila Quintero and Don Joaquín Blanco, on the night of October 23.[24]

While the tiny bloodstain on Aldama's hair ribbon led to his arrest and initial interrogation, Emparan and other judicial officials worked hard to manipulate the three prime suspects into confessing. The case was not solved by one genius working alone. Additionally, an assortment of other Mexico City residents, including Blanco's aunt and the managers of the local cockfights, contributed important evidence. The physical evidence was also damaging, most notably the massive sum of pesos found in Quintero's lodgings.

Commentators who focus on the bloodstain present their accounts of the Dongo murders in a knowing, self-congratulatory tone. In a way that hearkens to Sherlock Holmes, the resolution of a horrific crime from an almost invisible red dot assures readers that powerful, rational men such as Emparan do have control over the chaotic world around them. In classic True Crime fashion, the drop of blood proves that order can triumph over evil and mayhem, as long as effective law enforcement

---

[23] AGN, Mexico, Criminal Vol. 337, Exp. 2, Part 2, 39–40.
[24] AGN, Mexico, Criminal Vol. 337, Exp. 2, Part 2, 40, 43.

takes the right action in reaction to the physical clues and other data. This singular focus on the bloodstain underscores that the True Crime genre ultimately supports the status quo. As the texts that present this case have grown over the centuries, writers have created a template that demands an emphasis on certain plot elements. As such, every Dongo narrative provides the full story of the momentous drop of blood.

More than any other single clue, following the money trail helped Emparan find his culprits. The judge collected useful information by watching their facial expressions and body language. He also challenged the suspects' honor by suggesting that they lied to him. His next task was to obtain a full confession from all three of perpetrators. Emparan rapidly achieves this goal with the help of a pair of silk stockings.

9

Confessions

All three of the prime suspects in the Dongo investigation have previous experience with serious accusations. They show their understanding of the justice system with different degrees of sophistication and their responses to Emparan's questions are often aggressive or evasive.[1] Quintero is the first to confess but he downplays his guilt. In response, Emparan pressures him with irrefutable physical evidence and plays him off of the other witnesses. The judge doubles down on these tactics while interrogating both Quintero and Blanco, especially after Aldama provides a detailed account of the massacre.

In the process of multiple interrogations, the other two perpetrators narrate different versions of the events, even as they have sworn, once and for all, to tell the truth. Combined with the death scene described in Chapter 1, these confessions come together to create a shifting kaleidoscope of the crime. Finally, faced with bloodstains on each of their belongings, Quintero, Blanco, and Aldama can no longer avoid the truth. They admit that they were all responsible for the killing on the night of October 23, 1789, but not before Emparan's court collects more evidence and they are called in for more questioning.

What tips Quintero into confessional mode are the twenty-three money sacks containing over twenty-one thousand pesos found in his rented lodgings, and the fresh blood splattered throughout his room, on objects and the door. How can he deny his guilt when challenged with this evidence? He cannot, but at first he tries to lessen it.

---

[1] The classic source for analyzing the rhetoric of confessions is Zemon Davis, *Fiction in the Archives*.

Quintero starts his first "true" confession by saying that Aldama conceived of the idea of a "considerable robbery." He concedes that all three men agreed to the plan. They visited Dongo's house a total of three times. The first two times ended up serving as reconnaissance. Only on the last occasion did the servants allow them to enter, due to a ploy which Aldama explains in his full confession. Quintero insists that he "was forced and obligated to contribute to the homicides." Supposedly feeling misgivings after his accomplices bullied him into taking part, he claims that he killed no one, but simply guarded the door:

> He confesses this to discharge his conscience, because he knows that he only has to give an account to God and His Majesty. The Lord knows that he resisted but they vilified him, calling him a coward, because he did not help with the wounds. The same Lord also knows that he consented because of his needs [for money?].[2]

Even though he claims, in this version of events, that he just stood at his post at the door, somehow Quintero knew that his co-conspirators began the massacre by killing the servants who slept on the first floor. Then they walked up the stairs to the mezzanine and killed the cashier. Lastly, they murdered Dongo, his coachman, and his page. During this session of testifying, Quintero does not provide any further details regarding the events that took place during the massacre.

Emparan next asks Quintero about the money and other objects found in his lodgings. The confessant states that Aldama drove the coach to Quintero's rooms only once to drop off all of the money bags there. He also admits that he recognizes the stick found in his room that has marks on it. He claims that he does not remember if he, too, took part in the weapon practice alongside Blanco and Aldama. Quintero also offers the first description of the murder weapons: "Three machetes, or 'mountain knives,' well-sharpened. Aldama or Blanco organized the weapons and gave one to Quintero, but he did not use it. The other two also took all three weapons away [after the massacre], and he does not know what they did with them."[3]

After a few more questions, Quintero claims he has no more information, and he is dismissed. Emparan then calls Aldama back into his chambers.

Before the second confessant narrates his version of the events, Emparan asks Aldama a few introductory questions. The judge first interrogates him about the stolen goods and the murder weapons. Aldama mentions that

---

[2] AGN, Mexico, Criminal Vol. 337, Exp. 2, Part 2, 40.
[3] AGN, Mexico, Criminal Vol. 337, Exp. 2, Part 2, 41.

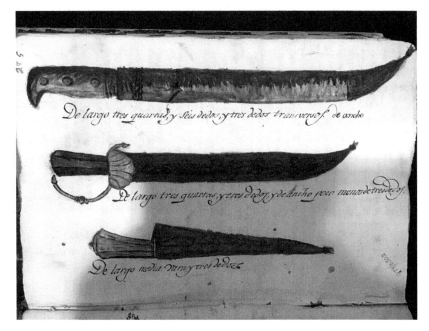

FIGURE 9.1 Murder weapons. Retrieved from the Archivo General de la Nación, Mexico City. Photo by Ismael Pardo.

Blanco hid Dongo's gold watch under some stones at the opening of a drainage pipe as they made their getaway. Then, contradicting Quintero's statement, Aldama testifies that in fact he gave Quintero five pesos to buy the murder weapons, although he does not know where Quintero went to buy them. Aldama also clarifies where the machetes ended up after the crime. As the killers fled the scene in Dongo's carriage, they approached the tobacco factory in the Santa Catalina *barrio*.[4] They knew that a guard patrolled this area. Their fear of the watchman observing them prompted the killers to discard the weapons by throwing them in the canal that passed nearby under two bridges.[5]

In response to this information, a group of *alcaldes* and other judicial functionaries head out at 9:30 p.m. on the night of October 30 to investigate the precise locations that Aldama mentioned in his confession. They first go to the Puente de Amaya, the bridge specified by Aldama. One court

[4] Aldama refers to the older location of the factory in the northern edge of the central city, before it moved to Mexico City's southwest corner at its peak in the 1790s.

[5] AGN, Mexico, Criminal Vol. 337, Exp. 2, Part 2, 44.

representative orders three men, referred to only as *indios*, to descend into the canal and look for the weapons. One of these laborers emerges with a twenty-seven-inch-long machete with a wooden handle, along with a shorter knife measuring about seventeen inches in length. Next the officials sent the indigenous men underneath the Puente de Mariscal, where they find another machete, this one about twenty-five inches long with an iron handle. The group then proceeds to the street near the "old" tobacco factory. The same indigenous men lift up some stones and find a gold watch with a shattered glass cover. For the three hours of physical work required to track down these important evidentiary objects, the *indio* laborers receive one peso each from the court.[6]

With this growing collection of physical evidence on display in his chambers, Emparan applies more pressure on his prime suspects, and uncovers more details about their planning process. Aldama insists that Quintero initiated the plans for robbery, another contradiction of the older man's confession. According to Aldama, it was Quintero who first suggested the home of a wealthy man where Blanco used to work as a servant as a likely spot to steal some money. When these plans fell through, Blanco suggested robbing Dongo. He claimed that this house contained the fantastical sum of three hundred thousand pesos, an obvious exaggeration, and very few servants. Inspired by these ludicrous claims, the three men began to stake out Dongo's establishment on the night of Wednesday, October 21. They saw Dongo leave in his coach with his driver and page. A few men lingered in the street outside the house, so they did not make any further moves to ambush.

Throughout Aldama's narration, he centers himself as the leader at the scene of the crime, even if Blanco and Quintero played important roles in dreaming up the plan for targeting Dongo. Perhaps to dissuade them from striking too soon, Aldama testifies that he warned his accomplices: "Gentlemen, we can do nothing now. We need to watch what happens. By chance, if those three men were in the street [during the robbery], they would see the fight, make a commotion, and then we would be lost."[7] In this and his other statements, Aldama presents himself as the intelligent strategist of the group.

Not waiting for Dongo to return on this first reconnaissance mission, the co-conspirators leave and come back the next night. On the second visit, they carefully observe that the coachman stepped off his vehicle first,

---

[6] AGN, Mexico, Criminal Vol. 337, Exp. 2, Part 2, 33; Criminal Vol. 338, Exp. 1, 28.
[7] AGN, Mexico, Criminal Vol. 337, Exp. 2, Part 2, 46.

waiting for a servant inside the house to open the door to the coach house. Then Dongo disembarked. Observing this series of events helps the killers plan effectively so they can dominate over their victims more easily the next night.[8]

Finally, Aldama details the massacre itself. He says that he, Quintero, and Blanco began their murder spree after Aldama knocked at Dongo's main door between 8:15 p.m. and 8:30 p.m. on Friday October 23. An intimidated elderly doorman allowed them to enter, because Aldama, in his ongoing obsession with law enforcement, claimed to be the neighborhood *alcalde*. This ruse allowed him to gain entry to the locked-up building, in theory guarded by two doormen assigned to keep suspicious visitors out.

Once the door opened, Quintero shoved past Blanco and Aldama. He threatened the doorman with his weapon, demanding to know the location of the other doorman. The older servant stated that his fellow servant was upstairs, serving Don Nicolás. The three intruders then instructed him to call the younger servant. When the *mozo* arrived downstairs, Aldama continued speaking as if he were the local *alcalde*. He justified his entry into the house by claiming that he was investigating a fictional theft. He shouted to the younger doorman, "Come here rogue, tell me where you hid the two thousand pesos that you stole from your master." Perhaps it is no coincidence that two thousand pesos was the exact amount that Aldama had been accused of stealing in an earlier theft/homicide incident.[9]

Immediately after asking the question, Aldama tied up the porter, leaving Blanco to "take care of him," with rapid and fatal cutting blows to his head. Meanwhile, Aldama proceeded down the corridor in the entryway to the patio. He ordered Quintero to tie up the older servant. They quickly killed him with slashes across his skull. As the three men brutalized the four male servants scattered around Dongo's patio, Aldama encourages his accomplices with the word "*dale*." This word means many things, including "give it to him" and "go ahead." Then Aldama grabbed the Indigenous messenger by the arm, and both he and Blanco sliced open his head.

The depth of the wounds examined on the morning of October 24 indicate that the three murderers put all of their physical strength into each machete swing. The cut piece of wood in Quintero's rooms shows that they practiced their technique and tested their strength repeatedly before the massacre, perhaps to gauge how quickly they could make

[8] AGN, Mexico, Criminal Vol. 337, Exp. 2, Part 2, 47.
[9] AGN, Mexico, Criminal Vol. 337, Exp. 2, Part 2, 24, 47.

a killing blow. Aware of all the people present in the house, they cannot allow their victims to make any exclamations of surprise or pain before they died.

While the choice of attacking their victims' heads makes sense for the purpose of a quick and quiet death for Dongo's servants, it also resulted in massive bloodshed, staining their clothes and flooding the patio. Although not a modern forensic scientist, Emparan knew enough about different kinds of blood spatter to challenge the explanations that the killers made in their previous statements. Quintero and Aldama had claimed various reasons for the stains on their clothes and hats, including nosebleeds, taking snuff, the blood dripping from cocks injured in fights, or drops flying off men getting whipped as they paraded down the city streets.

Today we have more technology to analyze what kinds of weapons caused blood pools around the Dongo establishment and the droplets on the murderers' clothes. When the investigators entered the building, they observed what modern experts call low- and medium-velocity spatter. Low-velocity spatter, which travels only a few feet per second, refers to a situation where the drops of blood pooled around the victims after they fell on the ground. Nosebleeds and injured roosters passing over one's head could also create these large drops of blood. These kinds of blood-stains simply result from the effects of gravity.[10]

In contrast, smaller spatters result from violent actions. The force of the machete cuts caused the medium-velocity spatter which gave the killers away to the careful observer who noticed the bloodstain on Aldama's hair tie. As noted, this drop was not even as big as a lentil. Today crime scene investigators measure medium-velocity spatter as between one and three millimeters in diameter. The bloodstains on Aldama's hair tie may not have come from a person whom he killed. Instead, this blood traveled around twenty-five feet per second from an attack executed by Blanco or Quintero, only a foot or two away from where Aldama stood. The stains also could have come from castoff blood as the killers removed their weapons from their victims' heads.[11] As Aldama raised his arm above or even behind his head, spatter may have sprayed on his own hat and hair. Although it is possible that medium-velocity spatter could derive from the public lashings that Aldama allegedly attended, this would require him to walk very close to the whips.

---

[10] Tom Farmer and Marty Foley, *A Murder in Wellesley* (Boston, MA: Northeastern University Press, 2012), 51–52.

[11] Farmer and Foley, *A Murder*, 51–52.

Because the Dongo killers did not use guns, the investigators do not find
high-velocity spatter. This fact also explains why Emparan and Luzero
describe the patio as blood drenched, but did not mention blood-covered
walls, the kind seen in modern crime scenes. The patios and chambers
were probably too large for the blood from machete wounds to travel that
far of a distance.[12]

Returning to Aldama's detailed narration of the events, after murdering the servants on the first floor, the three men proceeded up the stairs.
Quintero and Aldama killed Don Nicolás as he slept in his bed, acting so
quickly that their victim had not time to reach for the harquebus leaning
on the nearby wall. Meanwhile, Blanco watched the door.

They continued to move around the rest of the house, still pretending
that they were looking for the imaginary stolen two thousand pesos.
Finding Dongo's cook, laundress, and maids working in the kitchen,
Aldama said to Quintero, "Your grace, go to the door, and do not let
these people out. I will examine them one by one." Aldama then dragged
the maid to another room and killed her. He repeated this process with
another woman. Very quickly Quintero and Aldama murdered all four of
the female servants.[13]

Then they went downstairs to the entryway to wait for Don Joaquín
Dongo to return home. When he arrived, Aldama continued his *alcalde*
ruse one last time. He said, "Señor Don Joaquín, Your grace has this place,
which has now been overrun. Your grace must go with these gentlemen,
and I will deal with your servants here." Dongo stepped away, but before
he walked up the stairs, Aldama perceived that the homeowner was
suspicious. Later Quintero and Blanco told Aldama that it appeared that
Dongo started to draw a weapon, so they killed him. Aldama took the
opportunity to murder Dongo's page. With everyone in the house dead
and dying, Aldama opened the door leading into the coach house where
Dongo's driver had just entered. As a group, they killed the coachman.[14]

With all possible witnesses eliminated, Aldama, Blanco, and Quintero
proceeded to rob the house. They searched Dongo's body and found three
keys in bags that he carried on his person – the very same keys that
a neighbor's servant would find discarded on the street early the next
morning. One key opened a wardrobe on the mezzanine, which contained
nothing that the killers wanted so they moved. Another opened a file

[12] Farmer and Foley, *A Murder*, 52.
[13] AGN, Mexico, Criminal Vol. 337, Exp. 2, Part 2, 48.
[14] AGN, Mexico, Criminal Vol. 337, Exp. 2, Part 2, 48–49.

cabinet, where they encountered more sets of keys. They jumbled all of the keys together and lost track of them. Giving up on the keys, the killers searched the office where Dongo and his relatives worked. They took the time to unwrap several packets of silk stockings from China, dropping the empty wrappers on the floor. Next they found eight thousand pesos under the counter in this room. But they knew that the largest treasure rested securely in the next room. They had to break down that door to access another thirteen thousand pesos, which they loaded into Dongo's carriage. The group drove the carriage to Quintero's lodgings, where they left their loot. Then they abandoned the carriage near the dragoon barracks, where the corporal saw it approximately eight hours later. Finally, each murderer took around a hundred pesos as an initial compensation for their efforts.[15]

This is the money that Aldama used for betting and to redeem his pawned items on October 24. He performed these tasks and walked around the central city chatting with everyone he met about the Dongo massacre, while unwittingly displaying his victims' blood on his hair ribbon. These very unwise actions created a trail of evidence leading directly to his arrest and questioning three days later.

After Aldama finishes this complete and detailed confession, Emparan formally charges him with "the cruel and inhuman act of taking the lives of eleven people, with premeditation and treachery, surprising them when they were helpless and unprepared." This "depraved" crime will result in a "suitable penalty." Aldama resorts to the common defensive language of his "miserable and fragile nature" and asks that Emparan consider his family honor in the sentencing phase.[16]

Aldama's confession, of course, differs from what Quintero has admitted up to this point. Quintero had tried to lessen his guilt by claiming ignorance of the weapons' provenance and saying that he only guarded the door. To clarify the contradicting confessions, Emparan calls the two men into another *careo*, interrogating both of them at the same time. This tactic forces the older man to admit his full guilt. Without denials or further argumentation, Quintero confirms that he singlehandedly killed the cook, and that he recognizes the weapons displayed before him. He tries to minimize his culpability for purchasing these machetes and having them sharpened by noting that Aldama gave him the money for these

[15] AGN, Mexico, Criminal Vol. 337, Exp. 2, Part 2, 49–50.
[16] AGN, Mexico, Criminal Vol. 337, Exp. 2, Part 2, 50.

tasks.[17] Eventually Quintero admits that it was he who convinced Aldama to take part in the massacre. As initiator, the older man carries the most guilt.[18] Like Aldama, he resorts to all of the verbal tactics available to him in an effort to soften the inevitable consequences:

He said that his human fragility, poverty, and the dire needs that he has suffered led him to this misfortune. He did not think beforehand that God always sees all. He carried out [the killings] with so much pain, so he begs God and the court for forgiveness and that they treat him with their customary piety and mercy, granting the privilege of his birth in determining his penalty.[19]

With these words, Quintero plays on the importance of Christian mercy on the part of the judge, as well as his own feelings of remorse. These tactics sometimes succeeded with the Novohispanic judiciary, but Emparan has no desire to pander to these killers' manipulations. Their crime against a respectable Spaniard and his dependents merits the most devasting penalty possible.

In an effort to convince all three of his prime suspects to fully admit their guilt, the judge then asks Quintero and Aldama about Blanco's clothes. Had he changed them after the murders? His two accomplices testify that Blanco did change his stockings because they were covered in blood. They explain that as they hid the bags of money in Quintero's rented rooms, Blanco put on silk stockings from China which he found among the looted goods taken from Dongo's house. Both killers willingly sign the *careo*, confirming its accuracy, which now leaves only Blanco to tell the truth.[20]

Although perhaps not as exciting as the legendary drop of blood, stockings feature more prominently as important pieces of evidence throughout this investigation. Witnesses mention the suspects' stockings in the physical descriptions that they provide for the court. The first investigators who enter Dongo's ransacked premises note that they discovered empty packets of Chinese silk stockings left behind by the killers. Quintero's lodgings also contained a cache of brand-new stockings. The final inventory of items relating to this crime lists thirteen pairs of stockings stolen from Dongo's house. Finally, a line of questioning about stockings allows Emparan to attain confessions from the unforthcoming Blanco.[21]

---

[17] AGN, Mexico, Criminal Vol. 337, Exp. 2, Part 2, 59.
[18] AGN, Mexico, Criminal Vol. 337, Exp. 2, Part 2, "Sentencia," 12–13.
[19] AGN, Mexico, Criminal Vol. 337, Exp. 2, 57–59.
[20] AGN, Mexico, Criminal Vol. 337, Exp. 2, Part 2, 51.
[21] AGN, Mexico, Criminal Vol. 337, Exp. 2, 6; Part 2, 2, 36, 51–58; Sentencia, 40–41.

Given his youth – in this court system, everyone under twenty-five counts as a legal minor – Blanco has a *procurador* (attorney) to defend him.[22] The court appoints Fernández de Córdova as his advocate. Coincidentally this *procurador* is Dongo's neighbor whose servant found the warehouse keys tossed on the street. Fernández de Córdova will feebly defend his client based on Blanco's claims to honor.

Emparan opens his interrogation of Blanco with a gesture toward the red-flecked stockings which the court has on display. The judge pressures him to confess by asking: "Do you know anything about these bloody gray stockings? The blood that stains them comes from the innocent victims whom you sacrificed last Friday night, at the house of Don Joaquín Dongo?" Blanco insists that he has never seen the stockings before.

In response, the judge tries the very effective *careo* tactic once again. He brings back Aldama and Quintero, asking them to go over their confessions, which they both confirm in the presence of Blanco. The judge notes that Blanco has a cut on his sleeve, grazing his left arm. Quintero admits that he accidentally cut Blanco's arm while he brought down his machete in the process of killing one of his victims. Emparan asks Blanco again, "Where were you Friday night after prayers?" The young man continues to insist that he spent the entire night at Aldama's house.[23]

Frustrated by his stubborn refusal to confess along with his accomplices, Emparan orders a functionary of the royal court, Captain Vicente Elizalde, to visit the house of Blanco's thirty-seven-year-old aunt. She lives near the Salto de Agua, in this era, a new fountain on the outskirts of the city center.

After swearing to tell the truth, Doña María Josefa Rodríguez admits that, through her deceased husband, she knows his nephew named Joaquín Blanco. The captain asks, "What clothes does he keep here [in her house]?" According to his aunt, Blanco has a very limited inventory of possessions including: three old jackets, worn-out satin breeches, one shirt, sheets, a blanket, pillows, and a saddle and spurs. When questioned if he also owned gray stockings, Blanco's aunt mentions that, yes, she embroidered a pair of gray stockings for him. She noticed that he wore this

---

[22] See Jacqueline Alba Romulado, "Importancia del procurador de la defensa del menor y la familia del estado de México en el procedimiento de controversia de violencia familiar establecido en el código de procedimientos civiles del estado de México, como coadyuvante del juez familiar sobre los efectos que tiene la sentencia para asegurar la paz y el orden familiar" (Ph.D. diss., Universidad Nacional Autónoma de México, 2013).

[23] AGN, Mexico, Criminal Vol. 337, Exp. 2, Part 2, 53–54.

FIGURE 9.2 Salto de Agua, eighteenth-century fountain near where Blanco's aunt lived. Photo by Inez Ayrey.

gift when he left the house the past Friday night, after an argument with her. Captain Elizalde then shows her the stockings that she embroidered, now soaked in dried blood, which were found in Quintero's lodging along with the sacks of money and other incriminating objects. Doña María Josefa and her laundress recognize them. The captain returns to the court with all of Blanco's clothes, including the incriminating, blood-stained stockings.[24]

With this evidence on display, Emparan brings Blanco back in for questioning. The young man confirms his previous testimony and continues to deny that he had taken any other part in the massacre. Showing

---

[24] AGN, Mexico, Criminal Vol. 337, Exp. 2, 55–57.

him the stockings again, Emparan asks him to explain how they did not belong to him, even if his aunt and their washerwoman said that they did. Blanco starts to become desperate. He demands to hear the women make this assertion in his presence. The judge ignores this request. Blanco then tries a new tactic: confessing that he only guarded the door and did not kill anyone.

Believing that the confrontation over the bloody stockings has weakened Blanco's resolve, Emparan brings Aldama and Quintero back into the chamber. Once again, they certify the accuracy of their own previous confessions. At this point, Blanco finally admits that he took an active role in the massacre. The judge then formally accuses Blanco of committing these atrocious crimes, "with no fear of God ... sacrificing defenseless innocents in his rage." Blanco now fully admits that he understands "the gravity and atrocity of his crimes, committed due to the suggestions of his accomplices."[25] Perhaps because of his youthful ignorance, he does not add any rhetoric about his fragility, unlike his older co-defendants. He can also count on his advocate to speak for him at the right moment. Blanco's signed confession allows the court to proceed to the sentencing phase of the process.

[25] AGN, Mexico, Criminal Vol. 337, Exp. 2, 57–58.

PART IV

CHARACTERS

10

Dongo

This man had all the strength of maturity. He had passed through the spring of his life and was at the zenith of his existence. In personality, he was not arrogant, but he did not disdain the best. At first glance, his physiognomy appeared to have a severe aspect. This impression softened as soon as he communicated or voiced a command. His broad, smooth forehead showed the signs of intelligence. His black, large, slanted eyes had an intense and dominating gaze. He had an aquiline nose. His lips and cheeks were hidden by a thick black and silky beard, as abundant as the hair on his head. Under the beard, his mouth appeared proportionate, with a thin upper lip. Even before he spoke, his appearance showed that he belonged to a distinguished breed, raised in an aristocratic cradle, with a loyal soul and a noble heart. He looked like one of those people who overflows with philanthropy and benevolence, on this earth to sooth life's sufferings, to console humanity's troubles, to relieve the needs of the helpless, a distinguished protector of the vulnerable. In a word: he was an illustrious viceregal philanthropist. He owned the house in which we find ourselves [Dongo's rural hacienda]. Everyone around him showed him respect and careful consideration.[1]

In the above lines, the novelist Manuel Filomeno Rodríguez introduces Don Joaquín Dongo as the ideal Novohispanic aristocrat. Rodríguez emphasizes that his caring paternalism assured his rightful place among the most important men in 1780s New Spain. Both this fictional version of Dongo and the real person possessed the essential characteristics of a man at the pinnacle of honor: wealth, piety, distinguished Spanish lineage, and charity. He also showed loyalty to the Spanish crown through his service to the Mexican viceroys. Dongo's ancestry and actions exemplify the ideals of the privileged few at the top of the eighteenth-century Novohispanic social pyramid.

[1] Rodríguez, *Los Asesinos de Dongo*, 26–27.

ANCESTRY

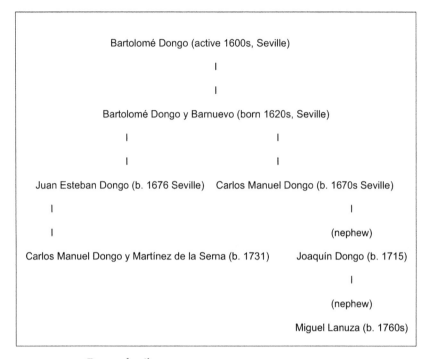

FIGURE 10.1 Dongo family tree
Note: *two dashes indicate father–son.*

Spaniards of Dongo's status took pride in documenting their ancestry
for several generations. Don Joaquín Dongo had many prominent relatives – a complex heritage to summarize – but his family lineage represented a key aspect of his identity. With a surname that may derive from
a town on the northwest shore of Lake Como, Dongo's family history
includes international trade, military service to the crown, and pious
bequests to Catholic charities.[2] Although possibly not a direct relative of
Don Joaquín Dongo, a prominent man with the last name Dongo lived in

---

[2] The lineage I am summarizing here focuses on Seville. Other Dongos had connections to
Spain, but appear to be more recently based in Italy, in contrast to Don Joaquín's direct
ancestors. See Archivo Histórico de la Nobleza, ES. 45168, AHNOB/1//OSUNA, C.1981,
D.105, *Carta de Felipe IV a Fray Daniel Dongo, Vicario general de San Francisco, como
contestación a otra de éste, con la que le daba cuenta de la visita hecha de su religión por
Italia y Nápoles, habiendo pasado a Sicilia*, 1650.

Spain as early as the late fifteenth century. In 1497, Fernando López de Dongo made a petition for *hidalguía*, or noble status, to the royal court and chancellery in Valladolid.[3] López de Dongo hailed from a tiny settlement near Lugo in the far northwest corner of Spain. This document assured that his descendants could claim aristocratic status for generations after his death.

Dongos appear in Seville dating back to the early seventeenth century. In this era Don Joaquín Dongo's great-uncle initiated the career path and the exalted status that his descendants would continue for the next 150 years. In 1644, a young merchant named Bartolomé Dongo y Barnuevo applied to the *Casa de la Contratación*, the royal administrative office for trade to the Americas, for permission to transport merchandise across the Atlantic to sell in New Spain. This particular Dongo remained based in Seville after this trip, in business with his relatives.[4] Sometime in the seventeenth century, he received the privilege of a *mayorazgo*, a rare royal grant of entailment that allowed nobles to pass down their property to a single heir, going against the standard Spanish inheritance laws.[5] A possible ancestor, a man named Juan Bautista Pluma Campo Dongo, owned a slave ship in the 1640s. This Dongo most likely set sail in Seville for the African coast and then unloaded his human cargo in New Spain.[6] Around the same time, the father of Bartolomé Dongo y Barnuevo made a testamentary donation of seventy-five thousand *maravedis* (a unit of currency) to a charity hospital in Seville. All of this indicates that

[3] Archivo de la Real Chancillería de Valladolid, *Ejecutoria del pleito litigado por Fernando López de Dongo, vecino de San Julián de Sante (Lugo), con el concejo, justicia y regimiento de San Julián de Sante, sobre hidalguía*, 1497. Again, there may be more recent Italian immigrants, including the distinguished scholar and royal librarian Antonio Dongo Barnuevo y Mesa (1663–1722), who published a poem dedicated to Sor Juana Inez de la Cruz in 1692. My guess is that he was a nephew of Bartolomé Dongo. See Francisco M. Carriscondo Esquivel, "Antonio Dongo Barnuevo y Mesa," https://dbe.rah.es/biografias/19567/antonio-dongo-barnuevo-y-mesa, accessed October 20, 2021. Arguably, this branch of the family appears higher ranking and more prestigious than their merchant relatives.

[4] Archivo General de Indias (AGI), Contratación 5427, N.1, R.12; Archivo de la Real Chancillería de Valladolid, Registro de Ejecutorias 2973, 68, 1675 lists Dongo y Barnuevo as a *vecino* (established resident) of Seville.

[5] The children disputed this. See Esteban Dongo Barnuevo, *Por D. Esevan Felix Dongo Barrionuebo en el pleyto con Don Ioseph Dongo Barrionuebo, su hermano sobre la propiedad del vinculo, y mayorazgo que fundó Bartolome Dongo, padre de los susodichos, del tercio y remaniente del quinto de sus bienes*, http://catalogos.mecd.es/CCPB/cgi-ccpb/abnetopac/O12110/ID5a432a39/NT1, accessed October 20, 2021.

[6] AGI, Contratación Registro de Esclavos, N. 7, R. 1, *Juan Bautista Pluma Campo Dongo, maestre del navío* Nuestra Señora de Guadalupe *a Nueva España o Tierra*, 1654.

seventeenth-century Dongos enjoyed wealth and prominence in the most important city for Spanish international trade.[7]

The Dongo y Barnuevo branch of the Dongo family also distinguished itself with service in the military. In the early eighteenth century, Juan Esteban Dongo documented his achievements as a Sevillian soldier in the *tercios* (military units) defending the Spanish fleet. Born in 1676 and the son of the merchant Bartolomé Dongo Barrionuevo (most likely the trader mentioned above), he served in this role from age eighteen until twenty-two. This Dongo then received a promotion to a "gentleman of the royal standard for the Captain of the *flota*," a job he did until 1702. He took part in the defense during the English and Dutch invasion of the port of Vigo, a defeat for the Spanish at the start of the War of Spanish Succession.[8] At age fifty, Juan Esteban Dongo married a woman of Sevillian descent whose parents had settled in Mexico. His wife bore a child named Carlos Manuel Dongo y Martínez de la Serna in 1731. In his late twenties and already having served in the Spanish infantry, this young Dongo received the honor of a knighthood in the Order of Santiago.[9]

Another important family connection for the murder victim Don Joaquín Dongo was most likely Carlos Manuel Dongo. This Dongo was the uncle and namesake of the Knight of Santiago mentioned above. He resided in Seville and was the younger brother of Juan Esteban Dongo. Both men were sons of the patriarch Bartolomé Dongo y Barnuevo. The elder Carlos Manuel Dongo received a royal license to go to New Spain in 1723 as well as further permission to bring an enslaved boy to the Americas in 1725.[10] This merchant must have traveled back and forth

---

[7] Archivo General de Simancas, CME 1412, 9, *Juro a favor del hospital de San Cosme y San Damián de Pobres Inocentes de la ciudad de Sevilla, de 75.000 maravedís*, undated, second half of the seventeenth century.

[8] AGI, Indiferente 136, N. 128, *Relación de Méritos y servicios de Juan Esteban Dongo, soldado*, 1704. For more on this battle, including Isaac Newton's involvement in the captured silver, see Henry Kamen, "The Destruction of the Spanish Fleet at Vigo in 1702," *Bulletin of the Institute of Historical Research*, vol. 39: 100 (1966), 165–173.

[9] Vicente de Cadenas y Vicent, *Caballeros de la Orden de Santiago, Tomo IV* (Madrid: Ediciones Hidalguía, 1979), 278–279. His mother had a *familiar* of the Holy Office of the Tribunal of the Spanish Inquisition in her lineage, a proof of her *limpieza de sangre*, that is, Christian, Spanish heritage. Original documents for the knighthood in Madrid, Archivo Histórico de la Nación, Exp. 7814, *Expediente para la concesión del Título de Caballero de la Orden de Santiago de Carlos Manuel Dongo Martínez, natural de México, Cadete del Regimiento de Reales Guardias de Infantería en España*, 1760.

[10] AGI, Contratación 5473, N.1, R.22, *Expediente de información y licencia de pasajero a indias de Carlos Manuel Dongo*, 1723; AGI, Contratación 5475, N.2, R.63, 1725.

from Seville to the New World several times because he again requested a license to bring a servant and merchandise across the Atlantic in 1729. At this time, he was unmarried, in his fifties, of medium height and very thin.[11]

Born in Seville in 1715, Don Joaquín Dongo most likely came to New Spain in the 1730s. He may have traveled with his uncle Carlos Manuel Dongo, but he would have enjoyed the connections provided by a larger network of relatives on his journey and as he established himself in Mexico City. Don Joaquín probably started his career as a humble clerk, learning the business from his relatives. Many successful Spanish trading houses followed this practice in the eighteenth century; nephews carried on the trading enterprise, while sons went on to more noble occupations.[12] Dongo's elder uncle Juan Esteban Dongo was already well established as a distinguished resident of the viceregal court city, but he had a wife and a young son at this time. The slightly younger uncle Carlos Manuel might have appreciated guiding young Don Joaquín as his protégé in business. Before he was murdered, Don Joaquín continued this family tradition by employing his Sevillian nephew Miguel Lanuza as a clerk. Don Joaquín married but never had children of his own. As a result, he focused his time and wealth on serving the crown and showing devotion to the Catholic Church.

PIETY

Although money did not represent the be-all-end-all goal for honorable men, it certainly aided in undertaking the expected tasks of a high-status resident of Mexico City. These included donations to the religious organizations that maintained social welfare institutions as well as the lively calendar of Catholic ceremonies and fiestas. Dongo led and donated to two prominent *cofradías* or lay organizations in Mexico City. One of his chosen *cofradías* was dedicated to the *Santísimo Sacramento y Caridad*. Only seventeen years after the conquest of Tenochtitlán, Spaniards founded the Caridad *cofradía* in the San Francisco church. In 1544, this organization fused with the Holy Sacrament sodality based in the

---

[11] AGI, Contratación 5477, N.41, 1729.
[12] D. A. Brading, *Miners and Merchants in Bourbon Mexico, 1763–1810* (Cambridge: Cambridge University Press, 1971), 102–104. Notice that Juan Esteban's son took the noble path.

cathedral to create the amalgamated *archicofradía*.[13] Although typically *cofradías* dedicated to the Santísimo Sacramento had open membership extending to all of the faithful living near any given church regardless of race, gender, or status, their leadership drew from the highest status men of the vicinity. Dongo also served as the treasurer for the *Congregación de Nuestra Señora de Guadalupe* until his murder.[14]

Dongo's last will and testament confirmed his faith in the form of pious bequests. Carrying out the tradition of "spiritual accounting," which existed among rich and powerful Spaniards since the sixteenth century, Dongo started to organize funding related to his eternal fate in 1767, at age fifty-two. His first testament included a request for three thousand pesos worth of masses for his soul and a donation of four thousand pesos to the poor in the city of Guadalajara. He left twenty-six thousand pesos for distribution among his relatives, especially his nephew Don Miguel Lanuza. Dongo changed his will twenty years later, reducing the funds bequeathed to his family. He chose to have the *archicofradía* serve as executor of his will and donated ninety-six hundred pesos to a school in Toluca, which enrolled indigenous and Spanish girls.[15]

SERVICE TO THE CROWN

Don Joaquín Dongo's most important leadership role derived from his terms as prior of the powerful *consulado*, an organization that may have exercised more power in Mexico than the viceroys themselves. Scholars characterize the *consulado* as "the principal political-economic nucleus of the viceroyalty."[16] This group, found by royal decree in 1592 and with a set of rules dating to 1597, represented the interests of the top hundred wealthiest merchants in New Spain.[17] Although these men dealt in

---

[13] Luis Arturo del Castillo Muzquiz, "La Nobleza y el Comercio en la Nueva España del Siglo XVIII: El Primer Conde la Cortina (1741–1795)" (Mexico City: UNAM, 2008), 239–242.

[14] Miguel Ángel Vásquez Meléndez, "El Miedo Persuasivo en la Ejecución de los Asesinos de Dongo," in *Los Miedos en la Historia*, eds. Elisa Speckman Guerra, Claudia Agostoni, and Pilar Gonzalbo Aizpuru (Mexico City: Colegio de México, UNAM, 2009), 335–336.

[15] Vásquez Meléndez, "El Miedo," 335–336.

[16] Sánchez Santiró, "Comerciantes, Mineros, y Hacendados," 171–172.

[17] For the regulations of the *consulado*, see Guillermina del Valle Pavón, "Apertura Comercial del Imperio y Reconstitución de Facciones en el Consulado de México: el Conflicto Electoral de 1787," in *Mercaderes, Comercio y Consulados de Nueva España en el Siglo XVIII*, ed. Guillermina del Valle Pavón (Mexico City: Instituto Mora, 2003), 259–290.

international trade and goods that circulated around the viceroyalty, they all lived in Mexico City. Regulations demanded that only overseas merchants above the age of twenty-five could serve on this body. In the classic style of the Spanish empire, the *consulado* formed a powerful corporate body, controlling New Spain's economy through its silver production. The *consulado* adjudicated on disputes between merchants relating to debts and *bienes de difuntos*, the funds and goods of the deceased, especially the process of their distribution to the appropriate heirs in Spain. This group also collected royal taxes, especially the sales tax, or *alcabala*, and paid for a range of public projects, as well as financing a militia regiment, known as *del comercio*, in the eighteenth century.[18] Merchants sat on the *consulado* for decades, and also served in other leadership roles in the viceroyalty. After entering this prestigious organization in 1749, Dongo served terms as a *diputado* (a lower-ranking office) in the 1760s, and moved up the ranks to prior in the 1770s. During this time, the *consulado* contributed three hundred thousand pesos to building a new shipyard and also developed more interests in the Cuautla de Amilpas region, where Aldama worked as a mine administrator.[19] Perhaps as a result of an election conflict in 1787, Dongo asked the king to relieve him of these duties in 1789, but did not live to see his petition granted.[20]

Dongo's service to the crown also extended to close dealings with the viceroys and their projects. In 1779, he organized Bucareli's funeral in the cathedral as one of two "noble gentlemen" who served as executors of the viceroy's last will and testament.[21] After Bucareli's death, Dongo continued two of the viceroy's favorite projects: strengthening the Acordada in the face of a perceived increase in crime and contributing to the defense of the Spanish empire.[22] Dongo led the rebuilding and

[18] Lyle N. McAlister, *The "Fuero Militar" in New Spain, 1764–1800* (Gainesville: University Press of Florida, 1957), 2, 31–32, 98.

[19] Bobb, *Viceregency*, 114, 245; Sánchez Santiró, "Comerciantes, Mineros, y Hacendados"; Valle Pavón, "Apertura Comercial," 274.

[20] Christiana Renate Borchart de Moreno, *Los Mercaderes y el Capitalismo en la Ciudad de México: 1759–1778*, trans. Alejandro Zenker (Mexico City: Fondo de Cultura Económica, 1984), 22–29, 240–241; Odette María Rojas Sosa, "El caso de Joaquín Dongo, Ciudad de México, 1789: un acercamiento a la administración de justicia criminal novohispana" (MA thesis., Universidad Nacional Autónoma de México, 2011), 106–107.

[21] *Elogios funebres, 1758–1782* (Mexico City: Zúñiga y Ontiveras, various years), 45:1. This collection includes dozens of printed pages of sermons and poems written in honor of Bucareli.

[22] Bobb, *Viceregency*, 240, 260–261.

renovation of the Acordada building in 1781, applying his "well-known zeal and intelligence to this project." An engraving on the new structure acknowledged his leadership.[23] During the war against Great Britain from 1779 to 1783, Dongo donated twenty thousand pesos to feeding the fleet fighting in the Caribbean.[24]

In stark contrast to their victim, Dongo's killers lived as rogues creeping around the edges of polite society. Until his final moments facing their sharpened machetes on the night of October 23, Dongo could rest easy in his secure position as an exemplar of Novohispanic masculinity, cushioned throughout his life by generational wealth and a network of successful relatives. He reportedly lived very quietly and respectably and, unlike the men who killed him, Dongo had not alienated his family with his behavior. On the contrary, he fostered a new generation of merchants by employing a young nephew in imitation of the mentorship that he most likely received from his own uncles in the 1730s. All of his publicly facing actions carried out the honorable model of his forefathers. Dongo's solid position at the very top of the Spanish empire's social pyramid provoked the viceregal authorities to act quickly and effectively to wreak a cruel vengeance upon his murderers.

[23] María Luisa Rodríguez Sala, *La Cárcel del Tribunal Real de la Acordada* (Mexico City: Instituto de Investigaciones Jurídicas, 2009), 341–346.
[24] Guellermina de Valle Pavón, "Contraprestaciones por los servicios financieros del Consulado de México y sus miembros: los fondos extraordinarios para la guerra contra Gran Bretaña, 1779–1783," *Revista Complutense de América*, vol. 41 (2015), 156–157.

11

Rogue Lives

Clasping his rosary as he sits on a wooden bench in the chapel attached to the royal jail, the friar bows his head and ponders the task at hand. He thinks about how his next confessants must feel at this moment. Unlike all of us other sinners, they know the exact time and place when they will take their final breath of air. These three men have only five days left of this earthly life. They will face the executioner on the afternoon of November 7, 1789, and it is now the early morning hours of November 2. The most distinguished judges call on this friar regularly, whenever they deal with violent offenders facing fatal repercussions for their crimes. He has a special skill for communicating with these men. He can probe underneath their combative and deceptive words, deep into their souls, by reminding them what they already know: The only real judgment comes from God. This life is brief and miserable, but the spirit lives on eternally. If the court has sentenced them to death, which is the case with the three men he speaks to today, he will comfort them with assurances that they will suffer only for a few more bitter hours on this earth. But if they do not confess every heretofore secret crime that they have committed and receive absolution now, they will certainly endure horrible pains forever in hell.

In 1789, fortuitously three desperate and brutal Spaniards came together. Unemployed, broke, and with little else to do, they met at taverns in the central city to plot a heavily armed home invasion. Day by day and hour by hour, in the weeks and months leading up to the crime, Aldama, Blanco, and Quintero made decisions that eventually fated them to become New Spain's most infamous killers.

The deaths of Dongo and his family shocked New Spain. But after a close examination of the lives of all three of the perpetrators, it does not seem so surprising that they resorted to brutality to satisfy their greed. Even their favorite hobby – gambling on cockfights – involved fighting and death for the purpose of winning money.

Years before the Dongo massacre, Blanco, Quintero, and Aldama traveled across the Atlantic to New Spain, imagining that they would find wealth and success like so many Spanish immigrants had done since Cortes stepped on the beach at Veracruz in 1519. Instead, they drifted through agricultural towns in the provinces, or skulked around the shadows of Mexico City's busy streets and bustling businesses, scamming off the hard work of the people who had the misfortune of meeting them.[1] They passed their days conning and intimidating their friends and relatives, before eventually turning to theft, robbery, and murder. All of them spent time imprisoned while under investigation for other crimes before they became suspects in the Dongo massacre.

After Aldama, Quintero, and Blanco told Emparan and Luzero everything that happened on the night of October 23, the convicted murderers had a few days left to consider the fate of their souls in the afterlife. All three of them took the sacrament of confession with a mendicant friar. This idea of a religious professional comforting individuals sentenced to death arose out of the long tradition of executions in early modern Europe. Over centuries, the Catholic Church and rulers negotiated how to carry out divine judgment in the earthly realm, especially as confessions moved from a public to a secret private setting. In this era, executions were based on the older tradition of a public expiation of sins, but the accused's confessions blended public and private. With the gallows in sight, many of the condemned did not mind revealing all of their secrets. Pious friars, priests, and laypeople viewed the religious rituals surrounding execution as a way to help the broader community expiate the grievous sins of their worst offenders. New Spain, led by reforms instigated by Charles V and Philip II in the sixteenth century, as well as an early modern trend in charitable organizations to minister to those sentenced to death, enthusiastically included religious ceremony as part of the spectacle.[2]

---

[1] For more on eighteenth-century rogues in New Spain, see Taylor, *Fugitive Freedom*. Although not killers, but instead fake priests, Taylor's fugitives lied and manipulated, passing their lives in and out of trouble with the authorities. See also Richard A. Warren, *Vagrants and Citizens*.

[2] Prosperi, *Crime and Forgiveness*, 44–45, 48–60, 127, 234.

Priests and friars normally maintained secrecy regarding what they heard during the sacrament of confession. In the case of the Dongo murderers, the friar convinced them to also declare their secrets to the notary, creating a formal legal document providing new information about crimes that had no previous resolution. Facing their imminent death, both Quintero and Aldama took this opportunity to finally confess to murders that they had committed in the past. The youngest killer, Blanco, had no new crimes to reveal, but his rogue life was very similar to the other two men – a series of bad decisions, lies, and plundering the resources of others, which finally escalated to murder.[3]

The biography of the oldest among these killers, Baltazar Dávila Quintero, shows a pattern of violence going back at least three decades. Quintero spent a significant portion of his adult life roaming around the Caribbean seeking his fortune. His final journey took him from Cuba to Mexico. Traveling from Veracruz inland, Quintero proceeded on to the viceregal capital, what was once Tenochtitlán.[4] He arrived there in disgrace, and soon faced the fatal consequences of his greed and cruelty.

BALTAZAR DÁVILA QUINTERO

Quintero grew up on the tiny island of El Hierro in the Canaries off the coast of Morocco. Castile conquered these islands over the course of the fifteenth century.[5] Some of those who testified in the Dongo investigation referred to Quintero as an *alférez*, or ensign. Quintero described himself as a *piloto* (pilot of a ship) and a militia sublieutenant in Tenerife, one of the larger Canary Islands. When he introduced himself to the court, he bragged that for the past thirty years, he had served the king of Spain many times with bravery and distinction in both the Canaries and in America.[6] If he had not turned to a life of crime, this occupation would prove his irrefutable status as a man of honor.[7] (Chapter 12 will delve more deeply

---

[3] AGN, Criminal Vol. 338, Exp. 1, 114–120.

[4] For the conquistadors' journey, see Camilla Townsend, *Malintzin's Choices: An Indian Woman in the Conquest of Mexico* (Albuquerque: University of New Mexico Press, 2006).

[5] Eduardo Aznar Vallejo, "La colonización de las Islas Canarias en el siglo XV," *En la España medieval, Tomo V* (Madrid: Universidad Complutense, 1986), 195–217.

[6] Here he followed the classic *probanzas de mérito* formula for arguing service to the crown. See Matthew Restall, *Seven Myths of the Spanish Conquest* (Oxford: Oxford University Press, 2003).

[7] AGN, Criminal Vol. 338, Exp. 1, 27–28, 45.

into Quintero's career on the sea and the claims to honor made by all three of the murderers.)

While piloting ships in the Caribbean, Quintero witnessed and undoubtedly took part in skirmishes. Violence became familiar and comfortable to him, even a natural way to access the funds that he needed. He demonstrated this with another murder that he committed two decades before the Dongo massacre. In his final confession, Quintero admitted to this additional murder on November 2, 1789, five days before his execution.

Quintero confessed that, in 1770, he arrived in Campeche with some items to sell. However, for no clear reason, he lost this merchandise and ended up in debt. One night as he walked through the city streets, he ran into a man named Antonio, of unknown surname, also from the Canary Islands. Knowing that Antonio owned or managed a store, Quintero reacted quickly and turned to violence to solve his financial worries. He reached for his saber and cut Antonio in the head two times – the same method that he and his accomplices used to rapidly and quietly kill everyone in the Dongo household nineteen years later. Antonio fell to the ground, dying from his wounds. Quintero took advantage of Antonio as the man bled to death, and rummaged through his pockets. He found the key to Antonio's store. Quintero unlocked the store and stole seven hundred pesos.[8] It does not seem that any judges investigated him for this crime. The killer simply walked away, relieved that he could now pay his debts.

While he had not faced any consequences for the murder of Antonio in Campeche, Quintero spent some of the next two decades imprisoned for allegations of a property crime against a relative. Once again, he denied his guilt in this case until this final confession. Instead, Quintero maintained that he had successfully defended himself against the unfounded accusation that he had stolen four thousand pesos from his cousin's wife, Doña Gertrudis del Castillo.

This crime remained unsolved for the five years leading up to the Dongo massacre, although it seems that Emparan had his suspicions about the *piloto*'s guilt. Early on in the investigation, the judge asked Quintero how he maintained himself so far from his homeland. This prompted the suspect to narrate his biography. He claimed that he came to Mexico for the sole purpose of providing records for members of his family who needed proof of their *limpieza de sangre* ("clean blood"). This term refers to Christian ancestry, without the "stains" of ancestors practicing other

---

[8] AGN, Criminal Vol. 338, Exp. 1, 117–118.

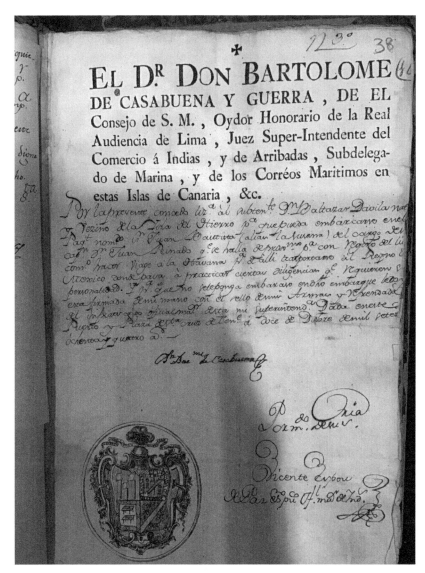

FIGURE 11.1 Document granting Quintero permission to travel to New Spain, 1784. Retrieved from the Archivo General de la Nación, Mexico City. Photo by Ismael Pardo.

religions, partaking in manual labor, or receiving inquisition convictions.[9] His cousin Cayetano Sánchez Quintero required documentation proving his "clean blood" in order for his two young daughters to enter the Santa Inés Convent. Quintero explained that he received this request in 1784, as he sat "resting" in his house in El Hierro. He decided to do this favor because he believed the "thousand promises that he would benefit" from bequests made in his cousin's last will and testament. Carrying out this family duty cost him, in total, over one thousand pesos. Even just acquiring the documents necessitated an initial expense of two hundred pesos.[10]

Once Quintero had the requested papers in hand, he secured official permission to travel to the Indies. He left the Canaries in December of 1784. Traveling on the *San Juan Bautista*, also known as *La Susana*, he crossed the Atlantic. He first stopped in Havana and then disembarked in Veracruz. His one-way passage to New Spain cost him 540 pesos, which he expected to receive back from his relatives when he wanted to return home. But upon arrival at his cousin's house in Tenango, in the region of Chalco (thirty miles southeast of Mexico City), Quintero found his cousin close to death. He passed on the necessary genealogical certifications to the girls' mother, Doña Gertrudis, completing his task as the family desired. But since the widow did not reimburse him for his expenses, Quintero could not buy his passage back to the Canary Islands. His poverty trapped him in New Spain.[11]

After leaving Tenango, Quintero claimed that he was surprised to find himself chased by men sent by Doña Gertrudis, who sought to reclaim four thousand pesos that she said he had stolen from her house. Quintero maintained that he only had nineteen pesos on his person at this time, all that remained from a twenty-five-peso loan that she had voluntarily given him. Despite protesting his innocence, he found himself under arrest and locked up in the Acordada jail in Mexico City. He suffered for more than six months in chains in a "horrible dungeon."[12] After three years of imprisonment, Quintero finally won the case. Afterward he maintained himself only due to the

[9] María Elena Martínez, *Genealogical Fictions: Limpieza de Sangre, Religion, and Gender in Colonial Mexico* (Stanford, CA: Stanford University Press, 2008); Linda Martz, "Pure Blood Statutes in Sixteenth Century Toledo: Implementation as Opposed to Adoption," *Sefarad*, vol. 55: 1 (1994), 83–108; Peter B. Villella, "'Pure and Noble Indians, Untainted by Inferior Idolatrous Races': Native Elites and the Discourse of Blood Purity in Late Colonial Mexico," *Hispanic American Historical Review*, vol. 91: 4 (2011), 633–663.
[10] AGN, Criminal Vol. 338, Exp. 1, 38, 41–42, 45, quote on 45.
[11] AGN, Criminal Vol. 338, Exp. 1, 38–46.   [12] AGN, Criminal Vol. 338, Exp. 1, 47–48.

charity of his friends.[13] Although he had been absolved of this theft, up until a few weeks before his second arrest for taking part in the Dongo massacre, Quintero continued to interact with the judiciary. He filed several petitions to regain his judicial privileges as a man who had served in the military.[14]

Five days before his execution, Quintero finally admitted to Doña Gertrudis's accusations. He confessed that he did steal a substantial sum of pesos from her which he guessed may have added up to four thousand. He justified the theft because she had not compensated him for bringing her the documents that she needed to help her daughters. He could not find any way to make a living in New Spain after leaving the Canary Islands. Quintero said that after he stole Doña Gertrudis's money, he buried it in a hole he dug on the outskirts of Tenango. Then the viceroy ordered his arrest, and he sat in jail for six months with no opportunity to make a statement. As soon as possible, he reached out to two of his acquaintances, asking them to bring him the buried money. Quintero said that he only received two pesos and some chocolate tablets from these so-called friends.[15]

In the months before the Dongo massacre, Quintero lived what he said was a very quiet life in a humble rented room. He routinely came home every night by 7:00 p.m. and avoided gossip and gambling dens. He survived on handouts from friends and he passed his time arguing for the reinstatement of his military privileges. He claimed that on October 23, he spent the entire day and night sick and unable to leave his bed. However, the owner of a *pulpería* a small grocery store that commonly gave loans to its clientele in the manner of a pawn shop, had passed notes between Aldama and Quintero in the week leading up to the murder.[16] Quintero claimed ignorance of this alleged plotting. Nor did he mention the other robbery schemes that he discussed with Blanco and Aldama at *vinaterías*.[17] An unemployed and disgraced adventurer who only knew how to attain his funds through acts of violence, Quintero had nothing else to fill his time leading up to the Dongo massacre other than planning his next crime.

---

[13] AGN, Criminal Vol. 337, Exp. 2, Part 2, 3, 5, 26–27.

[14] AGN, Criminal Vol. 338, Exp. 1, 55–58.

[15] AGN, Criminal Vol. 338, Exp. 1, 116–117.

[16] Francois, *A Culture of Everyday Credit*, 52–54; Deborah Toner, "Everything in Its Right Place? Drinking Places and Social Spaces in Mexico City, c. 1780–1900," *Social History of Alcohol and Drugs*, vol. 25 (2011); Matthew Scardaville, "Alcohol Abuse and Tavern Reform in Late Colonial Mexico City," *The Hispanic American Historical Review*, vol. 60: 4 (1980).

[17] AGN, Criminal Vol. 337, Exp. 2, 26–30.

FELIPE ALDAMA

The other two accused murderers, Aldama and Blanco, although a decade apart in age, both came from the Basque region of Old Spain, known as Vizcaya or Bizkaia (Biscay). Ambitious or bored and restless men from the remote locations where Blanco and Aldama were born and raised could escape to the port cities of Bilbao or Donostia-San Sebastian, only a couple of days on foot to the north.[18] All the way back to the sixteenth century, Basques have represented a significant and influential group in the population of New Spain and later Mexico. Numbering among the original conquistadors, they also emigrated over the centuries to work as craftsmen, sailors, and merchants.[19]

Born in 1757, Aldama came from a settlement that he referred to as San Juan Bautista. Today, no town of this name exists in this area. Only an abandoned church by the name of San Juan Bautista stands in ruins near the tiny village of Oiardo. This region of Vizcaya borders on a nature preserve full of waterfalls and hiking paths. One can find this church by traveling on quiet roads halfway between the town of Álaba and a village called Kexaa (Quejana), locations mentioned in Aldama's biographical details during the investigation. Undoubtedly, this region offered Aldama little in the way of material wealth, despite his claims to noble ancestry. By his early twenties, he had settled in the viceroyalty of New Spain.

In the days after the Dongo massacre, Emparan received a physical description of Aldama at the moment when he became a suspect due to the infamous "single drop of blood" seen on his hair ribbon. Observers described Aldama as of average height and weight and white-skinned. He had a close-cropped beard. He did not wear a wig, but wore his hair, which was dusted with gray, tied up in a bun. He had an aquiline nose and brown eyes. His typical clothing included a white hat and a blue cape, white stockings, a denim coat and matching breeches, and an additional layer of a military-style jacket, or *chupin*, of embroidered white silk.[20]

Emparan and Luzero first heard of Aldama as a "vagrant, of perverse habits [*hombre vago, y de perversas costumbres*] . . . with no profession or occupation." Palace gossips reportedly described Aldama as the type of man who "threw firecrackers at street sellers, bet heavily, and dressed too

[18] Xabier Lamikiz, *Trade and Trust in the Eighteenth-Century Atlantic World: Spanish Merchants and Their Overseas Networks* (London: Boydell Press, 2013).

[19] Juan Javier Pescador, *The New World Inside a Basque Village: The Oiartzun Valley and Its Atlantic Emigrants, 1550–1800* (Reno: University of Nevada Press, 2003).

[20] AGN, Criminal Vol. 337, Exp. 2, Part 2, 2.

well [despite the fact that] he had no job, nor any way of honestly making a living."[21] These descriptions indicate that his fortunes had fallen dramatically since his work as an administrator for the prosperous mine owner José Samper.

How did such a man pass his time in 1789 Mexico City? According to two employees of the "casa de gallos," Aldama spent much of his time during September and October betting on cockfights. Popular with many men, this *casa* hosted these fights every day except Sunday.[22] Aldama treated gambling on cockfights as if it were his occupation. He described sustaining himself by "trying his luck [*probando fortuna*] at the *casa de gallos*."[23] Perhaps he hoped for a big win to solve his financial worries. Instead, Aldama was stuck in a cycle of pawning his clothes and other items of value to bet on his chosen birds. When he had good luck, he bought back the items that he had pawned with his winnings. The money he won soon disappeared when his cocks lost, and the process started over again.[24]

Aldama was a familiar patron to the men who managed the *casa de gallos*. They saw him every day for several hours during the week before the Dongo massacre. During Aldama's typical day at the cockfights he might win fifty pesos in the morning, just to lose sixty-six pesos in the afternoon. His gambling style was to bet carefully when he was losing. When he had a winning streak, he doubled his bets up to a maximum of twenty pesos. Aldama testified that he spent the afternoon of October 23 once again at the cockfights from midafternoon until after evening prayers ended at six. An employee remembered him leaving that day after a loss of eight pesos. Aldama passed the next afternoon chatting with friends on the street, buying cigars, and returning once again to the *casa de gallos* to

---

[21] AGN, Criminal Vol. 338, Exp. 1, 68–69.
[22] On cockfights, see Sonya Lipsett Rivera, *The Origins of Macho: Men and Masculinity in Colonial Mexico* (Albuquerque: University of New Mexico Press, 2019), 30, 108, 134, 164; Claudia Parodi, "Ciudad lúdica: juegos, diversiones publicas, caballos, libreas, y otras galas novohispanas," in *Centro y Periferia: Cultura, Lengua, y literatura virreinales en América*, eds. Claudia Parodi and Jimena Rodríguez (Madrid: Iberoamérica, 2011); Viquiera Albán, *Propriety and Permissiveness in Bourbon Mexico*, 6; and for more recent history, Jerry Garcia, "The Measure of a Cock: Mexican Cockfighting, Culture, and Masculinity," *I Am Aztlán: The Personal Essay in Chicano Studies*, vol. 3 (2004), 109–138.
[23] AGN, Criminal Vol. 338, Exp. 1, 65.
[24] AGN, Criminal Vol. 337, Exp. 2, Part 2, 3, 5, 32–33. See Cope, *The Limits of Racial Domination*, 41.

gamble on the fights until the early evening. He also took the time to attend the theater on Sunday, one of his other regular diversions.[25]

Aldama did not always live this wastrel life. He had worked in reputable positions during his decade living in New Spain. Most prominently, he had administered a mine known as Santiago in the region of Cuautla, about fifty miles south of Mexico City in the modern state of Morelos which gave him indirect contact with the wealthy and powerful men who served on the Mexican *consulado*.[26] Surviving personal letters indicate that in the early 1780s, Aldama had a circle of friends and associates who corresponded with him over day-to-day issues such as borrowing his clothes or his horses.[27]

Everything changed for Aldama on a fateful day in 1785, when he killed a man called Julián Ramírez. The authorities had investigated him for years but absolved him of Ramírez's murder. In his religious and legal confessions given on November 2, 1789, Aldama finally explained all the details of his previous homicide:

As the two men rode along a deserted country road outside Cuautla, Aldama pondered the fact that Ramírez had two thousand pesos belonging to his master on his person. Craving the money, Aldama grabbed Ramírez's blunderbuss [*escopeta*], which they had both just used to shoot birds. He reached into his friend's saddlebags and took out two bullets. After loading the firearm, he aimed at a vulnerable spot just below Ramírez's ear and pulled the trigger, killing his friend in two shots. Aldama then tied up the other man's feet, and attached his head to his saddle. He dragged his friend several miles to the mouth of a mine. He then tossed the corpse and the horse's saddle, along with the *escopeta*, into the mine. Aldama loaded Ramírez's money onto his own mule, and rode back into town. Along the way he hid the money, returning later for it.[28]

A local official initiated the investigation, and later it moved up to the Acordada court. Aldama claimed that the murder investigation had prevented him from taking on any occupation. Other than winnings on the cockfights, he borrowed money from other men and family members to pay his expenses, which included two elderly servants and quite a well-equipped home, considering his lack of employment.[29] Like the others, Aldama filled his days gambling, loafing about town, and plotting to acquire funds without actually working. Having killed before, Aldama had no qualms about doing it again to loot Dongo's significant treasure.

[25] AGN, Criminal Vol. 337, Exp. 2, Part 2, 3, 5, 36–38; AGN, Criminal Vol. 338, Exp. 1, 24.
[26] AGN, Criminal Vol. 337, Exp. 2, Part 2, 8.
[27] AGN, Criminal Vol. 338, Exp. 1, 4–18.
[28] AGN, Criminal Vol. 338, Exp. 1, 119; part 2, 24.
[29] AGN, Criminal Vol. 337, Exp. 2, Part 2, 5, 8–9, 17–18.

JOAQUÍN BLANCO

Blanco stands apart from Aldama and Quintero. Although he had a criminal record and spent time imprisoned, his prior crimes were far less serious than his co-defendants. The youngest of the three killers by around a decade, all evidence suggests that Blanco committed murder for the first time on the night of October 23, 1789.

Born around 1767, Blanco also came to New Spain from Vizcaya. His hometown was Segura, not far from Gipuzkoa. This town sits between two mountainous regions, now designated as parks. On modern roads, Segura is less than sixty miles from Oiardo, near where Aldama was born. Not far as the crow flies, this distance would have required several days of arduous travel in the 1700s. However close their hometowns, Blanco and Aldama did not know each other in Vizcaya. They met in a tavern in the mid-1780s. They separated for around two years due to Blanco's arrest for theft, but later reunited and became very close friends.[30]

At around the age of sixteen, Blanco left Vizcaya, in hopes of connecting with his uncle and brother who lived in New Spain. He did not organize official permission for passage across the Atlantic, ignoring the passport system of the day. Instead, he felt that he could survive in the Americas just by bringing with him a letter of recommendation from an unspecified associate or family member based in Cádiz. With this guarantee of his character, in New Spain he sustained himself working in stores as a servant, including for a merchant called Don Ignacio Xavier de Alcoytia. He grew tired of his humble existence and began his life of crime in 1786.[31]

In late 1787, Blanco received a punishment of ten years forced military service in Puerto Rico for robbing his boss Alcoytia. In early 1788, Blanco traveled to Veracruz as part of a coffle of convicted criminals. For two months, he sat in the port, waiting for a ship to take him to Havana and then on to Puerto Rico. Although it seems that Blanco lived in comfort in a government official's house in Veracruz, he decided to desert his sentence. He fled the coast and returned to live with his widowed aunt, Doña María Josepha Rodríguez, in Mexico City.[32]

Since Blanco was related to his aunt only through her deceased husband, she did not feel the need to continue hiding him when the relationship turned combative. After a few weeks with Doña María Josepha, he

---

[30] AGN, Criminal Vol. 337, Exp. 2, Part 2, 19.
[31] AGN, Criminal Vol. 338, Exp. 1, 70–71.   [32] AGN, Criminal Vol. 338, Exp. 1, 70–71.

tracked down his brother, a miner in the boom town of Guanajuato. Blanco spent nine months there, but then heard from his aunt that the authorities in the viceregal capital were looking for him. He returned to Mexico City, and here the timeline becomes somewhat confusing. His daily routine focused on two activities: drifting around the city with his associates Quintero and Aldama, and plotting the execution of the Dongo murder. These pastimes overlapped with his interactions with the judiciary over his flight from the presidio sentence. Blanco claimed that he had good opportunities to work in the northern regions of the viceroyalty, either in commerce or the military. Perhaps he misrepresented his potential punishments for desertion, making them sound somewhat honorable.[33]

During the time that he was a deserter on the run, Viceroy Florez circulated Blanco's physical description. This document was dated only five weeks before Blanco took part in the Dongo murders. The "be on the lookout" described Blanco as white-skinned, with light brown hair, eyebrows, and eyes. He had a "regular" nose and a high, wrinkled forehead. Scars from a childhood bout with the pox marked his face. He may have looked even younger than twenty-three. Aldama described him as around eighteen or twenty years old.[34]

In the weeks leading up to the massacre, Blanco spent some nights living with his aunt, Doña María Josepha. They fought over his status as a fugitive from law enforcement. Doña María Josepha frequently locked him out of her house while she went on trips outside of Mexico City. She took these journeys to protect herself from Blanco's terrible temper.[35] In response, Blanco rented horses to try to track her down. When he could not find her, Blanco wandered around different restaurants and taverns, talking to his acquaintances and trying to find Aldama so he could sleep at his house. After he allegedly threatened to kill Doña María Josepha, she reported her nephew to a lawyer based in the local high court (the Audiencia). Taking the threats seriously, the lawyer told the Acordada judge about how Blanco had returned to Mexico City. Even after the authorities knew where to find him, Blanco enjoyed a few more days as a fugitive, with fatal consequences.[36]

---

[33] AGN, Criminal Vol. 338, Exp. 1, 70–77.
[34] AGN, Criminal Vol. 338, Exp. 1, 62; AGN, Criminal Vol. 337, Exp. 2, Part 2, 5.
[35] For related cases of gendered violence in Mexico City, see Lipsett-Rivera, *Gender and the Negotiation of Everyday Life in Mexico, 1750–1856* (Lincoln: University of Nebraska Press, 2012).
[36] AGN, Criminal Vol. 337, Exp. 2, Part 2, 14–16.

Despite these familial and legal conflicts and his lack of a stable home or job, Blanco claimed that he passed his time in the capital associating with reputable people, such as Carmelite friars. It is more likely that he spent his hours plotting with Aldama and Quintero. They discussed returning to rob Alcoytia's house, even killing him, because Blanco knew the layout from his time working there as a servant. However, these plans drifted "into the wind" because new occupants lived in the house now – members of the family of the Count of Valenciana, the owner of arguably the most productive silver mine in the world at this time. Although the files do not state it directly, it makes sense that anyone affiliated with Valenciana could afford to heavily guard their property. Tempted by Blanco's lies about Dongo storing three hundred thousand gold pesos in his warehouse, as well as another misunderstanding that this house only had one doorman and two maids to defend it, the three conspirators shifted their plans to the Calle de Cordobanes instead.[37]

Blanco spent the nights of Wednesday and Thursday, October 21 and 22, 1789, sleeping in Aldama's room in the *Alcaicería* because his aunt had locked him out of her house once again. On the night of the massacre, the two men slept side-by-side in Aldama's bed. A few nights later, Blanco spent some time in the Acordada jail. The authorities had finally caught up with him as a fugitive from his presidio sentence. At Emparan's command, on October 28, Blanco was transported in chains from the Acordada jail to the jail of the royal criminal court.[38]

The three rogue lives discussed in this chapter are not unique, as many men schemed, stole, and lied to get by in late 1700s Mexico. Thousands of other Spaniards with similar prospects emigrated to the Americas in this era. While most did not achieve wealth and success, only rarely did these fortune seekers descend to committing murder. The combined effect of Aldama, Quintero, and Blanco proved far more destructive than what each man did on his own. They ranged in age and had worked, however sporadically, in different occupations. Despite these differences, two fundamental aspects of their identities unified them: their willingness to kill to acquire funds and their deluded self-conception as reputable men of honor.

[37] AGN, Criminal Vol. 337, Exp. 2, Part 2, 12, 45–46.
[38] AGN, Criminal Vol. 337, Exp. 2, Part 2, 22, 44.

12

Motive: Honor

Scenes from October of 1789

Three Spaniards find themselves sleepless on this cool Mexico City night. The youngest, a sandy-haired man just past boyhood, paces back and forth on the street in front of his aunt's locked front door. His temper rises as he sees dark-skinned men filling their gourds at the popular Salto de Agua fountain across the street. They eye him suspiciously. Women with their heads covered in cotton blankets pass quickly with lowered eyes, avoiding coming too close. He struggles to control the rage that he feels toward his aunt as he remembers how she frequently locks him out of her house, forcing him to wander the streets like a vagrant, stared at by these Mexican barbarians.

A few blocks away, his older friend runs his fingers through his graying hair, catching his breath after his rooster loses another fight. Suppressing his anger, he hands over his last few pesos to the sweaty, grinning manager. Trying to breathe more steadily, in his mind's eye, he inventories his few remaining belongings. Does he have anything else to pawn? Maybe betting on one more fight means that he can pay his servants' wages, buy some food, and cover his rent for a few more days. Lost in thought among the crude shouts of other betters gambling on the bloody cockfight, he wonders: Who in Mexico City might have cash and how could he put his hands on it?

And in a cramped, windowless room, a grizzled veteran stretches out on his shabby cot, staring at the knife in his hands. He had killed for money before and he has no qualms about killing again. His family had stolen everything from him, hadn't they? And here he is, stuck in this dry, dusty city, teeming with drunk and rowdy mobs. After a life of adventure on the seas, laughing in the face of English sailors, he can no longer stand to beg his friends for crumbs. He needs to take action and find money, no matter what he has to do to get it.

Aldama, Quintero, and Blanco must have felt a deep and unbearable contradiction whenever they reflected on their lives. From birth, each could claim many of the essential traits of honorable men. In theory, all three murderers possessed the ideal masculine qualities of their era. All of them enjoyed the honorific title "don," as did members of their families. Even for poverty-stricken Spaniards, the titles *don* and *doña* suggested status above the plebeian mob.[1]

But in 1789, in contrast to their inherited status, each of these men lived as a poor and dishonorable criminal. The escalating daily tension that they experienced between their privileged birth as white male Spaniards and their experience as outcasts ramped up in the summer and fall of that year as they struggled to find money and defend themselves from the repercussions of their previous crimes. From their point of view, only a windfall of cash could end their struggle between whom they believed themselves to be and their actual existence as rogues.

A massive viceregal paper trail, numbering in the hundreds of thousands of handwritten pages, documents Spanish understandings of honor. Repeatedly emphasizing one's personal honor represented an essential strategy for anyone involved in judicial procedures. Spaniards in the New World understood honor as both a personal characteristic and an inheritable trait, but also as the most useful tool for defending themselves against criminal accusations.[2] Some of the key proofs of honor included a record of service to the crown, wealth, family origins in the Spanish landowning aristocracy, and public gestures of Christian piety. Also essential was no documented evidence of Muslim or Jewish ancestry at least in the last few centuries. An honorable man also provided for and protected his family and any other dependents whom he might have, including servants, slaves, or hangers on.[3] All of these basic traits hearken

---

[1] Lipsett-Rivera, *Gender and the Negotiation of Daily Life*, 171–210.

[2] Mark A. Burkholder, "Honor and Honors in Colonial Spanish America," in *The Faces of Honor: Sex, Shame, and Violence in Colonial Latin America*, eds. Lyman L. Johnson and Lipsett-Rivera (Albuquerque: University of New Mexico Press, 1998), 18–44. I have explored honor and court cases in Germeten, *Violent Delights, Violent Ends*, 54–84.

[3] Ann Twinam, *Public Lives, Private Secrets: Gender, Honor, Sexuality, and Illegitimacy in Colonial Spanish America* (Stanford, CA: Stanford University Press, 1999), 33, 89–124. "For men, defending the sexual reputation of their women kin was important, but male honor also included much else, including competence in one's trade or office, the management of one's credit and debt relationships, and one's performance in the aggressive,

back to the values of medieval Spain and *Reconquista* (reconquest). At its root, Spanish masculine honor derived from a warrior ideology that linked material benefits to acts of violence.[4]

In the investigation of the Dongo massacre, the perpetrators' concerns for their honor played out in both obvious and subtle ways. First, of course, greed motivated these murders.[5] But the murderers' greed was not simply for material gain. Access to wealth in New Spain confirmed a man's honorable reputation, although riches alone did not prove reputation. One's possessions just provided the simplest method to visually demonstrate one's honor. In terms of material objects, clothing offered the most obvious way to show honor in public.

To their shame, these three killers walked through the streets, broke and unknown, wearing shoddy old clothes. Unlike other Spaniards claiming noble lineage, they could not display and confirm their status through their possessions and wealth. This lack of prestige no doubt haunted each of them as they passed lonely evenings in their cheap lodgings. It motivated them to beg, borrow, or outright steal money from their acquaintances and relatives. Because they could no longer tolerate their own poverty and dishonor, Aldama, Quintero, and Blanco killed eleven people for no other reason than to acquire pesos, albeit a treasure roughly worth over three million dollars in the twenty-first century.[6]

In a second symbolic assertion of honor, on their bloody spree in the Dongo mansion, the murderers killed their victims with vicious blows to their heads and faces. This obliterated their humanity in more ways than just ending their lives. Yes, this kind of wound quietly, quickly, and effectively killed one's opponent, but it also represented the destruction of the victim's essence, their head, the part of the body most connected to personal honor.

Lastly, the murderers resorted to honor as their only possible self-defense. Here, their claims to honor sound shameless and opportunistic. Once they admitted their guilt, Blanco, Quintero, and Aldama only had

---

competitive play that composed much of male sociability." Scott K. Taylor, *Honor and Violence in Golden Age Spain* (New Haven, CT: Yale University Press, 2008), 9.

[4] Burkholder, "Honor and Honors," 20–24.

[5] Javier Villa-Flores, "Reframing a 'Dark Passion': Bourbon Morality, Gambling, and the Royal Lottery in New Spain," in *Emotions and Daily Life in Colonial Mexico*, eds. Villa-Flores and Sonya Lipsett-Rivera (Albuquerque: University of New Mexico Press, 2014), 153, 163.

[6] This calculation is based on the salary of a solid working-class job in the 1790s. The nightwatchmen only made fifteen pesos a month. Their annual salary (if they held the job consistently and did not accrue costs relating to their work) was 168 pesos. I estimated that a security guard earns $25,000 in the twenty-first century.

their familial honor to offer as a kind of mitigating circumstance to convince Emparan to lessen their punishments. Their court-appointed advocate deployed the same tactic. An analysis of the killers' clothes and their other possessions, as well as their rhetoric of self-defense within the context of Spanish masculine values of honor, clarifies their motivations for the cruel annihilation of Dongo and his family.

CLOTHES

Maintaining an honorable reputation in this era required dressing properly.[7] Appearing in public wearing clothes that demonstrated poverty caused shame, even as some realized the shallowness of these worries. More than two hundred years before the Dongo massacre, an anonymous Spanish writer mocked how petty noblemen prioritized their dress and their public display of honor above finding an income that would at least prevent them from dying of starvation. The 1554 novella *Lazarillo de Tormes* exposes and critiques the hypocrisy of petty aristocratic honor. The narrator, Lázaro, a boy who endures a childhood serving several cruel and abusive masters, actually has to provide food for one of his employers, an impoverished gentleman who would rather starve to death with dignity than work. As Lázaro explains it: "They may not have a penny in their pocket but they've got to keep up appearances. There's nothing anybody can do about it. They're like that until they die."

But Lázaro himself falls into the trap of caring more about appearances than working a steady job. At first, he is happy when he receives the opportunity to work as a water carrier. After four years of hard work, Lázaro finally has enough money to buy some ragged used clothes and an antique sword. He confesses that as soon as he perceived himself as well-dressed, he had no reason to work anymore, so he quit.[8]

Aldama, Quintero, and Blanco made decisions that echo the stories of the morally bankrupt but honor-obsessed characters depicted in *Lazarillo de Tormes*. They wanted better clothes and respect for their noble family heritage, but they refused to work daily to sustain themselves. Just like the destitute but honorable gentleman whom the fictional Lazarillo de

[7] Lipsett-Rivera, *Origins of Macho*, 144–150; Lipsett-Rivera, *Gender and Negotiation of Everyday Life in Mexico*, 213–232; Burkholder, "Honor and Honors," 30–31. I have previously explored clothing, gender, sexuality, race, and colonialism in Germeten, *Violent Delights, Violent Ends*, 144–146, 220–223.
[8] *The Swindler and Lazarillo de Tormes: Two Spanish Picaresque Novels*, trans. Michael Alpert (New York: Penguin, 1969), 38, 57.

Tormes served, gossips described Aldama as dressing too well for his unemployed status.[9]

In fact, the killers' biographies reveal that they did not always suffer in disreputable poverty. While they all experienced moments of success as well as humiliating disgraces and failures, their status as men of Spanish descent meant that they enjoyed privileged lives. Their material possessions confirmed this status, even if at any moment they might pawn these items for a bit of cash. Consider how this contrasts to the poverty of indigenous people living in Mexico City, who often walked the streets in rags, appearing to observers of the time as shamelessly undressed and exposed.[10] In the months leading up to the Dongo murders, the killers were preoccupied with maintaining their clothes to a certain standard, and thus publicly asserting their honor.

Inventories of the killers' possessions provide evidence that all three made an effort to appear wealthy through their clothes and accessories.[11] The youngest and least established of the three, Blanco, owned very few items. But even in poverty, his scant belongings suggest a very pared-down gesture toward the Spanish masculine ideal. His wardrobe contained nothing more than three old jackets, two doublets, one pair of old satin breeches, and a shirt. He could count on his aunt and her female servant to keep these items clean and presentable, a luxury in itself. Unlike many people in this era, he slept on a bed outfitted with a set of linen sheets, a coverlet, and a pillow. Most importantly, Blanco had some disposable funds to rent a horse, outfit it with his own saddle, and ride it while showing off his spurs.[12]

But clearly these simple luxuries did not satisfy Blanco's ambitions. The cracks in his honorable façade grew in the month of October 1789. When Blanco began threatening his aunt's life, he lost the privilege of accessing her home and the labor of her servant. He soon earned a reputation for heavily covering his face and head in public, possibly a sign of shame or an attempt to hide his identity from the authorities, who sought him out due to his flight from his presidio sentence.[13] Blanco's conviction for theft from his master seriously damaged his honorable reputation. Other than

[9] AGN, Mexico, Criminal Vol. 338, Exp. 1, 68–69.   [10] Arrom, *Containing the Poor*, 17.
[11] Burkholder, "Honor and Honors," 30–31.
[12] AGN, Mexico, Criminal Vol. 337, Exp. 2, part 2, 54.
[13] AGN, Mexico, Criminal Vol. 338, Exp. 1, 68. Of course, this clothing choice parallels perceptions and goals of the *tapadas*, veiled women of the same era. See Laura R. Bass and Amanda Wunder, "The Veiled Ladies of the Early Modern Spanish World: Seduction and Scandal in Seville, Madrid, and Lima," *Hispanic Review*, vol. 77: 1 (2009), 97–144.

his birthright as a Spaniard, he had a weak claim to honor. Perhaps he hoped that money would solve this problem. His fellow perpetrators had much more to lose when they savaged the Dongo household.

ALDAMA'S PRECARIOUS FORTUNE

At age thirty-two, recently absolved of a homicide charge, Aldama possessed much more confidence than Blanco. He asserted his noble Spanish lineage when he spoke in Emparan's chambers, despite his insecure finances. At first glance, Aldama seemed to live as a man of honor by the standards of the day. He claimed the Marquis del Villar de Águila as a relative and the marquis financially supported his rogue cousin.[14] Decently dressed, he employed two elderly widowed servants who waited on him at his well-equipped lodgings. From the moment that Emparan first questioned him, Aldama described himself as "a notorious noble gentleman whose quality, if necessary, can be justified." Aldama then showed the judge a piece of paper, perhaps documentation of his *limpieza de sangre*. The defendant believed that these papers certified his noble status and obviously hoped that they would cause Emparan to view him less as a criminal and more as a peer. However, without much interest, the judge glanced at the paper and then instantly passed it back to Aldama.[15]

A mature man living independently in his own small household, Aldama possessed many basic domestic necessities. He owned sufficient articles of clothing suited to a poor but still dignified man who could claim at least a veneer of civilization. Aldama's rich friends and the Marquis del Villar probably funded his wardrobe so they would not have to associate with a man who appeared destitute. Socializing in this circle of acquaintances demanded that he make an effort to look presentable. Possessing a certain degree of vanity, Aldama owned a simple shaving kit and accessories including gloves, silk stockings, and neckties. While he had a bigger wardrobe than Blanco, all of Aldama's clothes were old. He had likely already pawned any newer items of value at the time of his arrest. Despite his precarious finances, Aldama could still afford to send out his linens to laundresses on the Calle de Tacuba. He could change his outfit every day or

---

[14] AGN, Mexico, Criminal Vol. 338, Exp. 1, 64. This individual was an important figure in Querétaro. See John C. Super, "Pan, alimentación y política en Querétaro en la última década del siglo XVIII," *Historia Mexicana*, vol. 30: 2 (1980), 262 n28; Michael E. Murphy, *Irrigation in the Bajío Region of Colonial Mexico* (Boulder, CO: Westview Press, 1986).
[15] AGN, Mexico, Criminal Vol. 337, Exp. 2, part 2, 5.

two, a luxury not enjoyed by the overwhelming majority of poorer residents of the viceroyalty. He had a respectable number of staples including at least four shirts and eight pairs of stockings. He also owned three pairs of breeches, two overcoats, at least three silk vests, and two suits.[16]

Judging by the items inventoried by court functionaries during the Dongo investigation, Aldama seemed far more learned and civilized than his co-conspirators. The quantity of his possessions suggest that he rented maybe three rooms – a bedroom, a kitchen, and possibly a bit of space set aside for his office or as working space for his servants. His furnishings seemed luxurious for this era. Unlike tens of thousands of Mexico City residents who lived in poverty, Aldama owned a bed outfitted with a mattress and pillows. His domestic space featured linens from Europe, a carved decorative table, tin candlesticks, and two decorative screens used to divide his space. If he wished, Aldama could sit down with a companion and eat from a small set of dishes that included a few pieces of china, crystal glasses, and Talavera serving bowls. He owned objects that implied he had a studious side, or at least could read and write with ease: a wooden desk made in Michoacán, a copper inkwell with drying sand, and various papers and notebooks. His possessions also suggested that he had a decent education, including scripts for two plays and a small book in French. Although he spent most of his time at the cockfights, if Aldama was in the mood for a less bloody evening, he could stay at home playing his flute, perusing his copy of the *Guía de Forasteros* ("Visitors' Guide") to learn about Mexico City, or reading his devotional books while glancing up at a silver-plated crucifix displayed on his wall.[17] The court even inventoried his Talavera chamber pot – surprisingly an object that not everyone could afford in the viceregal era.[18]

A short inventory of Aldama's belongings, dating back to his first arrest on suspicion of homicide in 1785, survives within the Dongo case file. It is interesting to note that at that time he also owned a small French book and a white velvet cape, both of which also were listed in the 1789 inventory. However, by the time of the Dongo massacre, Aldama had pawned or lost a silk ruff, copper cutlery, two guns, and of course 250 silver pesos. Aldama probably stole the guns from his previous victim and the money was left over from the theft that precipitated the killing.[19] Aldama's

[16] AGN, Mexico, Criminal Vol. 338, Exp. 1, 25.
[17] Villa-Flores, "Reframing a 'Dark Passion'," 148–167.
[18] AGN, Mexico, Criminal Vol. 338, Exp. 1, 29.
[19] AGN, Mexico, Criminal Vol. 338, Exp. 1, 1.

possessions, which imply a slightly more cosmopolitan life than those of his accomplices, support his own assertions that he had the intelligence to make the strategic decisions in the planning and execution phases of the October 23 massacre.

QUINTERO'S LOSSES

Until the mid-1780s, Quintero, the oldest among the killers, enjoyed by far the most honorable path through life. He defined himself by his decades working as a seafaring pilot.[20] How he dealt with challenges relating to his clothes, and, to a lesser extent, other possessions, shaped his fate. As explained in the Chapter 11, Quintero journeyed to Mexico to document his family's honor and "blood purity." His willingness to serve his family in this way underscored his honorable reputation at this time. He spent a great deal of money preparing to make the trip in style, far beyond the cost of his transatlantic voyage and organizing the documents that his cousin needed.

In his confessional autobiographic narrative, Quintero justified the theft of four thousand pesos from his cousin's widow because she would not reimburse him for his passage to New Spain or the initial money that he spent to acquire family genealogical documents. While significant, these costs represented only part of the one thousand pesos that he spent on his travels. In fact, when Quintero arrived in New Spain, he had the appearance of a very rich man.

To start, Quintero's wardrobe demonstrates that he enjoyed the extremely rare privilege of enough clothes to dress in different ensembles every day for more than a week.[21] The existing inventories do not provide many details, so we can only imagine that he dressed much like other well-off men in the eighteenth century. He wore suits with short, form-fitting pants, white stockings highlighting his calves, and high heeled buckled shoes. Finely embroidered linens were on display underneath his carefully tailored coats. Quintero's matching suits of clothing included two military uniforms. Wearing these, he could proudly show off his rank as a militia sublieutenant. He also had two satin outfits, one red in color and the other blue, both trimmed in gold thread. Three other suits came from England,

---

[20] AGN, Mexico, Criminal Vol. 338, Exp. 1, 44.

[21] Rebecca Earle, "Luxury, Clothing, and Race in Colonial Spanish America," in *Luxury in the Eighteenth Century: Debates, Desires and Delectable Goods*, eds. Maxine Berg and Elizabeth Eger (New York: Palgrave, 2003), 219–227.

described as *prusiana* perhaps due to their blue color. These outfits featured embroidered decorations made from a Dutch fabric called *pontibi*.[22]

Wealthy individuals in the Spanish viceroyalties displayed their empire's reach by the impressive global provenance of their clothing. Even Quintero managed this imperialistic message, albeit in a limited way. He boasted English suits with Dutch detailing and his linen undergarments came from Brittany. The simple fact that he traveled with a dozen white shirts places him among the elite in terms of clothing. Even his underwear was made of Breton and Dutch linens. He also enjoyed the incredible luxury of two weeks' worth of woven stockings, including six pairs made of silk, possibly from China.[23]

Beyond these impressive wardrobe staples, Quintero traveled with a large collection of additional luxuries, some of which clearly asserted his honorable status. His accessories ranged from six embroidered ties to three pairs of satin breeches, two pairs of long pants, and two hats. Inarguable proof of his honorable masculinity included a cane that symbolized his rank as a sublieutenant in the Tenerife militia; a highly decorated silver sword weighing close to one-and-a-half pounds; a book documenting his noble genealogy, decorated by eight family coats of arms and silver letting; and a large red leather attaché case full of his service records, his correspondence, and other important papers.[24] The loss of these files hurt him deeply. Like Aldama, he could have used them to prove his stature to the court.

A set of marine maps and seven diaries of his past journeys testified to Quintero's professional achievements. Some of the other luxuries that crossed the Atlantic Ocean with him were a shaving kit, a book narrating the life of Saint Anthony, firearms and their paraphernalia, a set of silver cutlery, and his own bedding, napkins, and towels. A man who owned all of this, and could afford to transport it from the Canary Islands to a small town in New Spain, obviously proved his social and economic stature through his material wealth.[25]

But by the summer of 1789, Quintero no longer had access to any of these material objects. All of them remained in his dead cousin's house, jealously guarded by the widow who insisted that Quintero had robbed her of four thousand pesos. In response to her accusations, Quintero petitioned the court with a bitter litany of lost resources. He explained that, while languishing in jail due to the charge of theft, he came close to starving to

---

[22] AGN, Mexico, Criminal Vol. 338, Exp. 1, 43.
[23] AGN, Mexico, Criminal Vol. 338, Exp. 1, 43.
[24] AGN, Mexico, Criminal Vol. 338, Exp. 1, 43.
[25] AGN, Mexico, Criminal Vol. 338, Exp. 1, 43, 55.

death. In his desperation, Quintero sold many of his possessions at only 5 percent of what he paid for them. Every time he lost one of these items to feed himself, his acrimony increased. He could see that he was gradually shedding the material signs of honor – which equated to his self-conception and sense of worth and rank in his society. For example, upon arriving in New Spain, Quintero spent 160 pesos on a horse outfitted with the necessary accoutrements of a saddle, bridle, boots, and spurs. While incarcerated, he sold all of this for only thirty-one pesos. His beautiful gold-embroidered satin suit, bought for forty-four pesos, went for only three pesos. Wasting away in jail, Quintero sold everything that he could, from silver shoe buckles to silk stockings. He even parted with a silver reliquary and a rosary from Jerusalem with a silver cross, important physical representations of his dutiful Catholic piety.[26]

As he gradually lost every symbol of honor that he owned, Quintero became more and more enraged. In the summer of 1789, when he finally got out of jail, he submitted the inventories of his belongings to the Acordada. From his perspective, the "malignant" accusations of his cousin's widow left without dignity. As Quintero described it, "my extreme poverty is so notorious that it does not need more proof ... than the sight of my naked body and [the fact that I am living on] handouts."[27]

Quintero seemed to spend most of his time in the months before the Dongo massacre interacting with the court, plotting, and hiding out in his small, dark rented room. He either dwelled on his past successes, remembering how he ordered porters to load up his berth with all of his expensive goods and how he traveled across the Atlantic in relative comfort, or he pondered his losses. Don Joaquín Dongo and his family would suffer the consequences of Quintero's overpowering rage. Before his death, Dongo still possessed all of the wealth that Quintero no longer had. More importantly, the elderly man enjoyed an untainted honorable reputation. Aldama, Quintero, and Blanco did not. This infuriating contrast fueled the brutality of their deadly machete cuts.

DISHONORING THEIR VICTIMS

Without doubt, Dongo demonstrated many of the traits of the ideal Spanish man of honor. While never a soldier, he volunteered his resources and time to serve the viceroy and the city where he resided. His charitable

[26] AGN, Mexico, Criminal Vol. 338, Exp. 1, 41–42.
[27] AGN, Mexico, Criminal Vol. 338, Exp. 1, 49, 53.

acts proved his devout Christian piety. He supported at least eleven dependents living and working in his home and business – the ten victims of the massacre and his young nephew Don Manuel Lanuza, who fortuitously slept at his own house the night of the crime. Dongo's physical appearance checked all the boxes for demonstrating his wealth in public: he displayed expensive accessories, such as his gold watch and shoe buckles, and he rode out in his own carriage, driven by a male servant in livery, a definitive sign of aristocratic status.

Before the week of October 23, 1789, Dongo could feel secure in his own home – in a sense, a man protecting his castle. He employed two doormen to guard his home and his weaker dependents, including the four murdered women domestics and an elderly servant. His many servants, including the Indigenous messenger from his rural property, epitomized the kind of large entourage that a Spanish man of status was expected to maintain. To brutally kill a man who represented the ideals of their society suggests that Aldama, Quintero, and Blanco felt a destructive rage against these values. Dongo flaunted the ideal characteristics that they lacked, and so they annihilated him.

Of those living in the Dongo household, only the man of the house Don Joaquín and his relative Don Nicolás Lanuza came from Spain. The other men and women were most likely born and raised in Mexico. Despite working as servants, their connection to Dongo's household allowed them to enjoy a much more dignified if humble reputation than did Aldama, Quintero, and Blanco. The fact that serving women, lackeys, doormen, a coachman, and an Indigenous errand boy lived in significantly more comfort and stability than these three rogue Spaniards may have contributed to the killers' murderous rage.[28] Protected by Don Joaquín Dongo, each of the non-elite victims dressed well, sometimes in livery that proved that they belonged to this prestigious household. In their well-maintained clothes, affiliated with a prestigious wealthy man, they held their heads high on the street. When they went out, they had ample money in hand to buy whatever supplies the Dongo household needed. Although poor, menial, and in some cases, Indigenous or possibly of African descent, the nine servant victims could proudly claim a plebeian version of honor.[29]

[28] Warren, *Vagrants and Citizens*, 86.
[29] See Richard Boyer, "Honor among Plebeians," in *The Faces of Honor: Sex, Shame, and Violence in Colonial Latin America*, eds. Lyman L. Johnson and Lipsett-Rivera (Albuquerque: University of New Mexico Press, 1998), 152–178.

While a desperate need for honor and money motivated the massacre, the killers demonstrated a particularly dishonorable brutality when they killed each victim with a deep cut to the head. The head symbolized the person's identity in early modern Spain, as it does now, so an attack on someone's head meant an attack on their personhood. The many references to head wounds in Novohispanic criminal investigations suggest that aggressors purposefully injured their opponents' bodies in a way that most humiliated them. When Aldama, Blanco, and Quintero destroyed the heads of fellow Spaniards like Dongo and Lanuza, they symbolically attacked their positions of authority. In the cases of cutting their victims' faces, which they did to two of the servants, the killers attacked the place where they emoted and expressed their personalities. Face cutting also had a sexual element – as revenge for a perceived rejection, or to make a person too ugly for future lovers.[30] Dongo's cook Ignacia suffered a long cut to her face – perhaps she spoke up or somehow infuriated her killer more than any of the other victims.

SERVICE TO THE SPANISH CROWN

Although they offered the easiest way to assert honor, material possessions arguably represented the weakest proof of status in this society. Service to the monarch and family lineage had far greater value for personal reputation and as a defensive tactic in court. Of the three killers, only Quintero could confidently claim a distinguished record of service to the crown. The other two had nothing more than their family backgrounds and Spanish ancestry to attest to their honor.

Up until the early 1780s, as suggested by his lavish travel preparations, Quintero apparently lived as a distinguished and prosperous man in the Canary Islands. His stable life and his career accolades derived from the several years that he spent piloting ships in the Caribbean during the naval conflict between Spain and England. To be clear, although the two careers could intersect, the occupation of pilot sometimes differed from that of a captain. The *piloto* physically helmed the ship, while the captain may or may not carry out this task. The pilot was part of a crew, not necessarily the "master" of the ship. A pilot could also differ from a navigator.[31]

---

[30] Lipsett-Rivera, *Gender and Negotiation of Everyday Life in Mexico*, 147–151, 172–198; Taylor, *Honor and Violence*, 46–51, 107–114.
[31] Joseph M. H. Clark, "Veracruz and the Caribbean in the Seventeenth Century" (Ph.D. diss.: Johns Hopkins University, 2016), 120.

Although Quintero did not specify dates, his brief testimony suggests that he participated in the Spanish defense of Havana, possibly when the British besieged it in 1762 during the Seven Years' War. Piloting a fast and agile "sloop [*balandra*]," Quintero bragged about his successes in safely transporting hundreds of Spanish soldiers. At the direct request of the president of the high court located in Santo Domingo, Quintero made eight embarkations in service to the Spanish crown. The British may have come close to capturing his sloop on three occasions, but he survived the conflicts with the help of Spanish troops. As a privateer, he claimed that he seized several enemy vessels, including a twenty-four-gun frigate.[32]

Beyond his accomplishments during the war in the Caribbean, Quintero described two other incidents when he once again heroically risked his life in service to the crown. He narrated that in 1767, he suffered in a Veracruz sickbed. Upon hearing that the outgoing mail had arrived in the port, he jumped into action despite his fever. He claimed that he delivered all of the private correspondence and official government documents to Havana without receiving any compensation. Quintero also testified that he piloted a frigate safely to port soon after, safely transporting a cargo of over five million pesos.[33]

Returning home from his adventures in the Caribbean, Quintero's fortune peaked in the years from 1782 until 1785. In the summer of 1782, the governor of the Canaries officially named Quintero as "captain of the port," due to his "skill, good conduct, and maritime experience." Six months later, Quintero received an appointment as a sublieutenant in the provincial militia of the island of El Hierro.[34] However, in late 1784, Quintero made the decision to come to New Spain, which eventually ruined his life.

Although Quintero felt ashamed by the loss of his material possessions, he presented his entire identity as centered on the personal honor that he gleaned from his service to the crown as a *piloto*. His military persona so permeated his sense of self that he chose not to take an oath on the cross, as most witnesses in court did, but swore "under his word of honor."[35]

Perhaps even more shameful to Quintero than his long imprisonment or his poverty was his loss of military judicial privileges [*fuero*], a clear indicator of honor.[36] This dishonor came about due to the investigation

[32] AGN, Mexico Criminal Vol. 338, Exp. 1, 49.
[33] AGN, Mexico Criminal Vol. 338, Exp. 1, 50.
[34] AGN, Criminal Vol. 338, Exp. 1, 35, 37.
[35] AGN, Mexico, Criminal Vol. 337, Exp. 2, 26.
[36] McAlister, The *"Fuero Militar"* in New Spain.

initiated by his cousin's wife over the disappearance of four thousand pesos from her house. Throughout the summer of 1789, Quintero desperately tried to restore his judicial privileges in petitions to the Acordada judge. While highlighting his bravery as a pilot in the Caribbean, he stressed that all of his accomplishments were an effort to serve the king not to increase his own merit. For Quintero, his honor mattered more than life itself. As he explained:

I have been disgraced because [Doña Gertrudis] accused me of theft. [I was] imprisoned in a shameful prison full of evildoers. Although [I have been] absolved, this is not enough for my public satisfaction in Spain. Everywhere I go, people will forget all of my merits. I did not receive the satisfaction that corresponds to my noble status . . . . Without honor there is no life. I no longer have my honor and I also lack everything, including my good reputation. It would be better for me to pass away . . . . Living in infamy makes death more palatable than the sweet delights of life.[37]

Quintero kept pushing for the reestablishment of his *fuero* into October of 1789, just weeks before he helped kill Dongo and his family. The final response to his numerous petitions happened only on November 2, five days before his execution. Directly from the pen of Viceroy Revillagigedo came the decisive words: "Quintero does not enjoy any *fuero de guerra* whatsoever."[38] The experienced pilot must have felt an unbearable frustration as a result of this shameful decline in his status.

HONOR AS SELF-DEFENSE

Although Quintero could not count on the judicial privileges earned through his past military service, he and the other two murderers did have access to a court-appointed advocate named Don José Fernández de Córdova. This individual worked to defend impoverished litigants or those under the age of twenty-five, who were treated as minors within the Spanish judicial system.[39] In a halfhearted defense of all three of them, made in one short statement, Fernández de Córdova did not attempt to lessen the seriousness of their crime. He admitted that the "execrable and terrifying" murders "shocked nature." Instead of minimizing their actions, the advocate defended Aldama, Quintero, and Blanco with assertions of their families' honor.[40]

---

[37] AGN, Mexico Criminal Vol. 338, Exp. 1, 50–51.
[38] AGN, Mexico Criminal Vol. 338, Exp. 1, 59.
[39] Lipsett-Rivera, *Origins of Macho*, 18–19.
[40] AGN, Mexico, Criminal Vol. 337, Exp. 2, part 2, 20.

Fernández de Córdova stressed that the killers' executions, especially if they were sentenced to hang, brought dishonor to their "innocent" families. He described them as *"hijos dalgo* [sons of something – i.e., minor nobility]," with "notorious lineage and recognized houses." Despite the "accident" of their "privileged" birth, their actions "violated their heroic ancestry," a suggestion that they descended from the warrior aristocracy. Fernández de Córdova implied that "two wrongs don't make a right," when he discouraged Emparan from sentencing the killers to any shameful form of execution, such as hanging, which would "detract from their families' refined honor." In sum, Emparan should consider how his actions "stained" the honor of the murderers' families.[41]

Lastly, Fernández de Córdova called on the classic excuse of "fragility." He begged for Emparan to treat Aldama, Quintero, and Blanco with compassion and mercy because these men had acted desperately. They only thought of their current needs, without pondering the future problems that their deeds engendered.[42] All and all, the advocate offered a very weak defense, which failed utterly. As a neighbor of Dongo, Fernández de Córdova may have felt quite demotivated to defend thieves and killers who had violated both the safety of their shared neighborhood and the honor of a prosperous and well-reputed Spaniard.

On the surface, simple greed explains the Dongo massacre. Deeper analysis suggests that Aldama, Quintero, and Blanco craved money not just to live comfortably but to reestablish themselves as men of honor. They had to somehow resolve the insufferable contradictions of their failed lives. A particular kind of self-loathing shaped by the values of their time and place may have pushed them to their wits' end. But as they acted on their uncontrollable and murderous ire, they terribly miscalculated the repercussions of their crimes. They killed in the late eighteenth century, not in the eleventh century or the sixteenth century. They murdered a rich and established man and all of his dependents in cold blood in the wealthy center of the largest city in the hemisphere, not in the process of battling a hated enemy warrior in a frontier outpost. The Dongo killers acted like *conquistadores*, but they chose the wrong target and would not reap the rewards enjoyed by the celebrated *Reconquista*

---

[41] AGN, Mexico, Criminal Vol. 337, Exp. 2, part 2, 20–21.
[42] AGN, Mexico, Criminal Vol. 337, Exp. 2, part 2, 20–21.

heroes. Instead, the viceregal authorities felt no qualms matching the brutality of the criminals. The Dongo massacre roused the retributive rage of a cruel and powerful state. The late eighteenth-century viceroyalty of New Spain protected its innocent subjects and wreaked vengeance on wrongdoers with the very real threat of judicially sanctioned death sentences, carried out hundreds of times in gruesome performances in Mexico City's central plaza.

PART V

CONSEQUENCES

13

Ceremonies of Death

1800

The old halberdier pages through his notebooks. Before he became too tired for the task, he wrote down every important event that he witnessed over the course of the last three decades. Now age sixty-seven, he feels that he has very little time remaining. He wonders if anyone will ever read his chronicle, poorly written by a man of arms with very little education. His thoughts now turn to his earliest and happiest memories: squinting in the blazing hot sun of Granada, eating sweet, wrinkled oranges out of his mother Ana's hands, his parents laughing as he tried to lift his father Bernabé's sword for the first time. He left them forever forty-six years earlier to come to New Spain and make his fortune. Great wealth did not find him, but he also did not fall into a life of misery or crime like many other immigrants. Instead, he spent most of his life in and around the palace on the Plaza Mayor holding his halberd, standing patiently still for hours, observing the activities of twelve different viceroys as a member of their official corps of guards. Scenes pass through his mind's eye, jolting him away from peaceful thoughts of the dry earth that he played in as a child. His cramped hands turn to the first pages of his diary. The words he reads take him back to the time when he guarded Viceroy Bucareli:[1]

On Thursday, the 22nd day of August, 1776 in Mexico City, Felipe Santiago, alias ... *casado*, a black man, and Anastasio Basilio, a *mestizo*, were taken out of the Acordada jail for garroting as highwaymen. They were the first to be executed [after a period of incarceration in] this new jail.[2]

---

[1] González-Polo y Acosta, *Diario*, 18–19.
[2] González-Polo y Acosta, *Diario*, 30. It is not clear if the word "casado" here is the man's alias or a statement that he was married.

The halberdier remembers how strong he felt all those years ago, energetic enough to sit at his desk, sharpen his pen, and write in his journal even after long days spent on his feet. Now he can barely stand up for a few moments without fatigue. As comfortable as he can make himself in his narrow bed, he keeps reading.

1776 – STATISTICS

José Gómez Moreno started his diary with anecdotes relating to the strange occurrences that seemed to happen so frequently in late eighteenth-century Mexico City. Freak accidents, fires, murders, kidnappings, and assaults were not uncommon. While he certainly showed a fascination for the oddities of the day – from balloons to the viceroy's wig – the halberdier paid special attention to the 246 executions that he witnessed over the course of twenty-two years, an average of just over eleven per year. Some years saw more hangings, garrotings, and burnings than others. Annual executions peaked in 1790, with a total of thirty-two in the first full year of Viceroy Revillagigedo's reign. The years with the fewest deaths were 1797 and 1798, when urban residents witnessed only three each year. Not all of these executions came as a result of crimes within Mexico City – the Acordada court dealt with the serious problem of bandits roaming the highways outside of the capital. The *Real Sala* or royal criminal court tried other serious offenses from throughout New Spain. Lastly, military tribunals sentenced soldiers (see Table 13.1).

In the first year of his diary, Gómez took time to write down more detailed information about the prisoners whom he saw put to death. He listed their full names and race. This level of detail tapered off over the decades. In total, Gómez only mentioned racial designations in thirty-four of his descriptions of executions – twenty-one *españoles*, ten *indios*, two

TABLE 13.1 *Court and execution events*

Court	Number of Executions
Acordada	90
Real Sala	35
Military	2
No Information	6
Total	133

negros, one *mulato*, and one *mestizo*. Four women were executed during these decades. The halberdier probably watched all of these violent spectacles first hand, possibly even while serving as one of the viceroy's guards. However, Gómez most likely did not have access to the offenders' written case files, so he may not have known the race labels officially assigned to them and made assumptions on what he saw in their last few seconds before execution.

Gómez would have heard their crimes called out by a town crier at the ceremony, though he only noted this information in his diary sporadically. Other than the highwaymen mentioned above, other crimes in Gómez's 1776 entries include one nineteen-year-old Spaniard accused of killing his master and another man convicted for killing eight people and wounding another thirty. (See Table 13.2 for all of the crimes listed in the memoirs.)[3]

The diary's first few entries mention ten executions staged during the course of 1776. These took place on five different days as each event might include more than one death. From 1776 to 1798, 246 convicts died at 133 different ceremonies. Multiple executions on one day must have added to the agonizing suspense endured by the victims. Gómez showed some understanding of this feeling in his entry for November 28, 1776, when the Acordada court organized the hanging death of five men. Two of

TABLE 13.2 *Crimes resulting in executions, 1776–98*

Crime	Executions
No Crime Specified	196
Highway Robbery	19
Spouse Murder	8
Homicide	7
Bestiality, Sodomy, Rape	8
Robbery and Murder	5
Robbing Military Captain	1
Theft of Sacred Items	1
Forger	1
Total	246

[3] Gómez, "Diario," 7–8. This edition appears to be the first printed version of the journal.

these prisoners were brothers who had previously served as dragoons. The halberdier observed that the man hanged last had to wait for ninety minutes while watching his four companions die. Gómez believed that "his preparation and good attitude gave good signs for his salvation."[4]

1777 TO 1779 – METHODS OF EXECUTION

The three years from 1777 to 1779 saw a total of thirty-two executions, as well as the sudden death of Viceroy Bucareli in April of 1779. The new viceroy, Martín de Mayorga Ferrer, observed four men garroted and two hanged only three weeks after he started his new appointment in August of that year. Throughout his diary, Gómez nearly always listed the method of execution – most commonly hangings (127) and garrotings (99).[5] Three soldiers were *arcabuceando*, that is, killed by shooting with a harquebus. Additionally, two men were burned to death for offenses relating to sex acts. These burnings took place either with other men, presumably their lovers, or with animals, for those accused of bestiality.

Although garroting, according to custom, represented the method suitable for elite prisoners, no clear pattern emerges connecting class and race to the method of execution.[6] On March 30, 1778, an Indigenous man whom Gómez described as *"alocado y manco* [insane and one-armed]" died by garroting. In September of the same year, a Spaniard with the honorific title "Don" died by the more humiliating punishment of hanging, despite his "many distinguished relatives in this city."[7] In only one entry in his entire journal, Gómez points out that the men executed were "distinguished subjects." These three men, all given the honorific title "Don" and including a doctor, rode mules dressed in mourning (*enlutados*) and wore black clothes themselves en route to the gallows. Although Gómez does not explain the scene fully, he wrote that two higher-ranking judicial officials put masks on the executed men, "because the executioner would not touch them." His meaning is unclear, but this hesitancy may have been connected in some way to the hanged men's elevated social status.[8]

Although the customs regarding rank and punishment did not seem to apply consistently, it is very clear that offenses that the judiciary considered

---

[4] Gómez, "Diario," 13–14.

[5] Gómez leaves out the details of the method of execution in some cases, which is why these totals do not add up to 246.

[6] Prosperi, *Crime and Forgiveness*, 18, 144.   [7] Gómez, "Diario," 41, 49, 72.

[8] González-Polo y Acosta, *Diario*, 313.

more serious resulted in more brutal consequences. The authorities showed their vindictive rage at murderers and highwaymen by applying multiple posthumous desecrations upon their cadavers. After at least forty of the executions, judicial officials ordered more punishments on the corpses by carrying out one or more of the following acts: burning (three), *arrastrado* or dragging (six), and *descuartizado* or quartering (fourteen). In some cases, it is not clear which painful method of execution caused death. This is especially true for the punishment known as *encubado*.

In eighteenth-century Spanish, the term *encubado* literally means to put something in a barrel or a cask.[9] However, in the context of Gómez's journal, *encubado* refers to the Latin method of execution known as the *Poena cullei* ("the sack penalty"). Ancient sources explain that parricides suffered this particular punishment. The murderers were "sewn into a leather sack, in company with a dog, a monkey, a snake, and a rooster, and ... thrown into the sea or a river."[10] In 1769, a judge in Quito suggested that a man who had allegedly killed his wife deserved to die by this punishment, throwing the sack in a river near the scene of the crime. However, the judge recommended that instead he would die by hanging or garroting, because "not only has [*encubado*] been abolished in the Catholic Kingdoms of Spain, but also in the more distant kingdoms."[11] Apparently this prohibition did not apply to late eighteenth-century Mexico City, where prisoners condemned to death experienced "the punishment of the sack" at least seventeen times.

Gómez noted his first two observations of a sentence of *encubado* in 1779. He did not present a clear chronology of the execution, so it is unknown if the prisoners drowned while in the sack with the animals or if the executioner tied them up and threw them in a canal or Lake Texcoco after their deaths. Mexican judges followed Roman traditions when they chose this particular penalty. In seven cases, a sentence of *encubado*

---

[9] John Stevens, *A New Spanish and English Dictionary* (London: George Sawbridge, 1706), 165, accessed at https://www.rae.es on July 31, 2021.

[10] Richard A. Bauman, *Crime and Punishment in Ancient Rome* (New York: Routledge, 1996), 30.

[11] Ann Twinam, "Drinking, Gambling, and Death on a Colonial Hacienda: Quito, 1768," in *Colonial Lives: Documents on Latin American History, 1550–1850*, eds. Richard Boyer and Geoffrey Spurling (Oxford: Oxford University Press, 1999), 197. This alleged uxoricide ended up dying when his mule fell off a cliff into a river *en route* to his sentence to forced military service in Chile.

applied to individuals who had murdered members of their families. For example, on May 12, 1779, an Indigenous man named Lorenzo Martin died by *encubado* and quartering as a punishment for killing his wife.[12] Gómez observed that only one clergyman, an Augustinian friar, in the entire city spoke his language, Mazahua, and could therefore administer his final confession. Less than two months later, another Indigenous man faced *encubado* for an unknown crime, but this time the bizarre punishment occurred after his death by hanging.[13] Nine other convicts received the sentence of *encubado* with no crime specified, but most likely they had killed family members. Judges from the Acordada or the royal criminal court added *encubado* to the spectacle along with an array of other punishments, including dragging, garroting, and quartering. These multiple forms of torture or posthumous desecration, when applied to a single individual, conveyed a powerful message of the authorities' wrath against the accused.

The crimes that Gómez listed for convicts who were *encubado* range from a man accused of strangling and poisoning his mother-in-law to a highwayman convicted of "terrifying the kingdom" and killing seven travelers.[14] Three women received an *encubado* sentence, although the *Diario* provides details for only two of them. For one of the women, María Murguia, Gómez noted that she died in possession of 18,000 pesos, perhaps repeating some gossip that was circulating around the city. After her death by hanging, Murguia's body continued to move, which caused rioting among the spectators. Priests came running up with holy oil to anoint her for last rites. But this frightening occurrence did not stop the executioner from continuing the ritual of dragging her body and then putting it in the *encubado* sack. The judge sentenced Murguia to this suite of punishments because she allegedly killed her husband with the help of her lover.[15] Only five months after Murguia's prolonged execution, another woman was hanged and *encubada* for killing her husband. Her lover died the same way, and also suffered the added humiliation of *encubado*.[16]

[12] Victor Uribe Uran, *Fatal Love: Spousal Killers, Law, and Punishment in the Late Colonial Spanish Atlantic* (Stanford, CA: Stanford University Press, 2015), 117–150, 209–239.
[13] González-Polo y Acosta, *Diario*, 60, 62.   [14] Gómez, "Diario," 154, 354.
[15] Gómez, "Diario," 172.
[16] González-Polo y Acosta, *Diario*, 128; Uribe Uran, *Fatal Love*, 176–208.

1780 TO 1784 – DESECRATING CONDEMNED BODIES

During the era of Viceroy Mayoraga, and later his successor, Matías de Gálvez, 1780 to 1784, the number of executions increased to a total of fifty-five, and many involved prolonged bloody spectacles. It seems that in most cases the Novohispanic judiciary imposed extra punishments such as *encubado* after a convict had already died by hanging or garroting to underscore how crime led to ritual exclusion. They justified these posthumous desecrations by applying them to offenders who defied the most important values of the time, most notably the sanctity of marriage or sexual norms. After conviction for a crime as serious as killing one's husband or wife, the viceregal judges dramatically demonstrated that the perpetrator no longer deserved membership in the human community and possibly had forfeited their right to any chance of eternal life beyond the infinite torments of hell. Their heirs also no longer possessed any right of access to their bodies. The public spectacle of the punishments implicated spectators in the tortures and executions, implying that the urban populace consented to these acts, and thus agreed with their leaders' acts of vengeance.[17]

Some desecrations – including burning and dissection – made it very difficult to give any remaining body parts a decent burial. Instead, from the point of view of the state, condemned bodies "should disappear forever."[18] However, in most cases, it seems that even the worst offenders enjoyed the privilege of sacred burial in line with the Catholic Baroque emphasis on a "good death."[19] Lay charitable organizations took on the mission of collecting the body parts that were left behind in plazas used for executions and gathered them for burial, if at all possible.[20] Not surprisingly given the value placed on the mutilated limbs discarded in the plazas, Gómez expressed shock in 1780 when learning for the first time that a cadaver ended up "brought to the university in order to [dissect] its

---

[17] Thomas A. Abercrombie, "Affairs of the Courtroom: Fernando de Medina Confesses to Killing His Wife," in *Colonial Lives: Documents on Latin American History, 1550–1850*, eds. Richard Boyer and Geoffrey Spurling (Oxford: Oxford University Press, 1999), 54–76; Prosperi, *Crime and Forgiveness*, 62, 66, 309–310.

[18] Prosperi, *Crime and Forgiveness*, 67.

[19] See Susan Schroeder, "Jesuits, Nahuas, and the Good Death Society in Mexico City, 1710–1767," *Hispanic American Historical Review*, vol. 80: 1 (2000), 43–76.

[20] This task began in the era of the Black Plague, when no one wanted to deal with dead bodies. Prosperi, *Crime and Forgiveness*, 82–83, 124, 309–311. It also functioned to remove the temptation of the people taking souvenirs to use for a magical purpose.

anatomy."[21] Because this and the other dissection he mentioned both took place after the convicts were *encubado*, it is likely that both men had killed members of their family.[22]

Crimes relating to sex acts that the authorities viewed as "unnatural" also led to extreme punishments and desecration of the offenders' corpses.[23] Gómez narrates three executions for alleged sodomy and five for bestiality (grouped in Table 13.2 with the one execution for rape for a total of eight). In two of these deaths for sex-related offenses, the accused died by burning, the traditional punishment for sodomy in Spain and its territories.[24] The first took place on February 17, 1780. The victim was a man named José Antonio, alias *el Callejon* (the alley). The second execution actually involved two burnings – a man accused of bestiality as well as his *burro* – a pointless cruelty that offended Gómez.[25] A similar spectacle took place in 1786, when the authorities sentenced a mare to die by burning and burned the body of the perpetrator after garroting him. On the same day, another two men died by the same punishment and with the same posthumous destruction of their corpses. In this case they were alleged "sodomites," which, including the execution in 1780, added up to a total of three men killed for sodomy.[26] A final spectacle of this kind took place in 1787, when two men accused of bestiality died by garroting. Afterward, their bodies were burned along with another *burra*.[27]

1785 TO 1788 – BODY PARTS ON DISPLAY

In the late 1780s, Mexico City's leaders perceived an increase in homicide and robberies. They blamed this crime wave on the mass influx into the capital of rural migrants fleeing famine and disease in the countryside. As a result, the viceroys Bernardo de Gálvez, Alonso Núñez de Haro, and

---

[21] On corpses used for anatomical dissection, see Jonathan M. Weber, *Death Is All Around Us: Corpses, Chaos, and Public Health in Porfirian Mexico City* (Lincoln: University of Nebraska Press, 2019), 79–122; Hernández Saenz, *Learning to Heal*, 35–37, 86–87, 92–94.

[22] Gómez, "Diario," 85. The second anatomy took place in 1783. González-Polo y Acosta, *Diario*, 111.

[23] See Zeb Tortorici, ed., *Sexuality and the Unnatural* (Oakland: University of California Press, 2018) for essays on the idea of unnatural sex in the eighteenth-century Iberian empires.

[24] Christian Berco, *Sexual Hierarchies, Public Status: Men, Sodomy, and Society in Spain's Golden Age* (Toronto: University of Toronto Press, 2006).

[25] Gómez, "Diario," 79, 188. Tortorici, *Sins against Nature*, 124–160.

[26] González-Polo y Acosta, *Diario*, 186.

[27] González-Polo y Acosta, *Diario*, 182. Another execution for bestiality took place without the animal punished – the "muchacho" died by hanging. González-Polo y Acosta, *Diario*, 164.

Manuel Antonio de Flórez executed a total of fifty-nine convicted criminals between 1785 and 1789.

Throughout the decades that Gómez kept his diary, the judiciary occasionally chose to reinforce and extend the message of the execution ceremonies by displaying the body parts of executed men in the locations where they had committed their crimes. This action, meant to literally embody the New Testament directive to "cut off the part of the body that causes the sin" (Matt. 5:30), provoked fear and disgust in the capital city's residents.[28] At times they protested the exhibits of corpses and body parts. These popular reactions resulted in the authorities taking down the gruesome exhibits – including decomposing whole cadavers, or just their heads or hands – from public spaces.

Gómez first mentions this practice in his entry for March of 1779. As punishment for raping two girls, the executioner hanged a man and then displayed his body on the street called La Palma for three days, after which the accused received a decent burial in the nearby parish church. Given the abhorrence of this man's offense, Gómez does not record any protest against this display. He also comments that this is the first time an entire corpse was shown in public, although of course this only means in his own personal observation.[29] In 1783, the man mentioned above who killed his wife and mother-in-law suffered hanging, *encubado*, dissection, and lastly, the removal of his head for public viewing in the location where he committed his crime in Huamantla.[30] This four-part spectacle certainly would have convinced spectators that their society forbade uxoricide, despite its popularity as a plotline in classic theatrical productions.[31]

In two cases (not including the Dongo execution process, which will be discussed in Chapter 14), Gómez described how protests against these displays of cadavers or body parts led to their removal. In 1786, the executioner hanged three men of Spanish-descent for an unspecified crime. One of their heads was put on display in front of the cathedral, at a spot where the Eucharist passed as it entered the sanctuary. Immediately someone, perhaps a religious leader, demanded the head's removal. But two Acordada guards standing near the head refused to move it. Gómez

---

[28] Prosperi, *Crime and Forgiveness*, 22.

[29] González-Polo y Acosta, *Diario*, 56. The halberdier also believed that this crime had not occurred in the past, which could probably be disproven in criminal records.

[30] González-Polo y Acosta, *Diario*, 111.

[31] At least thirty-one *siglo de oro* plays had uxoricide as a key plot device. See Matthew D. Stroud, "The Wife-Murder Plays," in *A Companion to Early Modern Hispanic Theater*, ed. Hilaire Kallendorf (Leiden: Brill, 2014), 91–103.

reports that this caused an argument and "a bit of a riot, until finally it was taken down and buried."[32] The same thing happened in 1789, when the executioner placed the heads of three hanged men in iron cages for the crime of stealing sacred objects from a church. In this case, a group of priests demanded the removal of the heads and influenced the Acordada judge to give them a decent church burial.[33]

These protests suggest that while spectators flocked to watch executions, they may not have approved of this level of brutal state-sanctioned vengeance in all cases. Another clue to the public response to the death sentence comes from Gómez's entry for April of 1786. He writes that Viceroy Bernardo de Gálvez pardoned three men whom the Acordada had sentenced to death. The viceroy granted these pardons in the name of the king, and the people reacted by crying out "Long live *el señor* Viceroy Gálvez!"[34] This incident offers a rare example of anyone successfully challenging the authority of the Acordada.[35]

1789 TO 1796 – THE MOST VENGEFUL YEARS

In the eight years from 1789 to 1796, Mexico City witnessed the Dongo massacre, the simultaneous transition from the reign of Viceroy Flórez to Revillagigedo, and a total of eighty-two executions. Perhaps as a direct response to the shocking eleven murders on October 23, 1789, in the next calendar year the number of executions in Mexico City peaked at thirty-two, promoting Revillagigedo's reputation as the "avenger of Justice [Justitiae Vindex]."[36]

Gómez observed on several occasions that ominous events took place during or just after executions – including on the day of the triple killing of Aldama, Quintero, and Blanco. All of these strange happenings added to the visceral brutality of the execution spectacle. For example, at the moment that the executioner hanged a man in March of 1789, a shack roof crashed to the stones of the Plaza Mayor, injuring a number of

[32] González-Polo y Acosta, *Diario*, 162.   [33] González-Polo y Acosta, *Diario*, 205–206.
[34] González-Polo y Acosta, *Diario*, 156. Charles R. Cutter, "Judicial Punishment in Colonial New Mexico," *Western Legal History*, vol. 8: 1 (1995), 115–130, notes that pardons took place to celebrate events in the life of the royal family.
[35] Terán Enríquez, *Justicia y Crimen*, 85. Crimes that never allowed for royal pardons included sodomy, murdering a priest, premeditated arson, insults to the king, and blasphemy, among others.
[36] Andrés Cavo, *Los Tres Siglos de Méjico Durante el Gobierno Español* (Mexico City: Navarro, 1852), 218 n168.

Indigenous spectators. In June of 1790, the executioner planned to hang seven men, but his rope broke on the second one, possibly a man who had stolen a lamp from a church. Although the prisoner was already close to death, the authorities set up a pole to garrote him. Less than a year later, another rope broke during a hanging. Both the executioner and the prisoner fell off the platform, but the man was forced to climb the platform again for his death by hanging. The most prolonged death occurred in the summer of 1792, when a Spanish soldier named Basilio González survived his hanging by a few days, even able to drink water afterward. Revillagigedo ordered a second attempt to hang him, but González finally died a few days before this plan was put into effect.[37]

Gómez and other viewers of the executions commented on the locations of the killings, objecting to executions occurring in sacred spaces, such as when the gallows' steps faced directly into the cathedral for a hanging in September of 1789. Gómez also expressed discomfort with the staging of executions in different locations around the city. In these years, they took place for the first time in the Plaza de Tenespa, three different smaller plazas (Our Lady of Loreto, Juan Carbonero, and the Vizcainas), and another small plaza in front of the *pulquería de Mixcalco*.[38] As the majority of these executions in new locations took place during Revillagigedo's first year as viceroy, they suggest an effort to spread the message of an intimidating state which did not tolerate criminality.

As the epicenter of royal authority in New Spain, Mexico City provided the venue for executions of offenders who had committed crimes in other parts of the viceroyalty. Afterward, their body parts were returned to these other regions for display, spreading the threatening tone of Revillagigedo's early months across the landscape. Gómez gives an example of this messaging with his first entry for 1791:

On the 19th of January of 1791 in Mexico [City], they took the famous bandit captain Pillo Madera out of the Acordada jail to [administer] justice to him. This thief had scared the entire kingdom, in particular the Diocese of Puebla. He was garroted, dragged, and *encubado*. In the afternoon, they put his entire body in a box and took it to Puebla, where he was hanged on the gallows for 24 hours. Afterwards [his body was tied to] a stick until it was naturally consumed. He killed seven people, but the most infamous was killing his pregnant wife. As such, they

---

[37] González-Polo y Acosta, *Diario*, 202, 220, 232, 244.
[38] González-Polo y Acosta, *Diario*, 207, 217–218, 221, 235, 242.

investigated eight deaths and 28 assaults by him alone, without his gang. This was justice, the viceroy being the Count of Revillagigedo.[39]

A similar process occurred in 1792, when the body of an unnamed offender was taken to Querétaro after he was garroted. Viceroy Branciforte followed Revillagigedo's harsh stance on highwaymen, as evidenced by the executions in late August 1796. On this day, five men were hanged and quartered. Later, Gómez reported "their remains along with their heads were displayed on the highways of Guadalajara, where they attacked their victims. Their innards [*tripas*] were buried in the cemetery of Santa Veracruz."[40] After this extended demonstration, the number of executions tapered off, at least according to the halberdier's diary.

1797 AND 1798 – THE FINAL YEARS

The halberdier felt his age in 1797 and 1798. He watched at least two more men die by garroting and two by hanging, bringing the total to over 246 executions since he started his diary in 1776.[41] As he faced moments of both pride and challenges in his career and his health declined, a network of godchildren sustained Gómez. He described arresting a soldier, perhaps a friend of his, and a serious fall that he took during these years as the low points of his life. Meanwhile, the city suffered from more natural disasters: a drought and an epidemic of smallpox. The populace turned to the Virgin of Remedios to help them through these crises.[42] Through all of these ups and downs, the halberdier commented only briefly about the change in viceroys, as Branciforte passed on the office to Miguel José de Azanza in May of 1798. With little energy to put his pen to paper, Gómez concluded his diary after describing Azanza's mass of thanksgiving and welcome held on June 26, 1798.[43]

---

[39] González-Polo y Acosta, *Diario*, 229–230.

[40] González-Polo y Acosta, *Diario*, 243, 313.

[41] On April 25, 1798, a man left the Acordada jail for a sentence, but no specifics are provided. González-Polo y Acosta, *Diario*, 325.

[42] For more on the use of images to deal with disasters, see Paul Ramírez and William B. Taylor, "Out of Tlatelolco's Ruins: Patronage, Devotion, and Natural Disaster at the Shrine of Our Lady of the Angels, 1745–1781," *Hispanic American Historical Review*, 93: 1 (2011), 33–65; Taylor, *Theater of a Thousand Wonders*, 172.

[43] González-Polo y Acosta, *Diario*, 318–326.

1800

His eyes burning and his hands almost unable to turn the last page, the halberdier sighs as he reads one of his final entries:

On April 26, 1798, the *india* Ascencia Marcela Galicia was taken out of the royal jail for her execution. She had not been seen since February 6, 1771. There was so much confusion because they garroted her, then dragged her, and later hanged her, and afterwards she was *encubado*. The only thing missing was to quarter her so that she would feel all of the weight of the law.[44]

Exhausted, he closes his eyes and his head falls back on his pillow.[45]

[44] González-Polo y Acosta, *Diario*, 325.
[45] José Gómez Moreno died on February 1, 1800. González-Polo y Acosta, *Diario*, 329.

14

Punishment

From the case file, sentencing phase of the Dongo murderers:

The sentence for the homicide of Don Joaquín Dongo, prior and consul of the royal court of the consulate of this kingdom, six servants, and four maids and the robbery of 21,634 pesos from [Dongo's] warehouse and house. Don Baltasar Quintero also committed homicide and stole 670 pesos in Campeche from Antonio of unknown surname, a merchant and traveler. Aldama also committed homicide on Julian Ramírez in Cuautla, stealing more than 2,000 pesos [that the victim carried belonging to] his master, Don José Máximo Samper . . . .

The inmates Don Baltasar Dávila Quintero, Don Felipe Aldama y Bustamante, and Don José Joaquín Blanco are condemned to leave the royal jail dressed in black robes and hoods. They will be taken to the gallows where they will suffer the capital punishment of garroting. Afterwards, their three right hands will be cut off. One of them will be fixed with spikes on the building in the Calle de Águila, where they hid the [items stolen from Dongo during the] robbery. [One hand will be nailed to] the part top of the wall, and the other two on the doors of Don Joaquín Dongo's house. No one should dare remove [these hands] under pain of death. The [murder] weapons will be broken on the gallows by the hands of the executioner. . . . Likewise, any assets that can be found will be confiscated, and applied to [judicial] costs. Any remaining funds will go to [Dongo's] heir, which is the Archicofradía . . . .

This sentence is confirmed in the royal courtroom. . . . The three prisoners were immediately placed in the chapel of the royal prison.

November 5, 1789

PREPARATIONS

After the royal court issued the above decree, Aldama, Quintero, and Blanco each signed their death sentence on two separate occasions.[1]

[1] AGN, Criminal Vol. 337, Exp. 2, Sentencing, 22.

Next, Luzero and a group of craftsmen made the complicated arrangements required to pull off the sentence of triple execution.

Information about the preparations, which took place during the few days between the sentencing and the executions, comes from a final accounting of the costs of the trial process. Luzero and other court officials made a special point of acknowledging the difficult work accomplished by a number of people over the course of the two weeks between the crime and the execution. Many worked through "sleepless nights" on this "anguishing process." Elite men like Luzero and Elizalde received compensation for every petition they wrote or task they completed as a matter of course. Due to the extremely disturbing nature of the Dongo massacre, the documents underscore the "seriously fatiguing and worrisome" effort made by the judicial subalterns, even down to the labors of the doormen who worked extra hours in Emparan's chambers.[2]

Notary Luzero had the task of personally organizing the execution, including overseeing the details involved in building the stage for the event, renting the animals that carried the perpetrators to their death, and accessing the appropriate black fabric needed for what essentially functioned as the costumes and sets in this drama.[3] He worked tirelessly to complete these tasks within twenty-four hours of the murderers' sentencing.

Luzero hired a carpenter called Master Torres to build the scaffolding, who presented the notary with a bill for forty pesos. At least fourteen men worked on this construction project, including the master carpenter, four journeyman carpenters, and up to nine laborers. All of these men worked through the nights of November 5 and 6, earning a kind of overtime or hardship pay. Luzero recorded detailed accounts of each of their wages, as well as the cost of every piece of wood, tool, and nail required to build the temporary structure. The work on the platform required setting up three poles for the process of garroting Aldama, Blanco, and Quintero. Luzero even wrote down the minuscule three-real cost of purchasing the three nails used to affix the murderers' hands above the doorways of Dongo's house and Quintero's rooms.[4]

[2] AGN, Criminal Vol. 337, Exp. 2, Sentencing, 23, 32–35.
[3] For more on notaries' various duties, see Kathryn Burns, *Into the Archive: Writing and Power in Colonial Peru* (Durham, NC: Duke University Press, 2010), 20–41; Tortorici, *Sins Against Nature*, 14.
[4] AGN, Criminal Vol. 337, Exp. 2, Sentencing, 26, 42–43.

Animals, fabric, and crowd management all played important roles in the buildup to the executions.[5] Luzero arranged the rental of three old mules for transporting the killers from the jail to the plaza, at a total cost of ten pesos. He also rented four horses for the judicial officials who took part in the procession to the scaffold. The notary purchased fourteen yards of black woolen or baize cloth needed for draping the platform. He rented the black robes and hoods worn by both the condemned men and their mules, as well as the chains that prevented any chance of their escape. The ceremony required chairs for the officials and stands for the spectators. Local troops and their sergeant watched over the crowd to prevent rioting.

Lastly, the unnamed executioner received payment for his work. He charged three pesos each to execute Aldama, Quintero, and Blanco. Each of his three assistants earned the small compensation of four reales, or a half-peso. Perhaps due to the extra work required for cutting off the killers' hands and nailing them above the two doorways, the total cost demanded by the executioner for his work and that of his team added up to sixteen pesos. Staging the execution cost a total of 155 pesos. The belongings and money confiscated from the killers helped cover the bill for carrying out their own deaths.[6]

EXECUTIONS

Less than forty-eight hours after signing two copies of their own death sentences, at 11:00 a.m. on November 7, Aldama, Quintero, and Blanco met the judicial official Don Antonio Fonseca in the royal jail's chapel. Wearing black robes and hoods, they mounted three black-draped mules and began their grim parade, as they took part in this "orderly and solemn" ritual, which had a strong religious tone.[7] The assembled crowd listened to a trumpet blasting as the killers passed through the central city streets and heard a town crier loudly proclaim the Spaniards' despicable crimes. The procession

---

[5] This event has similarities to the preparation that went into an auto-da-fé in the Spanish viceroyalties. See Kamen, *The Spanish Inquisition: A Historical Revision*, 4th ed. (New Haven, CT: Yale University Press, 2014), 255–260; Alejandro Cañeque, "Theater of Power: Writing and Representing the Auto de Fe in Colonial Mexico," *The Americas*, vol. 52: 3 (1996), 321–343.

[6] AGN, Criminal Vol. 337, Exp. 2, Sentencing, 26, 34, 42–45.

[7] Prosperi, *Crime and Forgiveness*, 145.

moved along the Calle de Cordobanes, passing Dongo's house as it approached the viceregal palace.[8]

In front of the palace, and in view of the cathedral, Aldama, Quintero, and Blanco dismounted their mules and climbed up the black-shrouded platform erected for the purpose of their executions. They each sat down on one of the three stools prepared for their garroting. Remaining in a seated position, they placed their necks close to the pole that ran parallel to their spines. The anonymous executioner first strangled Quintero, then Aldama, and lastly Blanco. He left their corpses on display for several hours. After the garroting, the executioner also broke the *bastón* (stick) that Aldama had used to facilitate his entry into the Dongo establishment as he pretended that he carried an official staff. Then the executioner publicly destroyed the three machetes wielded during the massacre.[9]

Luzero officially confirmed these symbolic acts in his account of the ceremony. He added the observation that "innumerable people" attended the triple execution.[10] Neither Luzero nor the halberdier Gómez, also in attendance, attempted to summarize the crowd's mood. This lack of details suggests that nothing particularly interesting or unusual took place among the spectators. The general public may have felt subdued or vindicated. A later writer described the popular reaction as follows, possibly a fictional description intermingled with Luzero's words:

The innumerable people that attended the execution remained fearfully silent, mixed with compassion and joy for the triumph of justice ... which assured the tranquility of the kingdom.[11]

Perhaps the perpetrators took advantage of this last possible moment to perform a conventional demonstration of their honor, assuming a penitential demeanor as they made their final journey through the city streets.

---

[8] This account of the execution comes from Luzero's narration in AGN, Criminal Vol. 337, Exp. 2, Sentencing, 25–26 and González-Polo y Acosta, *Diario*, 209.

[9] AGN, Criminal Vol. 337, Exp. 2, Sentencing, 25–26; González-Polo y Acosta, *Diario*, 209.

[10] AGN, Criminal Vol. 337, Exp. 2, Sentencing, 25–26; González-Polo y Acosta, *Diario*, 209.

[11] Carlos María Bustamante, *Los tres siglos de México durante el gobierno español, hasta la entrada del ejército trigarante* (Mexico City: Navarro, 1852), 194. These lines included hero-worshipping tributes to Viceroy Revillagigedo.

El drama de la ley. (Nov.ᵉ 7 de 1789.) pág. 574.

FIGURE 14.1 Illustration of the execution of the Dongo murderers. Illustration in *El Pecado del Siglo*.

POSTHUMOUS ARRANGEMENTS

In the evening of November 7, the cadavers of Quintero, Aldama, and Blanco returned to the jail for the removal of their right hands – the embodied symbol of their crime and the hand that symbolized goodness, in contrast to the left or *siniestra* (sinister) hand.[12] Other than their hands, the men's corpses received honorable treatment. Covered in burial clothes, which took the form of the religious habit of Saint Fernando, they were displayed in a chapel later in the evening of their execution. On the morning of November 8, in line with the Catholic belief in the importance of a "good death" and charity toward those condemned to death by secular law, the elite lay brotherhood *archicofradía de la Santa Veracruz* buried the three bodies in the church of the same name. Observers described their funeral as magnificent and well attended.

To twenty-first-century eyes, there is a jarring disconnect between the religious ceremonies and the gruesome execution scene. However, the murderers had made their final confession, although they were not permitted the final sacrament of extreme unction by which the pious prepared for a "good death." Catholics in the early modern era resisted the idea that sovereigns had the power to condemn individuals to hell – which would be their certain fate if they were executed without the confession ritual. Burial in sacred ground assured that their bodies would be resurrected when Jesus Christ returned at the end of time. Secondly, the burial symbolized "the dead person's peace with Christ and the reconciliation between the condemned and community." Although there is no account of the crowd's reaction, it is possible that the spectators prayed during the execution, and they certainly must have when they attended the funeral.[13]

Back in the brutal world of secular vengeance, the ceremonies of viceregal justice barely paused after this momentous resolution of the Dongo massacre. Residents of the city watched another display of judicial violence only two days later, when five men received two hundred public lashes.[14]

The aftermath of these murders dragged on for another several weeks. The executioner nailed Quintero's hand to the doorway of the building where he rented his accommodation, and where he had hidden the stolen

---

[12] Cope, *The Limits of Racial Domination*, 39.

[13] Lay interest in taking part in this charitable task began in the fifteenth century, forming powerful brotherhoods who played the important role of comforters to the condemned. The Jesuits believed strongly in this mission. Prosperi, *Crime and Forgiveness*, 46–48, 76, 118–119, 137–145, 216, quote on 58.

[14] AGN, Criminal Vol. 337, Exp. 2, Sentencing, 27; González-Polo y Acosta, *Diario*, 209–210.

money. Presumably the hand remained there until it rotted away to bones and eventually dust – no documents attest to the reactions of others who lived here or saw Quintero's appendage as they walked past. But the horrific sight of Aldama and Blanco's hands, nailed above the two entrances to Dongo's house, caused some controversy.[15]

The display of the killers' hands served as a threat to the populace – a warning of the repercussions of heinous crime under the regime of the Spanish viceroys. Over the passing of the next few weeks, the hands disintegrated down to their bones in full public view. Carrion birds might have grabbed pieces of the flesh to speed up the process or leave it to the maggots. Passersby avoided the entire street if they could, or turned their heads in disgust or terror if they had to walk down the Calle de Cordobanes. This situation became intolerable for the owners of the building, who happened to be the *archicofradía del santísimo sacramento*, a prestigious lay brotherhood based in the cathedral. The building located at 13 Calle de Cordobanes had housed a very wealthy merchant, with ample space for an office and a warehouse. As such the *archicofradía* typically earned seven hundred pesos annually from its rent.[16] This massive sum represented about six times what most of the humble city residents earned for an entire year of work.

Tired of losing money on the empty premises, the leader of the *archicofradía* begged the court to authorize the removal of Aldama and Blanco's hands. He explained that his organization intended to use this income for charitable purposes. For the moment, no one was renting the house "due to the horror and dread that the house inspires in the public." No one would consider paying a substantial amount to live in a house marked with such a grotesque symbol. Anyone, especially elite people who could afford seven hundred pesos a year, would feel dishonored to inhabit this cursed space. As a result, the *archicofradía* lost out on earning funds that might help someone in need. The authorities conceded that the hands had served their purpose – to punish the criminals and "vindicate the populace." They allowed for their removal on December 27, along with the hand of another criminal, which had been displayed on the gallows for almost two years.[17] In the nineteenth century, aristocrats would feel comfortable enough to live in this building again.

---

[15] AGN, Criminal Vol. 337, Exp. 2, Sentencing, 25.
[16] AGN, Criminal Vol. 337, Exp. 2, Sentencing, 36.
[17] AGN, Criminal Vol. 337, Exp. 2, Sentencing, 36, 49; González-Polo y Acosta, *Diario*, 211.

The judiciary also had to tie up a few additional loose ends by responding to the actions of the women involved in the investigations. On
November 7, as Quintero sat in the chapel awaiting his execution, his
cousin's widow made a petition to Emparan. Doña Gertrudis confirmed
the fact that Quintero stole four thousand pesos from her when she left
him in charge of her house. Ten days later, the authorities arrested and
imprisoned him. She commented that he could not have spent all of this
money so rapidly – he must have hidden it. The widow desperately needed
the money back. But the court could not produce any funds to help Doña
Gertrudis.[18]

Although issues relating to Dongo's property dragged on for years, the
final concerns in the immediate aftermath of the crimes related to
Aldama's two elderly servants. Emparan angrily concluded the Dongo
investigation by noting that these women, by lying to the court on numerous instances including during face-to-face *careos*, "impeded the discovery of the truth in such an arduous case, of such great interest to the public
[good?]." For this dishonesty and misplaced loyalty to their employer, the
judge sentenced them to four years *recogida*, that is, living in a semi-
religious institution enclosed with other women.[19]

The archival record notes another set of issues relating to Dongo's
death: the status of one of his valuable properties. In 1793, the surviving
nephew and heir Don Miguel had to deal with a petition from his uncle's
family in Seville regarding the sale of the Veta Grande mine near
Zacatecas.[20] Don Miguel's mother Doña Michaela made this petition in
the name of her two children who remained with her in Spain. Many other
relatives may have also desired access to the murdered man's wealth.
From his location in Mexico City, as Dongo's designated heir, Don
Miguel argued that his uncle treated him as a loving father, and had left
pages in his 1787 last will and testament blank to allow for future
contingencies, including the need to improve the mine under discussion.
The case became very complex and may have continued in additional
deliberations by the high court.[21]

[18] AGN, Criminal Vol. 337, Exp. 2, Sentencing, 29. Another man claimed that Quintero
owed him a hundred pesos, and the killer had twenty pesos when he was arrested. Like the
widow, he seemed to receive nothing. AGN, Criminal Vol. 337, Exp. 2, Sentencing, 38.
[19] AGN, Criminal Vol. 337, Exp. 2, Sentencing, 49. Nancy van Deusen, *Between the Sacred
and the Worldly: The Institutional and Cultural Practice of Recogimiento in Colonial
Lima* (Stanford, CA: Stanford University Press, 2001).
[20] AGN, Real Audiencia Vol. 157, Exp. 9.
[21] AGN, Real Audiencia Vol. 157, Exp. 9, 63–74.

Partially due to the Dongo massacre, the viceroy, the judiciary, and other commentators perceived this violent city as spiraling out of control in the late 1780s. They reacted with harsher and more frequent death sentences for offenders, reaching a peak number of annual executions in the early 1790s.[22] Revillagigedo also conceived of a new semi-professional cadre of nightwatchmen who would in theory increase official surveillance of Mexico City's streets to prevent future murders and home invasions. With this reform, New Spain took a small step toward what might be called "modern" policing, although its effectiveness is certainly open to debate.

[22] Cutter, "Judicial Punishment."

15

Law Enforcement Reform

Illumination is very useful, because darkness engenders enormous crimes: not only because it covers them, but because it encourages criminals to commit them. For this reason, [public lighting] has been adopted in Europe in the most organized cities. This capital has even more justification to follow this example because its population is undoubtedly very numerous, and very corrupt.

Commentary in support of Mexico City public lighting, 1777

The eighteenth century saw a series of reforms in judicial structures and practices, including the creation of the Acordada and the division of the capital city into *cuarteles*.[1] These reforms may have contributed to more draconian approaches to justice in New Spain, as evidenced by an increasing number of corporal punishment sentences in the late 1780s and a peak in executions in 1790. This year also represents a watershed in the history of the Novohispanic judiciary due to the creation of Mexico's first salaried corps of nightwatchmen. Arguably, the shock of the Dongo massacre motivated Revillagigedo to create this new institution. As stated by a nineteenth-century commentator:

This horrendous crime made it clear to Revillagigedo that he found himself in a horrible position. Mexico was a den of thieves. To free the population of them, he had to adopt a form of never-before-seen police vigilance, which afterwards he succeeded in achieving.[2]

Even with this apparent clear causality, the idea of better surveillance at night had percolated in Mexico City since the mid-eighteenth century.

[1] See Bailey Glasco, *Constructing Mexico City*, 1–16; Lozano Armdendares, *La Criminalidad*, 24–26.
[2] Carlos María Bustamante, *Los tres siglos de México*, 195.

European models also inspired viceregal reformers. After decades of debate over how to prevent nocturnal dangers, the capital city eventually turned to publicly funded and organized street lighting as a possible deterrent for murderers and robbers. The maintenance of over one thousand new lanterns became the task of a corps of ninety-nine men known as "lantern guards [*guarda faroleros*]."

As the quote at the start of this chapter indicates, even a dozen years before the Dongo murders, residents perceived an increase in criminal activity and hoped that illuminating the streets at night would help.[3] This justification for the lighting project combined with arguments that the viceregal capital was an important court city that should maintain standards set in Europe. Local commentators were well aware that efforts to brighten European cities such as Paris, Amsterdam, and London extended back to the 1660s. In the Old World, kings, princes, and town governments viewed street lighting as beautiful and a way to control who inhabited the city streets and what activities took place during the night.[4] Both in terms of beautification and crime prevention, in the 1770s the authorities expressed their belief that New Spain should imitate Europe and impose more surveillance on their allegedly vice-ridden urban population:

> It should be enough to remember that in the courts and populous cities of Europe, the most energetic activity of judges and their superiors has not achieved avoiding crimes and excesses in the dark of the night, [but instead] they remedy them with the lighting of their streets, because the transgressors fear the eyes of their neighbors, those who pass them, and the magistrates. These powerful reasons [apply] everywhere, and they have greater strength in Mexico because of its multitude of inhabitants that lack a good education that would turn them away from vices, and create a fear of justice.[5]

The imperial authorities perceived public lighting as a way to improve the behavior and morality of a large segment of their urban subjects.

In response to these opinions, in late 1783, Viceroy Gálvez called on locals' sense of pride and competition with European cities to mandate that they pay for their own street lighting:

[3] AGN, Ayuntamiento Vol. 107, Exp. 1, 1777, 45.
[4] Craig Koslofsky, *Evening's Empire: A History of Night in Early Modern Europe* (Cambridge: Cambridge University Press, 2011), 130–145; Wolfgang Schivelbusch, *Disenchanted Night: The Industrialization of Light in the Nineteenth Century* (Oakland: University of California Press, 1995), 86. Paris's 1667 street lighting was a response to the Fronde revolt. See Germeten, *Enlightened Patrolman*, for the complete history of both the lighting project and the lantern guards.
[5] AGN, Mexico, Ayuntamiento Vol. 107, Exp. 1, 1777, 52.

In all of the great cities, the illumination of their streets has been viewed as convenient, both for the comfort of their inhabitants, as well as the prevention of disorder …. I have resolved, that within four months from this date, that anyone with the wherewithal to contribute must install lanterns on their streets.[6]

The presumption that private homeowners would willingly pay for this reform showed a poor understanding of Mexico City's urban culture and the lack of support for reforms of this kind. As such, the debate over how to light the city continued throughout the entire tumultuous 1780s. Only a handful of elite residents who truly bought into Enlightened urban beautification participated in the project.

By mid-1785, homeowners in select areas funded lighting on the following streets: "San Francisco, Empedradillo, Tacuba, Donceles, Medinas, Santa Clara and its alleyway, Canoa, Esclavo, Manrique, Pila Seca, San Andrés, and Santo Domingo up to the Santa Ana parish," allegedly "without any resistance from anyone."[7] These streets, some of which retain these names to the present day, formed a rough rectangle of approximately six blocks by three blocks, located to the immediate west and ranging a bit to the northwest of the cathedral. Adjacent to the sacred center, this district hosted prestigious friaries such as San José Real, and the convents of the Belemitas and Santa Clara. Of course, these several lighted blocks bordered on but did not include the Calle de Cordobanes. Located directly north of the Plaza Mayor, Dongo's house lacked a lantern in front of it. If the lanterns were still maintained on the streets listed four years later, his residence would have sat only seconds away from a slightly brighter neighborhood. It is debatable if his murderers would have been deterred by the feeble illumination emitted by these lanterns.

Both Viceroy Matías de Gálvez and his son and successor Bernardo died suddenly before seeing much success in the prolonged plans for privately funded lighting. From December of 1786 to May of 1787, the Audiencia took over until the arrival of a new viceroy. Frustrated with the lack of compliance to previous orders regarding installing lanterns, the court issued a new mandate:

Many streets remain without light due to the insensibility of their residents to the common good, and their own. It can be observed that some of the first [lighted streets] are now dark again, and that the [number] of lanterns have been reduced because the residents make excuses for not continuing their contributions …. The idea of serving God should serve as a stimulus, as well as the obligation to attend to

---

[6] AGN, Instituciones Coloniales, Bando, Vol. 12, Exp. 67, November 6, 1783.
[7] AGN, Instituciones Coloniales, Ayuntamiento, Vol. 194, 1785.

the common good, and prevent the thefts, deaths, and abuses encouraged by night's shadows, to facilitate the security of houses and property, and the ability to travel on lighted streets.

This decree again called on the idea that residents cared about the safety of the city as a whole, almost as a Christian duty. Once again, this way of thinking did not fit with reality. The Audiencia threatened that neighbors who did not comply by early 1788 would have to leave their residences, a difficult penalty to carry out. Imagine how these leaders shook their heads in dismay when they heard about the Dongo murders, remembering their fruitless efforts only two years before.

With his entry into Mexico City coinciding with the Dongo investigation, Revillagigedo made up for lost time. By spring of 1790, he confirmed receipt of twenty thousand pesos from the *real tribunal del consulado*, previously led by Dongo himself, to pay "master tinsmiths" to construct of all of the needed lanterns, which ended up numbering 1,128 in the first phase of installation. Around the same time, in April of 1790, the viceroy decreed the establishment of a corps of lantern lighters, emphasizing the structure of their leadership, pay, and duties in his order.[8]

Revillagigedo decided that a small tax on flour would cover the costs of the lanterns and the lantern guards. In proposing this tax, it seems that he had the Dongo massacre in mind, because he argued that "the wealthy and those of middle rank," would happily pay much more for "the imponderable benefits that lighting offers, which interests everyone, because they count on it for the security of their persons and the wealth represented by their families and houses." As Revillagigedo explained:

[Street lighting] would restore the tranquility that decent men lacked. It will contain the habitual or careless delinquent, preventing evil deeds from coming to pass . . .. It will provide the inestimable comfort of street transit without danger. This very populous capital, with a growing number of all kinds of residents, cannot rest without establishing the good order of governance [*el buen orden de policía*], and lighting is a fundamental to everything, as it strikes at the root of the worst crimes, planned by day and executed at night.

Continuing the theme of "defense and caution," the viceroy specified that the new corps of patrolmen would help prevent "the frequent robberies, assaults, homicides, and other crimes that take place in the darkness." Revillagigedo argued that "[these acts already] have declined since their

---

[8] AGN, Mexico, Instituciones Coloniales, Ayuntamiento Vol. 219, 106–107, March 10, 1790; AGN, Mexico, Instituciones Coloniales, Bandos Vol. 1, Exp. 60.

establishment."[9] When read with the Dongo murder in mind, arguably the viceroy chose all of this verbiage to address the fears many must have continued to feel for their safety in 1790.

These new nightwatchmen attempted to carry out their duties for the remaining three decades of New Spain's existence. On a nightly basis, they lighted the lanterns installed on their assigned beats. They arrested thousands of intoxicated individuals who spilled out of taverns selling *pulque* from early evening through to the early hours of the morning.[10] They also had ancillary tasks which came up on occasion. Like the very rudimentary police that they were, the lantern guards had a kind of primitive first responder role in Mexico City. They helped with basic healthcare emergencies at night and sometimes played the roles of priest, surgeon, midwife, doctor, and fireman. They even carried out a fatherly role in taking children into custody, including both orphans and the children of parents who asked for their help, and dealing with other personal welfare issues that took place on the street, including those that resulted from fighting and severe intoxication. These tasks added to their more basic duties of keeping an eye out for open houses and unlocked doors.

The populace regularly rejected the authority of these new street patrols. Mexico City residents showed their disdain in many ways, including insults, mockery, sarcastic comments, resisting arrest, tearing their capes and shirts, physically beating the guards, and, most frequently, breaking the glass of their handheld lanterns. These incidents demonstrate the widespread opposition to the new patrols and suggest a simmering sense of rebellion against law enforcement. The lantern guards also often lacked oil to fill their assigned lanterns, leaving streets dark all night, and irritating the city's homeowners, who felt that the individual men failed in their most basic task. Lastly, off-duty military men and military patrols often violently clashed with the nightwatchmen from their foundation in 1790 to the final years before independence from Spain.

Mexico City follows patterns seen in North Atlantic cities around this time period, which justified law enforcement reforms as an approach to a perception of increased crime and a greater need for public safety. Revillagigedo and his fellow elite leaders feared the influx of "unproductive, unattached, and unemployed" migrants into Mexico City in the 1780s as a threat to the "social order." Other cities around the Atlantic also experienced "the rapidly multiplying poor of cities whose size had no

[9] AGN, Mexico, Instituciones Coloniales, Bandos Vol. 15, Exp. 94, 1790.
[10] Toner, *Alcohol and Nationhood*; Scardaville, *Crime and the Urban Poor*, 208–271.

precedent in Western history."[11] However, historians of policing have questioned the perceived and actual "problems of crime, riot, and disorder." By some analyses, an increase in professional patrols took place in times of relative orderliness in urban life, not the opposite.[12] Criminalizing the poor, especially their leisure activities, and showing official success through extensive documentation of crime and punishment operated within the rhetoric of bolstering the imperial project in New Spain.[13] Like the frequent public whippings and executions, the paper trail initiated by the nightwatchmen demonstrated the viceroys' strong hand in dealing with what they portrayed as barbaric, hard-to-control subjects.

Although no other famous mass murder occurred in the remaining decades of the viceregal era, overall, the new public lighting and the institution of the nightwatchmen roundly failed in its ulterior motive of controlling the Mexico City masses. It may have even provided rowdy nocturnal drinkers with a ready target for demonstrating their hatred of the viceregal judiciary, offering them an opportunity to put into practice small rebellious acts against petty authority figures. Scholarship on early nineteenth-century Mexico City suggests that violence, theft, and robberies did not decline from the previous decades and perhaps even increased.[14] The existence of a new patrol introduced more armed men to the urban streets, which caused escalating conflicts, and, in at least one case, murder. And less than two decades after the creation of the lantern guards, New Spain began the violent process of transitioning to the independent Republic of Mexico. Ultimately this attempt at increased nocturnal surveillance and displays of corporal punishment, hangings,

---

[11] Allan Silver, "The Demand for Order in Civil Society: A Review of Some Themes in the History of Urban Crime, Police, and Riot," in *Theories and Origins of the Modern Police*, ed. Clive Emsley (Farnham: Ashgate, 2011), 25–26; Clive Emsley, ed. *Theories and Origins of the Modern Police* (Farnham: Ashgate, 2011), xii.

[12] John Styles, "The Emergence of the Police: Explaining Police Reform in Eighteenth and Nineteenth-Century England," *British Journal of Criminology*, vol. 27: 1 (1987), 17–20; David H. Bayley, "The Police and Political Development," in *Theories and Origins of the Modern Police*, ed. Clive Emsley (Farnham: Ashgate, 2011), 71–79; Ruth Paley, "'An Imperfect, Inadequate and Wretched System'? Policing London Before Peel," in *Theories and Origins of the Modern Police*, ed. Clive Emsley (Farnham: Ashgate 2011), 414.

[13] Adam Malka, *The Men of Mobtown: Policing Baltimore in the Age of Slavery and Emancipation* (Chapel Hill: University of North Carolina Press), 55–64. For a detailed analysis of both police history in the United States and theories about policing, see Kristian Williams, *Our Enemies in Blue: Police and Power in America* (Oakland, CA: AK Press, 2013).

[14] Lozano Armendares, *La Criminalidad*, has a great deal of data to support this supposition.

and garrotings, did not lead to stability for the viceroyalty. The viceroy and his judges and executioners were not able to control some of the momentous happenings that took place in the days and months after November 7, 1789. Already shocked by the ongoing killings, the populace would witness even more incomprehensible events in the next three years.

PART VI

INTERPRETATIONS

16

Violent City

On the 11th of this month, the mail from Spain arrived in Mexico, and in it came the news about the marriage of the infante Don Luis and the king's decree which said that if his brother carried out this marriage, it would be outside of Spain and its dominions, along with other bad statements.

On the 21st of August of 1776 in Mexico, in the Royal Customs House, the Señora Doña Ana María de Uribe was on a balcony that crashed onto Encarnación Street, without knowing how, she fell into the street and died. Her brains spread out on the stones. This lady was the widow of the Señor Don José Alfaro, of the Royal Audiencia, and that gentleman also died suddenly, so both the man and wife had pitiful deaths. She was buried in the San Francisco Church, after dying on Wednesday.

First entries in the diary of the halberdier José Gómez, 1776

The Dongo massacre, the backstories of the perpetrators, and the execution of Aldama, Quintero, and Blanco offer the most famous examples of how violence and entertainment intertwined in late eighteenth-century Mexico City. Texts dating to this era chronicle the multitude of other spectacles that displayed the viceroys' vindictive justice in the form of corporal punishment and executions. These spectacles sent out a strong message from the authorities regarding the values that they wished to promote. They expected the urban crowds to watch, hear, and smell the consequences of lawbreaking in New Spain.[1] It is no surprise that a man so close to a dozen viceroys kept the closest account of officially sanctioned violence.

[1] Vanessa Schwartz, *Spectacular Realities: Early Mass Culture in Fin-de-Siècle Paris* (Oakland: University of California Press, 1998), 4–6.

The diary of the halberdier José Gómez, discussed earlier, sounds at times like a tabloid, voyeuristically narrating the most scandalous crimes of the day in addition to the executions he witnessed. He was, most likely, not writing his entries with a reader in mind, so he included what were, to him, the most noteworthy events from the 1770s to the 1790s. As seen in the above quote, Gómez juxtaposed events in the lives of the monarchs with the explicit and gory details of surprising deaths.[2] Gómez narrated both kinds of news in a gossipy tone. It is likely that in addition to events he personally witnessed, he also documented the most popular gossip of the city. He described trivial occurrences such as a diverting night at the theater in almost the same breath as he reported the loss of Spanish territories in war or devastating natural disasters. These juxtapositions suggest that good and bad news blended together as information spread around the city, drawing the attention of the writer.[3] In reading this text and others, including the Dongo case file itself, readers to the present day also find entertainment in these accounts.

Even as it veers from observations as serious as mass murder to as trivial as the feathers on the horses pulling the viceroy's carriage, the *Diario* paints an overall portrait of a violent viceregal capital.[4] Throughout the city, bloodshed marked many of the streets and plazas – and not just on execution days. Gómez's other notations mapping out this habitual violence include depictions of murders, sex crimes, riots, public whippings, unplanned killings of criminals on the streets by law enforcement, bullfights, judicial spectacles such as "feathering" criminals, and the common sight of hundreds of men setting out on a forced march to distant locations to serve out their punitive sentences working in presidios. Some months included multiple events from this list occurring within a matter of a few days. While not all of these scenes narrated by Gómez include death, they do recreate late eighteenth-century Mexico City's milieu of interwoven pain and entertainment.

JUDICIAL SPECTACLES

Executions by hanging, garroting, and burning ranked among the most violent events staged by the viceregal authorities, but Mexico City residents also witnessed frequent nonlethal punishments. Although not often as bizarre as their decision to impose "the punishment of the sack," the

---

[2] González-Polo y Acosta, *Diario*, 29.   [3] González-Polo y Acosta, *Diario*, 39–40, 55–56.
[4] González-Polo y Acosta, *Diario*, 208.

judiciary had a few other creative approaches to demonstrating its intimidating might in prolonged, uncomfortable performances in the urban streets and plazas. On at least seven occasions in two decades, men and women were *emplumados* (feathered), paraded through the streets, and put on display for a few hours on a centrally located platform, before they started their incarceration. According to Gómez, these defendants suffered this penalty due to a conviction as *alcahuetas* or *alcahuetes* – an Arabic-derived term meaning procuring others into sex work. While Spanish laws did not expressly forbid solicitation for oneself or other forms of transactional sex, they had sanctioned against *alcahuetando* for centuries.[5] Gómez reported that the first time that this spectacle occurred, it created a never-before-seen scandal in the city, as three perpetrators known as *La Grilla, Cantaloro,* and María Jesús Barrera (no alias), sat out in a rainstorm for hours *emplumados*. It almost seems as though the authorities were trying to continue drawing popular attention to their spectacles by introducing new punitive methods.

While *emplumado* punishments happened rarely, city residents likely became accustomed to seeing groups of men and the occasional woman receiving the sentence of two hundred lashes, another long performance as the prisoners walked through the city streets. The authorities organized mass spectacles of this kind at least sixty-six times during the twenty-two years covered by the halberdier's diary. Although this represents only half the number of execution events (133 in same timeframe), many more people suffered public whippings than death sentences. At times the city streets would be crowded with what must have looked like excruciating parades as dozens of people received their sentences of lashings. The numbers of individuals whipped at one time ranged from a single man to eighty.[6] The number of public lashing events hit their peak in the years just before executions also reached their maximum annual total (see Table 16.1).

[5] Gómez, "Diario," 9–10, 32–33, 120, 207, 309–310, 451–452, 465. For more on this topic, see Nicole von Germeten, *Profit and Passion: Transactional Sex in Colonial Mexico* (Lincoln: University of Nebraska Press, 2018). These cases show that women often earned money this way in partnership with their husbands. See also Eukene Lacarra Lanz, "Legal and Clandestine Prostitution in Medieval Spain," *Bulletin of Hispanic Studies*, vol. 79: 3 (2002), 265–285; Eukene Lacarra Lanz, "Changing Boundaries of Licit and Illicit Unions: Concubinage and Prostitution," in *Marriage and Sexuality in Medieval and Early Modern Iberia*, ed. Eukene Lacarra Lanz (New York: Routledge, 2002), 158–194; Mary Elizabeth Perry, "Deviant Insiders: Legalized Prostitutes and a Consciousness of Women in Early Modern Seville," *Comparative Studies in Society and History*, vol. 27: 1 (1985), 138–158; James A. Brundage, "Prostitution in the Medieval Canon Law," *Signs: Journal of Women in Culture and Society*, vol. 1: 4 (1976), 825–845.
[6] Gómez, "Diario," 8, 268.

TABLE 16.1 *Lashing processions in Mexico City, 1785–9*

Date	Number of Convicts
May 1785	13
August 1785	27
December 1785	24
May 1786	42
June 1786	32
September 1786	18
January 1787	16
April 1787	80
June 1787	17
August 1787	13
September 1787	8
December 1787	23
February 1789	13
April 1789	12
August 1789	18

While a low-level judicial functionary carried out the sentences of lashings, the sight of public whippings was not unfamiliar to observers. In religious contexts, penitential self-flagellation in public had featured as a common practice for centuries all around the Spanish empire.[7] In a sense, these forced marches presented a familiar sight, although with an important difference – traditionally devout Catholics whipped themselves voluntarily as part of Holy Week processions or on other holy days. In late eighteenth-century New Spain, reforming leaders criticized public lashings for religious purposes as a barbaric, uncivilized embarrassment. But in effect, with the sentence of mass corporal punishments, they repeated and secularized what had functioned as a popular pious expression in Europe since at least the era of the Black Death.[8] Also in the late eighteenth century, government reformers sought more control of other aspects of public life that the Catholic

---

[7] Patrick Vandermeersch, "Self-Flagellation in the Early Modern Era," in *The Sense of Suffering: Constructions of Physical Pain in Early Modern Culture*, eds. Jan Frans van Dijkhuien and K. A. E. Enekel (Leiden: Brill, 2009), 253–265.

[8] See Nicole von Germeten, *Black Blood Brothers: Confraternities and Social Mobility for Afromexicans* (Tallahassee: University Press of Florida, 2006), for more on race and penitential practices in New Spain over the centuries.

Church had previously monopolized, most notably street illumination and burials.[9]

Coerced processions also took place when convicts marched together as they departed from the capital for their presidio sentences, forced military service in distant locations such as Acapulco, Veracruz, Puerto Rico or Havana. Up to five hundred men paraded out of the capital at one time, roped together in coffles. The movement of men sentenced to military or construction labor did not expose the crowds to gore and bloodshed, but this frequently occurring spectacle still represented an intimidating public demonstration of viceregal authority.

Another kind of incident also brought violence to the streets, although unplanned in this case: when criminals ran away from law enforcement. In 1781, a prisoner was shot as he tried to flee the royal jail. A more disturbing shooting took place inside of the San Miguel parish church, when a grenadier shot a man who caused a disturbance by bringing in drinking vessels full of *tepache* (a low-alcohol fermented fruit drink).[10] Taking into account these accidental killings, executions in the plazas around the city, coffles, and the frequent whipping processions, rarely a month passed in the late eighteenth century without some kind of spectacle hammering home the intimidating message against breaking Spanish laws. As they carried out all of these physical penalties, the viceroys and their underlings purposefully mapped out a geography of pain. Crowds experienced this at a visceral level as they watched accused criminals' fear bleed out on the stones of their city's streets and plazas. Of course, the Plaza Mayor served as the epicenter for these embodied rituals of violence.

VIOLENT CRIMES

In this city where ceremonial executions occurred on average once a month, alongside all the other forms of corporal punishment mentioned above, publicly sanctioned bloodshed represented part of the normal routine. The authorities justified these punishments by pointing to what they perceived to be an increase in crime.

Given this prevalence of officially sanctioned violence, it should come as no surprise that viceregal authorities were also sadistic in their personal lives. Six years before the investigation of the Dongo massacre, two men

---

[9] Pamela Voekel, *Alone before God: The Religious Origins of Modernity in Mexico* (Durham, NC: Duke University Press, 2002); Germeten, *Enlightened Patrolman*.
[10] González-Polo y Acosta, *Diario*, 80, 131, 173.

who later became deeply involved in this case faced sanctions for their own brutal behavior, due to a strange situation discovered on April 11, 1783. That evening, one of the city *alcaldes* made his usual rounds with a group of his men to patrol the city streets. Alerted by some sign, perhaps a noise or a tip from an informant, the roundsmen discovered a man tied up in a makeshift dungeon, blindfolded, and almost starving to death. Nearby, his captors had already dug his grave. Further investigation determined that a group of four thugs had imprisoned this man. Their justification for torturing him was that one of the perpetrators had an ongoing adulterous relationship with the victim's wife. Because he desired this woman all for himself, he asked three of his trusted friends to help him dispose of her husband in this cruel and prolonged way.[11] What kind of man would participate in such a nefarious plot?

As it happened, two of the perpetrators had prominent roles in the judiciary and by extension the government of Mexico City and the viceroyalty of New Spain. These important men were Rafael Luzero (also spelled Lucero), a chief scribe for the royal criminal court, and Vicente Elizalde, a captain who supervised the men who worked to carry out the tasks of the Acordada court. The third co-conspirator was a Lieutenant Rendon, affiliated with the dragoon regiment. As described in previous chapters, in fall of 1789, both Luzero and Elizalde worked continuously to help solve the Dongo investigation in a matter of days. The diarist Gómez recorded that in 1783 thirty dragoons chased down the adulterous lover who apparently formulated the above plan to slowly kill his rival. Due to the elevated social status of all three of his co-conspirators, it seems that they did not face a criminal trial. Instead, archbishop Alonso Núñez de Haro excommunicated them by way of a document posted prominently on the cathedral door. These were the kinds of ruthless men who implemented Spanish laws in Mexico City.[12]

Gómez noted only the highlights of the most scandalous crimes that took place during his career. Including the Dongo massacre, he narrated a total of seven shocking murders over the entirety of his twenty-two-year diary. At least two of these involved sexual relationships, another one related to family conflicts, and the motives of the three others remained mysterious, at least according to the information Gómez provided. Unplanned violence erupted in the viceregal capital alongside the planned executions and corporal punishments. The fact that seventeen judicial executions occurred the summer and early fall leading up to the Dongo massacre suggests that the

[11] González-Polo y Acosta, *Diario*, 113, 117.
[12] González-Polo y Acosta, *Diario*, 113, 117.

authorities' brutality certainly did not discourage Aldama, Quintero, and Blanco. Although Gómez wrote that the Dongo killings "were a greater spectacle than has ever been seen before or read about in stories," the other six cases show that this city of approximately 120,000 inhabitants had experienced similar scandals in the recent past.[13]

In October of 1780, the Mexico City dawn exposed the brutal murder of an entire small family, including two young children. Their mother, beaten to death, had managed a dairy in her home near the Balvanera chapel in the Franciscan friary. Within three days, the judiciary arrested the culprit, the woman's nephew, a twenty-one-year-old man named Luis González. Allegedly González slit the throats of his aunt's children. This horrific act inspired the harshest and most humiliating punishments that the Acordada court could imagine. First the perpetrator received two hundred lashes while walking the streets from the Mariscala bridge to the Calle real de Calvario, wearing a sign that stated his crime: "for having killed his aunt the *lechera* [milkmaid]." Two days later, less than a week after the murder, the executioner applied four different methods of killing González: in no clear order, the killer was dragged, hanged, *encubado*, and quartered.[14] With this spectacle, the judiciary only amplified the violence started by the killer.

Gómez also narrated crimes that defied heteronormative interpretations of love and desire, events that probably inspired intense gossip across the city. The first was a love triangle involving two women and one man that led to a murder plot in 1782. The impetus for the crime occurred when a married woman had a passionate affair with a woman described as "*amachada* [manly]," while the first woman's husband sat in a military dungeon. Allegedly the two women devised a plan to poison the unwanted imprisoned husband. They cooked up a jug of *champurrado* and sent it over to the jail. The husband generously shared this delicious, warm, spicy chocolate corn drink with two of his cellmates. All three ended up very ill, and one of them, not the husband, soon died in the San Andrés hospital. Gómez reported that the authorities arrested both women and imprisoned them in the Acordada jail, although he does not include any further information about their sentences and no women appear in the whipping processions for several months after this murder.[15]

A few years later, two men committed another murder likely also related to relationships that defied the conventional gender and sexual norms of the era. On Valentine's Day of 1784, the city once again woke to

---

[13] González-Polo y Acosta, *Diario*, 208. [14] González-Polo y Acosta, *Diario*, 75.
[15] González-Polo y Acosta, *Diario*, 100–101; Uran, *Fatal Love*, 176–208.

bizarre news – someone had beaten a man to death, then shrouded him in a hangman's outfit. The authorities found the body in an apartment on Calle del San Ildefonso. They took it to the royal jail and tracked down the dead man's master, who changed his shroud to the more appropriate and classic option of a Franciscan friar's habit. The master buried his servant with dignity the same evening, while law enforcement sought out his killers. According to Gómez, "they say that the murderers were Joaquín Quintana and someone called Berrio, effeminate men that here [in Mexico City] are known as *putos* or *jotos*."[16] Gómez did not explain the ultimate fates of these alleged murderers, but several men faced the executioner throughout 1784. Although unlikely due to the long delay, Berrio and Quintana possibly died by burning as "sodomites" on June 23, 1786.[17]

Another murder might have also had a sexual element. In Gómez's diary this incident serves to praise one of his fellow halberdiers. At 9:30 p.m. in early 1788, while the palace guardsman walked down the street in his leisure time, he heard screams and cries. Running into the house, he found four women who lived together suffering a surprise knife attack by a twenty-two-year-old man named José Cotilla, who was hiding under one of their beds. The halberdier arrested the culprit and took him to the royal jail, but not before the young man stabbed to death one of the terrified women. Just one week later, Cotilla died by hanging. Afterward, the executioner cut off both of his hands, displaying one on the pillory in the Plaza Mayor and attaching the other to the house where the murder took place. This hand remained on display for almost two years, until it was removed on December 17, 1789, the same day that the hands of the Dongo killers came down from the walls of the houses where they committed their crimes. Lastly, Gómez reported that by order of the king, the authorities tore down the gallows on this same day. Ultimately this was a pointless gesture, as executions peaked in 1790 under Viceroy Revillagigedo.[18]

UNSOLVED MYSTERIES

The years of 1788 to 1790 saw a range of unusual events, which left Mexico City's residents confused and on edge. Among these were the Dongo murders, dozens of executions, strange weather phenomena, and

---

[16] González-Polo y Acosta, *Diario*, 124.

[17] González-Polo y Acosta, *Diario*, 160; Berco, *Sexual Hierarchies*, 89–129; Tortorici, *Sins against Nature*, 84–124.

[18] González-Polo y Acosta, *Diario*, 186–187, 201.

the uncovering of an Aztec monolith, which struck a fear of pagan recidivism in the hearts of the authorities. Gómez narrates two puzzling mysteries that added to the city's sense of unease. In early 1789, the green and swollen bodies of a man and a woman were discovered in the basement of a doctor's house. To add to the strangeness of this incident, the couple appeared uninjured, as if they willingly had locked themselves in the room. Two of Gómez's fellow halberdiers guarded this room to prevent people coming to look at it, presumably for their own entertainment. (Several months later, the Dongo house also needed guards to protect the crime scene from voyeurs.) On the very same day as this inexplicable discovery, the Acordada paraded thirteen men on the street to receive their sentence of two hundred lashes. Not long after, the news of the death of Carlos III arrived in New Spain, and the court city went into mourning.[19]

The mysterious occurrences continued eighteen months later in September of 1790. At the start of the month, the authorities moved the enormous Aztec monolith they had just dug up in the central plaza to the nearby university. A few days later, the Acordada executed four men. Next, the Tribunal of the Holy Office of the Inquisition staged a seven-hour-long auto-de-fé for a man they viewed as "the evilest man." Later in the month, a Mercedarian friar murdered his superior and beat up another friar. Lastly, one of the other halberdiers made a series of strange discoveries in the palace. First, he found a basket sitting in a corridor, which contained a skull and a note to Viceroy Revillagigedo, which alluded to a man locked up in a room in the stocks, as well three dead bodies. The viceroy ordered an investigation into the note, resulting in the arrest of five men, but no further evidence about the information in the note.[20] Obviously the perpetrators meant to send a threatening or ominous message to the viceroy, but otherwise the incident remains mysterious.

RIOTS

Mexico City residents somehow did not internalize the intimidating message promoted by their leaders, who frequently manifested their angry and cruel vengeance in the name of justice. Apparently not cowed by all of the officially sanctioned violence, the urban population always seemed on the verge of

---

[19] González-Polo y Acosta, *Diario*, 200–202.
[20] González-Polo y Acosta, *Diario*, 223–225.

rioting.[21] Gómez mentions several *alborotos*, disturbances of popular unrest, in his diary. The first took place in 1781, when twenty-one prisoners escaped the royal jail to seek refuge in a variety of churches in the city. The authorities only rearrested fifteen of the fugitives, drawing them out of the sacred space inside the San Miguel and Santa Catalina churches.[22] As of 1774, the archbishop had forbidden that the more conveniently located cathedral provide refuge for fugitives due to its proximity to the royal jail and the Plaza Mayor where executions took place.[23] The halberdier does not explain why the people rioted on this day – perhaps in support of the convicts, or perhaps in fear that some remained on the loose. The fact that the judiciary succeeded in entering a church and removing individuals seeking refuge might have caused a violent reaction on the part of those who believed in the sanctity of these spaces and respected the authority of the clergy who allowed it despite the trend to limit the church's judicial authority in this era.[24] This particular riot, which Gómez ranks as a large one, might also indicate a protest against the harshness of the courts in this era, especially the Acordada.

An incident in 1787 also hints at the tension between church and state, and the competition for authoritative access to urban space. During April of this year, earthquakes terrified the city, leading to decrees against driving carriages too quickly over the broken cobblestones. The Catholic Church reacted to the natural disasters by organizing rogations for miraculous images and *novenas*. During the same weeks, hundreds of men paraded out of town for their forced military sentences, and thirty men left the Acordada jail for their lashings. As the men walked through the streets while feeling the bite of the whips, they passed by a carriage carrying the Eucharist en route to the cathedral. The driver called out "Does the church even matter?" For unexplained reasons, his words led to another riot.[25]

[21] Germeten, *Enlightened Patrolman*; Stephanie Merrim, *The Spectacular City: Mexico and Colonial Hispanic Literary Culture* (Austin: University of Texas Press, 2010), 195–246; Linda A. Curcio, *The Great Festivals of Colonial Mexico City: Performing Power and Identity* (Albuquerque: University of New Mexico Press, 2004), 97–120.

[22] González-Polo y Acosta, *Diario*, 78–79.   [23] Terán Enríquez, *Justicia y Crimen*, 84–85.

[24] Seeking refuge in a church was not uncommon in the Spanish viceroyalties. See Germeten, *Violent Delights, Violent Ends*, 25, 45–50, 90. For the changing judicial roles of the clergy from the mid-1700s, see William B. Taylor, *Magistrates of the Sacred: Priests and Parishioners in Eighteenth-Century Mexico* (Stanford, CA: Stanford University Press, 1996), 158–160. Flight from presidios and jails was also well known, especially given the huge number of men forced into military service. See Lozano Armdendares, *La Criminalidad*, 98–101.

[25] González-Polo y Acosta, *Diario*, 174–175.

One could almost sympathize with the authorities' attempt to figure out what would lead to a new outbreak of rioting among the city's population. At times, the people seemed to protest executions and whippings. For certain criminals, they supported the harshest possible measures. In 1783, viceroy Mayoraga chose to release a man who had allegedly murdered a soldier. Gómez observed that "this gave the city much to gossip about, because the dead man had not yet been buried."[26] Six months before the Dongo killings, the Acordada captured a famous bandit known as Paredes. His entrance into the city in captivity caused a disturbance. Gómez does not explain why, but notes that Paredes combed his hair very elaborately, and tied it up with a beautiful ribbon.[27] The halberdier seems almost proud of his adopted city on the one occasion when they showed the ability to calm their tendency to disorder. In early 1788, during a theatrical production called *Marta La Remolatina*, the audience broke out into an uproar due to the special effect of a column of fire on stage. Remarkably, everyone left the theater without injuries.[28]

Even though there was so much official violence in the city's routine, some individuals still wanted to stir the pot and cause disruption. In March of 1792, three men wandered all over the city, announcing that the viceroy had ordered that everyone must now water down, clean, and sweep the streets three times each day. Urban residents immediately reacted to the supposed command with widespread rioting. The perpetrators invented this mandate, so the authorities initiated a largescale manhunt to find them. The diary does not fill readers in on any further details regarding this prank, which fits into a 1790s pattern of mocking Mexico City's leaders.[29] This particular debacle seemed designed to critique Revillagigedo's campaigns to clean up the city.

BULLFIGHTS

The constant violence present in late viceregal Mexico City extended to officially sanctioned events involving animals. Previous chapters discussed the popularity of cockfighting and the burnings of animals

---

[26] González-Polo y Acosta, *Diario*, 112.   [27] González-Polo y Acosta, *Diario*, 201.

[28] González-Polo y Acosta, *Diario*, 187. For attempts to regulate the sometimes rowdy Mexico City theater in this era see Viquiera Albán, *Propriety and Permissiveness in Bourbon Mexico*, 27–96.

[29] González-Polo y Acosta, *Diario*, 241. See also Germeten, *Enlightened Patrolman* for the mockery and attacks experienced by nightwatchmen in this era.

victimized in bestiality cases, an act that Gómez viewed as pointless and cruel. The 1790s also saw contentious and brutal massacres of stray dogs.[30] Bullfights happened frequently as a ritual to celebrate important political events including the birth or marriage of royalty in Spain, or the entrance of a new viceroy into New Spain. Over the course of the 1770s to the 1790s, a few weeks of bullfights took place regularly at the end of January and into February, as well as in November and early December. Gómez attended the bullfights as part of his work duties as well as voluntarily for his own entertainment. The audience expected the animals to suffer and die during these events, so the halberdier did not mention these killings as newsworthy in his journal. However, he made a special point to report when the bullfighters died, which he described as a "misfortune."[31]

While violence was central to the experience of living in the viceregal capital, even bullfights might include more lighthearted elements to entertain the populace.[32] During the fall of 1785, Gómez reported a number of unusual additions to the bullfighting season, which he watched from a section of seating set aside for the halberdiers and paid for by the viceroy. The festivities began on October 11, when the crown regiment funded fireworks in honor of their patron Our Lady of the Pillar of Zaragoza. The next day Viceroy Bernardo de Gálvez's four-year-old son became an honorary grenadier, an occasion for opening up the palace to "all classes" for refreshments provided by the viceroy. On October 20, the bulls paraded out to the Plaza del Volador, just south of the palace. When the viceroy appeared in the afternoon, a very large balloon was released. Two weeks later, another balloon went up, described as "the best of all," as part of the party for the opening of the new Academia de Bellas Artes. So many balloons went up in these months that a poem circulated commenting on all of the trash that they created when they descended.[33] In November, the bullfights began and, in a rare innovation, on three different days, women fought the bulls, including a relative of the viceroy. Gálvez and his thirty-one-year-old wife Félicité de Saint Maxent, the

---

[30] Germeten, *The Enlightened Patrolman.*   [31] González-Polo y Acosta, *Diario,* 184–185.

[32] Viquiera Albán, *Propriety and Permissiveness in Bourbon Mexico,* 10–15; Christoph Rosenmüller, *Patrons, Partisans, and Palace Intrigues: The Court Society of Colonial Mexico, 1702–1710* (Calgary: University of Calgary Press, 2008), 47–48.

[33] As viceroy, Gálvez had a reputation as a young, vibrant innovator, interested in the French Enlightenment. The balloons may have also been viewed as having a military use. See Eliga Gould, "Review of *Bernardo de Gálvez: Spanish Hero of the American Revolution* by Quintero Saravia," *The William and Mary Quarterly,* vol. 76: 3 (July 2019), 597–600.

widowed daughter of a powerful New Orleans merchant, made many appearances at these events, traveling around the city in a distinctive carriage. Gálvez funded other dances and fireworks – including one display that burned up all of the vendors' tables in the Plaza Mayor. His wife attended bullfights without him and led dances on her own. In contrast to these lighthearted shows, eight men were executed on October 22 and thirty-nine men received two hundred lashes later in the month. At the end of November, another four hundred men paraded out of the city "on the cord" for their presidio sentences, on the same day as a festival in honor of the anniversary of the death of the previous viceroy, Gálvez's father.[34]

After Gálvez's untimely death at age forty in 1786, the city seemed less festive, at least according to Gómez's memoirs. The year 1788 saw a great deal of judicial violence as well as prolonged bullfights in January. Gómez's entries for January critiqued the "ugly" spectacles organized by the manager of the bullfighting ring, who chose to include other small animals in the event. The diarist often rated the bullfights as "very badly done" and observed that Viceroy Flórez chose not to attend during the two-week season. This particular month, residents of the city witnessed not only these cruel spectacles involving animals, but the knifing and execution of Cotilla, the young man who had hidden under a woman's bed and then killed her.

Overall, both officially sanctioned executions and murders became almost routine events in the late 1780s, a decade which ended with the Dongo massacre.[35] In the early 1790s, when the courts took their cruel vengeance dozens of times in reaction to a perceived increase in criminality, reminders of the violence of the Aztec past would literally rise up from the same plaza where 246 executions took place.

[34] González-Polo y Acosta, *Diario*, 145–150.
[35] González-Polo y Acosta, *Diario*, 187–188.

17

Omens

The 20th of December 1780 was a memorable day for Mexico. There was an earthquake at 8:30 in the morning, and on the same day, five men left the Acordada jail for execution.

On the night of the 14th of November, 1789 in Mexico, the northern sky filled with clouds that looked like fiery flames, which caused turmoil among the people. Several churches organized prayers [*rogativas*]. People were so scared and confused. Some begged for mercy; others prayed; women wept. In a word, this night [felt like] a judgment. Some people went to [the shrine of] Our Lady of Guadalupe, others to Calvario and other churches. In the streets, there was nothing but crowds of men, women, and boys, some crying and some praying . . ..

Diary entry by the halberdier José Gómez

The combination of violent crimes, gruesome and prolonged execution spectacles, and natural disasters created an atmosphere of tension and fear in late 1780s Mexico City. Scientists of the era identified the flaming clouds that Gómez described above as an aurora borealis. But most people at the time would not have read these scientific interpretations. Instead, shocking natural phenomena prompted a turn to their faith in the supernatural for explanations and remedies. This reaction drew from both European and Indigenous beliefs about the connection between the divine and the physical world. In both cultures natural features and events served to demonstrate that a "divine life force suffused the material universe" – miraculous springs for example existed in both Spain and Mesoamerica.[1] The "spirit and will" of supernatural forces "manifest[ed] in natural

---

[1] Davíd Carrasco, ed., *Aztec Ceremonial Landscapes* (Boulder: University Press of Colorado, 1999); Taylor, *Theater*, 140.

events," including earthquakes, storms, and floods.[2] Gómez himself communicated a sense of the ineffable links between human acts and natural phenomena (perhaps caused by unseen supernatural entities) in the first quote by juxtaposing an earthquake with the execution of five men. The skepticism of the European Enlightenment did not diminish the Novohispanic belief in miracles.[3]

Whether or not they used the halberdier's diary as a source, many accounts of the Dongo massacre and its aftermath include the aurora borealis as a concluding event in the narration – a signpost signifying the end of the murder story.[4] The implication, both in these later sources and in the strong emotions described above, is that powerful forces beyond human understanding in some inexplicable way reacted to the killings – both the eleven victims of Aldama, Blanco, and Quintero, as well as when the killers themselves were garroted. The popular reaction to the 1789 aurora borealis can be contextualized by examining the fearful months of natural disasters that led up to the Dongo massacres and the decades of tense buildup caused by dozens of earthquakes. While the secular government created spectacles of public lashings and executions to illustrate to the populace that the viceroyalty could control criminal activity, the church gathered the city residents together to create a communal response to weather and astronomical phenomena.

Gómez's anecdote depicting the popular reaction to the aurora borealis fits the standard Novohispanic response to natural disasters: to seek help en masse at churches and shrines.[5] Collective action by the church and the populace to beg for divine intervention in crisis situations happened often in the years from the mid-1780s to the early 1790s. In this short timeframe, Mexico City residents experienced shock after shock, starting with epidemics and flooding which lasted from 1783 to 1786. Two viceroys died due to illness, causing six unexpected changes in New Spain's leadership over the course of only five years. In the late 1780s, the city witnessed an increase in public corporal punishments and presidio sentences, along with earthquakes, floods, and hurricanes.

---

[2] The classic source for Spain's supernaturally charged landscape is William Christian, *Local Religion in Sixteenth-Century Spain* (Princeton, NJ: Princeton University Press, 1989). For these beliefs in the Americas under Spanish rule, see Martin Nesvig, ed., *Local Religion in Colonial Mexico* (Albuquerque: University of New Mexico, 2006); Taylor, *Theater*, 340, 560–562, quote on 126.

[3] Taylor, *Theater*, 98–99, sums up the "consolidation and growth" of miracle shrines in this era.

[4] See José de Cuéllar, *Sin of the Century*, trans. Nicole von Germeten, forthcoming.

[5] Taylor, *Theater*, 187–193, 317, 561.

During the most intense periods of seismic activity, Mexico City's church and state leaders prompted the populace to seek solace by staging ritual events.[6] For example, a strange series of weather events began on March 19, 1787, with a "hurricane of wind and dust, so that nobody could see anything in the streets."[7] This unusual wind returned a few days later, and then, on March 28, the first of several earthquakes shook the city for five minutes. The *Gazeta* reported that government officials immediately left their chambers and went out to the Plaza Mayor. Soon "crowds of people and families" also gathered in the same location.[8] Many buildings including the viceregal palace suffered damage. The prisoners in the royal jail panicked in fear of their lives. Troops allowed them to leave the building, and guarded the 220 inmates on the plaza, threatening to execute them on the spot if they tried to flee. Later they were housed in religious institutions.[9]

Many residents fled to the Villa of Guadalupe or the Sanctuary of Calvary. Even the most elite individuals chose to spend the night sleeping in Alameda Park or on the wide new streets such as the Paseo Nuevo, or they left the capital city. The high court mandated a two-week closure of theaters.[10] Additional patrols walked the streets trying to prevent looting. The military attempted to organize doctors and surgeons to help with the injured. As March ended, a hurricane and torrential rain continued to pound the city. On April 3, the cathedral and some of the most prominent convents suffered damages from a new quake, which destroyed the tower of the San Francisco church.[11]

Turning from practical responses to emotional reactions and the search for spiritual guidance in these disastrous weeks, Gómez described March 28, 1787, as "a day of judgment and confusion. Some prayed, some praised [God and the saints], most people cried out, others ran away, still others fell to the ground, and many women felt pains in their heart."[12]

Some of these panicked residents turned to church buildings for shelter. On April 13, the San José church began a *novena*, nine days of prayers and masses, "so that God would look down on us with merciful eyes, and cease this lamentable punishment." High court functionaries and other judicial and governmental officials attended, and also took part in

---

[6] For the ways that the supernatural manifested in or intertwined with Mexican earthquakes, see Taylor, *Theater*, 185, 205, 358, 420–422, 431, 448–451.

[7] Gómez, "Diario," 264.   [8] *Gazeta de México*, April 17, 1787, 3.

[9] *Gazeta de México*, April 17, 1787, 5.   [10] Gómez, "Diario," 264.

[11] *Gazeta de México*, April 17, 1787, 5–6.   [12] Gómez, "Diario," 264.

a prayer procession two days later. The statue of Saint Joseph accompanied the parade of "distinguished residents" who marched with candles in hand, displaying "as much illumination and devotion possible under the circumstances."[13] Despite the sacred rituals, another strong *temblor* (earthquake) struck the city on April 16. After this, the city enjoyed a respite from shaking earth for just over four months.[14]

Before long, the disasters began again. In September of 1787, another earthquake struck the city, followed by flooding. More *temblores* struck the city in November.[15] Nothing beyond standard bullfights, celebrations, and judicial spectacles occurred throughout 1788, but the year of 1789 promised to be a fatal one. Although New Spain did not receive the news immediately, the effective King Carlos III died at the end of 1788 after three decades as monarch. After learning this devastating information, for the entire month of March 1789 Mexico City occupied itself mourning the death of the king. All representatives of church and state participated in processions in mourning dress and church bells rang hundreds of times. The ceremonies in honor of the dead king continued all summer and into the fall, coinciding with repeated judicial spectacles as well as unforeseen natural disasters. During Holy Week in April, traditional processions were canceled due to thunder, lightning, and torrential rain which persisted for ten hours. In midsummer, another powerful earthquake struck the city, one of at least thirty-four documented in Gómez's diary (see Table 17.1).[16] Then came the Dongo killings, which coincided with Viceroy Revillagigedo's dramatic entrance into the city. It seems like the extreme violence of the Dongo murders and the execution of the perpetrators two weeks later on November 7 finally pushed the Mexico City populace to the edge, resulting in a dramatic response to the aurora borealis.[17]

An article in the December 1 edition of the *Gazeta de México* attempted to use examples of other similar celestial events to calm the public reaction:

A phenomena which rarely happens in lower latitude regions, like Mexico, gave the entire city the greatest consternation on the night of November 14. The people were

---

[13] *Gazeta de México*, April 17, 1787, 7.
[14] González-Polo y Acosta, *Diario*, 265–269. Gómez and the *Gazeta* knew about the simultaneous disasters happening in Oaxaca and Puebla. The coast of Tehuantepec experienced a tsunami on March 28, 1787, as reported in the *Gazeta de México*. See Gerardo Suárez, "El Gran Tsunami Mexicano de 1787," *Letras Libres* (September 2011).
[15] Gómez, "Diario," 281, 284.   [16] González-Polo y Acosta, *Diario*, 200–207.
[17] González-Polo y Acosta, *Diario*, 210.

TABLE 17.1 *Earthquakes in late eighteenth-century Mexico City*

December 20, 1780	March 28, 1787	April 13, 1790
February 15, 1781	March 30, 1787	April 20, 1790
January 20, 1782	April 3, 1787	March 2, 1793
May 22, 1782	April 8, 1787	December 19, 1793
September 29, 1783	April 16, 1787	February 19, 1794
June 26, 1785	June 21, 1787	March 7, 1794
March 3, 1786	September 4, 1787	March 8, 1794
April 3, 1786	November 7, 1787	July 18, 1794
June 26, 1786	April 5, 1787	December 5, 1794
July 1, 1786	June 27, 1788	April 8, 1795
October 28, 1786	July 6, 1789	August 29, 1795

dismayed to see a great part of our Northern skies illuminated. They screamed in the streets, anticipating burning up in the flames that their fear imagined.[18]

Observers described the lights as "whitish rays in a broom shape, which slowly spread." By 8:30 p.m., orangish lights appeared on the horizon, along with what appeared to be a thick dark pink smoke.[19] The *Gazeta* article tried to explain the cause of the aurora borealis and mentioned the frequency with which they took place in Europe and the Americas, extending this explanation to a long article published in the December 22 edition.[20] These articles formed part of a scientific debate that lasted for several months in Mexico City periodicals.[21]

Revillagigedo angrily suppressed the terrified popular reaction to the northern lights, commanding his secretary to write a statement that

[18] *Gazeta de México*, December 1, 1787, 8. This study and the one appearing the next edition was written by Antonio León y Gama, an astronomer and one of three Mexican scientists who studied the aurora borealis, including collecting letters about it from other parts of New Spain. María de la Paz Ramos-Lara, Héctor J. Durand-Manterola, and Adrián Canales-Pozos, "The Low Latitude Aurora Borealis of 1789," *Advances in Space Research*, vol. 68: 6 (2021), 2320–2331.

[19] Paz Ramos-Lara, Durand-Manterola, and Canales-Pozos, "The Low Latitude," 2325.

[20] *Gazeta de México*, December 22, 1787, 8–11. Most of this edition was dedicated to the celebrations in honor of the new king Carlos IV and ongoing mourning rituals for Carlos III.

[21] A. Luna and S. Biro, "La ciencia en la cultura novohispana: el debate sobre la aurora boreal de 1789," *Revista Mexicana de Física*, vol. 63: 2 (2017), 87–94. Another contributor to the debate was a clockmaker employed by the cathedral. See Heréndira Téllez Nieto and Juan Manuel Espinosa Sánchez, "La Astronomía Teórica Novohispana: Francisco Dimas Rangel y la Aurora Boreal de 1789," *Relaciones: Estudios de Historia y Sociedad*, vol. 30: 117 (2009), 183–210.

summed up the viceroy's disdain for his subjects. He described the Indigenous people of New Spain as fearful and ignorant, which contributed to their panicked reaction to the aurora borealis. In his view, they were influenced by "this or that fanatic" to fill the streets, crying and shouting in their distress. Viceroy Revillagigedo also expressed his dissatisfaction with the church response, which he believed fomented more panic among the populace. Multiple bells rang from church towers calling the faithful to pray for mercy. Street preachers added to the chaos with their doleful impromptu sermons. The brotherhood based in the San Agustín church had a procession with their statue of San Nicolás. Once again, crowds fled to the Villa of Guadalupe to appeal to its miraculous image. Hours later, "many people were still roaming about with burning brands, and praying in the streets." The viceroy imposed order by commanding soldiers to patrol to prevent looting and encourage everyone to return to their homes. He also demanded that the archbishop close the churches because "the cause deserved not the least dread."[22] Revillagigedo viewed the aurora borealis as a purely natural phenomenon. He seemed to believe that his forceful action would change the populace's ancient beliefs that connected unusual weather and celestial events to supernatural influences. Despite his efforts to impose an Enlightened interpretation, accounts of the Dongo massacre and its aftermath still deployed the shocking lights in the sky as a dramatic Gothic conclusion for these disruptive and deadly weeks.

A belief in the intertwining of nature and the supernatural influenced how residents of Mexico City reacted to the 1789 aurora borealis. However, surviving texts from the era concentrate on explaining the occurrence as purely physical. This event and the aftermath offer a typical example of the tension between officials and popular piety.[23] The same disconnect between the reactions of the urban masses versus disengaged intellectual analysis happened when workers uncovered three gargantuan carved stones in the Plaza Mayor in the next two years.

---

[22] Anonymous, "The Count of Revilla-Gigédo, Viceroy of Mexico," *Historical Magazine*, vol. 8 (April 1864), 146.
[23] Taylor, *Theater*, 108–110.

18

Artifacts

In the Plaza Principal in front of the Royal Palace, [workmen] lifting up some paving stones, removed an idol from [the era of] heathendom. The sculpture was a carved stone, with a skull on its shoulders. On the other side was another skull with four hands and carving on the rest of the body, but without feet or a head.

They took the stone which was in the Plaza Grande (an almanac for the heathen Indians) to the cathedral cemetery. We do not know where they will put it.

The stone that served as [a] sacrificial [platform] for the heathens was placed by the Holy Cross in the Cathedral cemetery, [on the side] that faces Empedradillo Street.

These few lines sum up the halberdier Gómez's thoughts on three momentous discoveries of Aztec monoliths in the Mexico City central plaza, now commonly known as the Zócalo.[1] The stones reemerged into the light of day after centuries underground due to Viceroy Revillagigedo's ambitious plans to renovate the plaza into a clean and organized space. He carried out this plan by removing market stalls, as well as trying to prevent flooding by installing and improving the stone paving in the Zócalo and the surrounding streets.[2] Workers on these projects uncovered dozens of artifacts, including the monoliths known today as the Stone of Tizoc, the Aztec Calendar Stone, and the Coatlicue statue. The artifacts emerged over the

---

[1] González-Polo y Acosta, *Diario*, 223, 235, 268.
[2] Bailey Glasco, *Constructing Mexico City*, 126–153; Toner, *Alcohol and Nationhood*, 61, 71; Toner, "Everything in Its Right Place," 30, 35.

course of sixteenth months, from mid-August of 1790 to mid-December of 1791.[3]

The quotes above suggest that Gómez was not particularly interested in or excited about the discovery of the three statues. However, these artifacts have played a strong role in the development of Mexican national identity over the last two-and-a-half centuries.[4] Scholars continue to debate the meanings of their complex and detailed carvings and their functions before the fall of Tenochtitlán. This important scholarship ranges from analysis of the late pre-conquest-era society and beliefs, to the implications of treating these stones as nothing more than objets d'art relegated to passive viewing in the national anthropology museum.

Contextualizing these discoveries within the tumultuous final years of the eighteenth century and the geographic space of New Spain's central plaza situates them in the centuries-long narrative of death in Mexico. Gómez jotted down the observations quoted above on September 4, 1790, July 2, 1791, and September 3, 1793. These dates suggest that the stones at least mildly interested the general populace for three years.

The Dongo massacre, twenty dozen executions, and other state-sanctioned violence took place in an area of central Mexico City measuring approximately two hundred square meters, precisely the same location as the sacred precinct of Tenochtitlán and where the three stones remained buried since the sixteenth or the early seventeenth century. Dongo's residence sat less than seventy-five meters to the north of the cathedral, well within the Aztec sacred precinct and only a stone's throw from the Templo Mayor. The building located on this spot before the Spanish destruction of Tenochtitlán was the Calmecac, a residence for priests as well as an educational institution for future leaders.[5] Although the answer might veer into the realm of speculation, this proximity raises the question – did the uncovering of the pre-conquest monuments affect how residents of Mexico City in the 1790s perceived the multiple layers of official violence occurring in and around their largest urban plaza?

[3] Leonardo López Luján, "La Coatlicue," in *Escultura monumental Mexica*, eds. Leonardo López Luján and Eduardo Matos Moctezuma (Mexico City: Fundación Commemoraciones, 2010), 133.

[4] Khristaan D. Villela, Matthew H. Robb, and Mary Ellen Miller, "Introduction," in *The Aztec Calendar Stone*, eds. Khristaan Villela and Mary Ellen Miller (Los Angeles: Getty Research Institute, 2010), 3.

[5] Caroline Dodds Pennock, "The Aztecs and the Ideology of Male Dominance," *Signs: Journal of Women in Culture and Society*, vol. 4: 2 (1978), 349–362; Caroline Dodds Pennock, *Bonds of Blood: Gender, Lifecycle, and Sacrifice in Aztec Culture* (London: Palgrave Macmillan, 2008), 72–73.

COATLICUE

*From terror to veneration, from disgust to fascination, Coatlicue has the
strange virtue of provoking the most contradictory reactions in viewers . . . .
The Coatlicue shows the dark side* [of the Mexica], *defined by monstrosity,
idolatry, and bloodthirstiness.*[6]

What we now call the Coatlicue statue generated a confused and overall
horrified and repulsed reaction in the first several decades after its discovery on August 13, 1790.[7] The statue was found by workers who were
digging an underground drainage trench in the southeast corner of the
Plaza Mayor and came upon a twenty-four-ton, over eight-foot-tall stone,
face down in a slightly tilted horizontal position, with the head buried
about a foot deeper than the feet.[8]

In a process similar to judicial investigations, a notary took statements
from witnesses to this discovery over the next several weeks. The *corregidor* and intendant Bernardo Bonavía y Zapata commanded a notary to
create a report that included the object's size and position to present to
Revillagigedo. This document began with a statement from the overseer of
the plaza renovation, José Antonio Cosío, and then added the perspectives
of José Damián Ortiz de Castro, an academic from the San Carlos academy who supervised the project. Ortiz de Castro described how "the
stone" was uncovered near a market of thirty-five small shops known as
the *Cajoncillos de San José*. Two business owners working out of these
cubbies (a peanut-seller and a haberdasher) confirmed that the laborers
uncovered the stone at around 9:30 a.m. In an incredible feat of engineer-
ing, by early September, the workers managed to create a scaffold and
pulleys to remove the stone from the ground and transport it a short
distance to rest by a door in the viceregal palace.[9]

---

[6] López Luján, "La Coatlicue," 115, 148.
[7] The perception of the statue's beauty versus its horror swung back and forth into the
twentieth century, all in relation to shifting imperialistic visions of Indigenous peoples. See
López Luján, "La Coatlicue," 118–122.
[8] Ann de León, "Coatlicue or How to Write the Dismembered Body," *MLN*, vol. 125: 2
(2010), 259–286; Jean Franco, "The Return of Coatlicue: Mexican Nationalism and the
Aztec Past," *Journal of Latin American Cultural Studies*, vol. 13: 2, (2004), 205–219;
Amanda L. Petersen, "The Ruinous Maternal Body 'Par Excellence': Coatlicue in the
Mexican Imaginary (From the Monolith to Elena Poniatowska)," *Letras Femeninas*, vol.
40: 1 (2014), 103–118; Cecilia F. Klein, "A New Interpretation of the Aztec Statue Called
Coatlicue, 'Snakes-Her Skirt'," *Ethnohistory*, vol. 55: 2 (2008), 229–250.
[9] López Luján, "La Coatlicue," 137–148, transcribes these documents and includes images
of the originals.

Bonavía and Revillagigedo corresponded over the next month about the appropriate location for the statue, agreeing that it deserved study at the nearby university. The *corregidor* observed that, due to its size, "it originated from before the Conquest," and that "very few monuments survive from those times." Revillagigedo agreed and added that the massive object should be conserved, measured, weighed, and sketched, in order to publish a report about its possible origins. The rector of the university confirmed that the monolith originated in "one of the Indian temples" and would be stored at this institution's new collection of Indigenous objects.[10] The stone moved once again to a position on a patio of the Royal University, at this time located near the Plaza de Volador.[11] As other discoveries took place, Bonavía continued to support their preservation in perpetuity. Although this was a relatively new approach to artifacts from pre-colonial times, Viceroy Bucareli had initiated the idea of storing ancient documents in the university.[12]

In contrast, the Dominican friars who led the Royal University did not want the Coatlicue in public view. A report from the early nineteenth century summed up their reasoning: "The Indians, who look with extremely stupid indifference on all of the monuments of European art, come with restless curiosity to contemplate their famous statue." Allegedly, the Indigenous residents of Mexico City had begun to worship the monolith, sneaking in when classes ended, falling on their knees before it or even stretching out on the ground full-length. They brought candles and other offerings. All of these actions seem plausible in the context of the quiet continuation of Indigenous practices that persisted long after the conquest.[13] Additionally, university students had broken off parts of the statue. As a result of this controversy, the friars reburied Coatlicue within the building so that only its hands could be seen, and they expressly forbade any Indigenous viewers.[14] This reaction demonstrates that, as Mexico approached three centuries of Spanish rule, "idolatry ... remained a political and devotional issue."[15]

---

[10] López Luján, "La Coatlicue," 146.

[11] López Luján, "El ídolo sin pies ni cabeza: la Coatlicue a fines del siglo XVIII," *Estudios de cultura náhuatl*, vol. 42 (2011), 203–232. This decision highlights the Enlightenment attitudes of Mexico City's elite in this era, as they began to value ancient artifacts as art.

[12] Antonio León y Gama, "A Historical and Chronological Description of Two Stones," in *The Aztec Calendar Stone*, eds. Khristaan Villela and Mary Ellen Miller (Los Angeles: Getty Research Institute, 2010), 61–62; Stace Graham Widdifield, "The *Aztec Calendar Stone*: A Critical History (1981)," in *The Aztec Calendar Stone*, eds. Khristaan Villela and Mary Ellen Miller (Los Angeles: Getty Research Institute, 2010), 227–228.

[13] Taylor, *Theater*, 146.   [14] López Luján, "La Coatlicue," 148–149.

[15] Taylor, *Theater*, 137–140, quote on 137.

Despite the fact that the Coatlicue statue was returned to the ground in the early nineteenth century, intellectuals in this era had begun to appreciate the value of "antiquities," inspired by recent excavations in Pompeii and near Toledo, Spain. The leading Novohispanic figure in this movement was Antonio León y Gama, a Creole astronomer born in Mexico City in 1735. His circle of intellectuals sought to correct the European vision of native Mexicans as barbaric and to represent ancient Mexican artifacts as being as valuable as those dug up in Italy. León y Gama wrote his first edition of the *Descripción histórica y cronológica de las piedras* in 1792. He believed that the Coatlicue monolith represented several conjoined divine images, with the front side showing a goddess called Teoyaomiqui who, in his opinion, collected the souls of slain warriors and sacrificial victims. To him, each of the different parts of the statue symbolized a different supernatural entity. He interpreted the hearts around Coatlicue's neck as bags of copal.[16]

León y Gama's interpretations faced suppression and debate in the local periodicals, the *Gazeta de Literatura* and the *Gazeta de México*.[17] Using the pseudonym Océlotl Tecuilhuitzintli, another Creole savant, Joseph Antonio Alzate y Ramírez, chastised León y Gama for making ignorant guesses about what the stone represented.[18] While the discussion continued for over a year, León y Gama held to his argument that learning about the Aztec past represented a duty to the Mexican *patria*. Two decades later, the new Republic of Mexico embraced this ideology.[19] President Guadalupe Victoria inaugurated a national museum in 1825, located in the Dominican-led university building where both the Coatlicue statue and the Stone of Tizoc sat since the 1790s. The new president's decision contradicted the friars' wish to keep Coatlicue buried within their premises.[20]

---

[16] López Luján, "El ídolo."

[17] López Luján, "El ídolo"; Jorge Cañizares-Esguerra, *How to Write the History of the New World Histories, Epistemologies, and Identities in the Eighteenth-Century Atlantic World* (Stanford, CA: Stanford University Press, 2001), 269–272.

[18] *Gazeta de México*, August 16, 1791, 8–11. See http://www.hndm.unam.mx/index.php/es/ for the article, accessed September 19, 2021.

[19] Shelley Garrigan, *Collecting Mexico: Museums, Monuments, and the Creation of National Identity* (Minneapolis: University of Minnesota Press, 2012), 96–100.

[20] Alfred Lopez Austin and López Luján, "The Posthumous History of the Tizoc Stone," in *Fanning the Sacred Flame: Mesoamerican Studies in Honor of H. B. Nicholson*, eds. Matthew Boxt and Brian Dillon (Boulder: University Press of Colorado, 2012), 439–460; López Luján, "La Coatlicue," 450–456; Ignacio Bernal, "La Historia Póstuma de Coatlicue," in *Homenaje a Justino Fernández*, ed. David Robertson (Mexico City: UNAM, Instituto de Investigaciones Estéticas, 1977), 31–34. Bernal notes

FIGURE 18.1 Early interpretation of the Aztec calendar stone. Retrieved from the Library of Congress.

THE CALENDAR STONE

I was inspired to show the literary sphere some of the great knowledge of art and science that the Indios *of the Americas possessed when they were heathens, so that the enemies of us Spaniards know how false it is to calumniate them for their irrationality or simplicity.*[21]

Antonio León y Gama, 1792

To León y Gama, the unburial of the Calendar Stone offered a superb example of Aztec learning and culture, demonstrating their civilization as advanced by current European standards. His 1792 report on the

---

that Coatlicue continued to suffer burials for a few more decades in the nineteenth century.

[21] Quoted in Matos Moctezuma, "La Piedra del Sol o Calendario Azteca," in *Escultura monumental Mexica*, eds. Leonardo López Luján and Eduardo Matos Moctezuma (Mexico City: Fundación Commemoraciones, 2010), 250.

Calendar Stone and the Coatlicue statue began with his musings on the potential "precious monuments ... jewels and treasures," hidden under the viceregal capital's soil. As noted above, his eagerness to convince Europe of Mexico's "enlightened" history was a proto-nationalist ambition for intellectuals like León y Gama.[22]

Before the Spanish invasion, the recently constructed forty-nine-thousand-pound disk may have sat in a horizontal position near the base of the Templo Mayor and served as a platform to exhibit extracted human hearts or perhaps a temporary resting place for sacrificial victims. After 1521, the Spanish let the Calendar Stone sit near the viceregal palace in a horizontal faceup position.[23] For several decades, the invaders tore down Aztec structures to change the Indigenous sacred precinct to a space that signified Christian domination. Sometime between 1554 and 1572, Archbishop Alonso de Montúfar decided to hide it again. It is even possible that workers flipped over the Calendar Stone and dragged it a short distance in order to serve as an enormous paving stone to stabilize the Plaza Mayor's mud. Fortunately, it was not broken apart like many other artifacts dating to before the conquest. These were often built into the walls of viceregal buildings, leading to their destruction or defacement.[24]

On December 17, 1790, only sixteen inches below the southwest corner of the Plaza Mayor, the Calendar Stone was finally unburied. Workers found it facedown and propped it up to a vertical position. Revillagigedo agreed with León y Gama that this monolith had educational value both for scholars and the general public. In July of 1791, it was moved into the care of the functionaries who looked after the

---

[22] León y Gama, "A Historical and Chronological Description of Two Stones," 50–80; D. A. Brading, *The First America: The Spanish Monarchy, Creole Patriots and the Liberal State 1492–1866* (Cambridge: Cambridge University Press, 1991), 462–465. Long after all of the intellectual debate of the 1790s had receded, Carlos María Bustamante, funded by the government of the Mexican Republic, republished León y Gama's reports in 1832. See Matos Moctezuma, "La Piedra," 251, 293.

[23] Frances Berdan, *Aztec Archaelogy and Ethnohistory* (New York: Cambridge University Press, 2014), 18–19.

[24] It is difficult to know when the Calendar Stone sustained the damage on its central face, especially the nose. A daguerreotype survives showing that this had already happened by 1839, and thus cannot be blamed on French or US soldiers when they occupied Mexico City later. See Villela, Robb, and Miller, "Introduction," 4, 16–17, 20; Elizabeth Hill Boone, "Templo Mayor Research, 1521–1978," in *The Aztec Templo Mayor: A Symposium at Dumbarton Oaks, 8th and 9th October 1983* (Washington, DC: Dumbarton Oaks, 1987), 19; Barrera Rivera, Álvaro, and Islas Domínguez, *Arqueología Urbana*, 33–34.

cathedral's other valuable statues and works of art. They displayed the stone in the church's atrium. Despite fears of "rustic and childish people ... injuring several of its figures with rocks and other instruments," it remained unprotected.[25] To León y Gama's dismay, the priests wished to rebury it facedown. Instead, it leaned against the western tower of the cathedral in a vertical position, where passersby nicknamed it "Montezuma's watch."[26] In 1885, this monolith finally moved to a more protected location in the *Salón de Monolitos* of the National Museum, now located in the building that had housed the viceregal mint.[27]

THE STONE OF TIZOC

The final monumental discovery of the late eighteenth century took place on December 17, 1791, when workers in the Plaza Mayor unburied another disk known as the Stone of Tizoc, which they encountered near the southwest end of the Zócalo.[28] Tizoc refers to the Aztec *tlatoani* ("speaker" meaning the ruler) depicted on the stone, who focused on expanding the Templo Mayor during his brief era in power from 1481 to 1486. His name, represented by a glyph of a leg marked by penitential self-mutilation, means "he who makes sacrifices," or even simply, "he who bleeds." Rumor has it that he died by poisoning.[29]

Despite his short reign, Tizoc made successful conquests on the Gulf Coast. The Stone of Tizoc commemorates these victories with fifteen images of the ruler grasping vanquished leaders by their hair. This disk, according to most scholars, served as a *cuauhxicalli* ("eagle vessel"), or a sacrificial stone used in the final moments of the lives of captured warriors. The Stone of Tizoc has a channel for blood carved into its top, as well as a stylized frieze of the sun in

[25] León y Gama, "A Historical and Chronological Description of Two Stones," 58.
[26] Enrique Juan Palacios, "The *Stone of the Sun* and the First Chapter of the History of Mexico (1921)," in *The Aztec Calendar Stone*, eds. Khristaan Villela and Mary Ellen Miller (Los Angeles: Getty Research Institute, 2010), 167–168.
[27] Matos Moctezuma, "La Piedra," 236–244; Gumesindo Mendoza and Jesús Sánchez, "Catalog of the Historical and Archeological Collections of the *Museo Nacional de México* (1882)," in *The Aztec Calendar Stone*, eds. Khristaan Villela and Mary Ellen Miller (Los Angeles: Getty Research Institute, 2010), 101–102.
[28] Barrera Rivera, Álvaro, and Islas Domínguez, *Arqueológica Urbana*, 56.
[29] Tízoc, "El que hace sacrificio," https://arqueologiamexicana.mx/mexico-antiguo/tizoc-el-que-hace-sacrificio-1481-1486, accessed August 29, 2021; Berdan, *Aztec Archaelogy*, 141–146.

concentric circles.[30] Although weighing in at only nineteen thousand pounds, well under half the weight of the Calendar Stone, Tizoc's memorial is only a few centimeters smaller in thickness. This solid structure suggests that it could hold the weight of men standing on it.

Like the other two monoliths, the Stone of Tizoc moved around a great deal after its construction in approximately 1486. Scholars believe that its original location may have been in the Xipe Totec Temple, south of the Great Temple. Buried soon after the fall of Tenochtitlán in 1521, the stone reappeared within a decade as the Spanish made their first attempt at building a cathedral. Several writers described it as placed by the western door of the original cathedral, a location of symbolic importance. This location seemed inappropriate to religious observers due to its function in of human sacrifice rituals. Sometime in the seventeenth century, the stone disappeared under the ground again, either intentionally or as a result of a 1629 flood.

When uncovered in late 1791, the Stone of Tizoc sat only a couple of feet underground, facedown. In early 1792, Bonavía told Revillagigedo that he would ask if the cathedral would display it. Although he had allowed the Calendar Stone to rest propped up on the church's wall, the dean of the cathedral did not want to exhibit this new monolith.[31] As a result, the Stone of Tizoc was reburied in the cemetery just to the east of the cathedral, this time faceup with its top exposed to the elements. The halberdier Gómez reported this event in September of 1793, with little excitement. For the rest of the viceregal era, only foreigners on scientific expeditions – Guillermo Dupaix and Alexander von Humboldt – took an interest in the Stone of Tizoc. Humboldt even received permission from the friars at the university to uncover Coatlicue for his research.[32]

After Mexican independence, more visitors began to study these three monoliths. Ironically, despite his disdain for Spain, one of these

---

[30] Emily Umberger, "A Reconsideration of Some Hieroglyphs on the Mexica *Calendar Stone*," in *The Aztec Calendar Stone*, eds. Khristaan Villela and Mary Ellen Miller (Los Angeles: Getty Research Institute, 2010), 241–242; Emily Umberger, "New Blood from an Old Stone, "*Estudios de Cultura Náhuatl*, vol. 28 (1998), 241–256.

[31] Eduardo Matos Moctezuma, "La Piedra de Tízoc y la del Antiguo Arzobispado," in *Escultura monumental Mexica*, eds. Leonardo López Luján and Eduardo Matos Moctezuma (Mexico City: Fundación Commemoraciones, 2010), 298.

[32] López Austin and López Luján, "The Posthumous History," 439–460; López Luján, "La Coatlicue," 150.

foreigners judged the Calendar Stone, Coatlicue, and the Stone of Tizoc in a very similar way to how they were viewed by the Catholic authorities during the viceregal era. Thanks to William Bullock, crowds in 1820s Piccadilly could visit his Egyptian Hall and observe these three monoliths – not the originals, but copies made from plaster casts that he assembled on a trip to Mexico in 1823. Once again, the university allowed the exhumation of Coatlicue, which Bullock called Teoyamique following León y Gama.[33] The Mexican government also supported Bullock's project. He published a catalog describing the forty-four items shown in the London exhibit. Bullock began his book suggesting that he had done the world a service by making these objects available to viewers three centuries after the conquistadors had destroyed so much of Indigenous Mexican culture. Bullock's catalog included lengthy quotes from Bernal Díaz del Castillo and Cortes's letters in an effort to decry the Spaniards for their destructive acts of conquest and their reburial of Coatlicue and the Stone of Tizoc. At the same time, the Aztecs were subject to his moral disgust for their practice of human sacrifice. He described Coatlicue as "horrible," "monstrous," "deformed," and with an "infernal purpose ... sanguinary rites, daily performed in its honor." In describing the Stone of Tizoc, he mentioned that thirty thousand sacrifices took place "at the coronation of the last emperor." In contrast, Bullock viewed the Calendar Stone as "a fine specimen of Mexican workmanship and knowledge."[34]

The fact that only the Aztec Calendar Stone remained uncovered from 1790 to the present day underscores the biases felt in Revillagigedo's era. The monoliths associated with Tizoc and Coatlicue reminded late eighteenth-century viewers of an Indigenous history and culture that they viewed as barbaric, while the Calendar Stone suggested advanced knowledge that called for deciphering and dissemination in Europe. Scattered comments regarding popular responses to the three objects express only fear of the populace harming them or that the stones might influence the Indigenous residents to fall back into beliefs viewed as idolatry and superstition. New Spain's leaders decided that the general population, due to their ignorance, did not deserve access to artifacts interpreted as

---

[33] López Luján, "La Coatlicue," 152–155.
[34] William Bullock, *A Description of the Unique Exhibition called Ancient Mexico* (London: Bullock, 1824), 2–4, 30–35. Also ironically, he does not quote the work of León y Gama, done during the viceregal era, because it is too "long, learned and hypothetical." Quote on 36.

either dangerous or very valuable as symbols of Mexico's advanced ancient past. Instead, the authorities, representing church, state, and the university, chose to rebury these reminders of how death had featured in Mexico City's ancient past. The Stone of Tizoc and Coatilicue disrupted how Novohispanic elites wanted to monopolize the drama and narrative of death in their capital city.

PART VII

TEXTS

19

The Anonymous Account

> Among the many examples of excesses and crimes which have taken place since the erection of this Mexican imperial court, there is none other as atrocious as the [murders] committed on the night of October 23, 1789, in this city, on the Calle de Cordobanes number 13, in the house of one of the most respected *republicanos*, an honored citizen and merchant, a prior of the consulate, Don Joaquín Dongo, by three Europeans of noble and distinguished birth.
>
> Anonymous account of the Dongo investigation

The identity of Dongo's killers did not remain a mystery for more than a couple of days, thanks to the untiring efforts and rapid responsiveness of several viceregal judicial officials. Although the massacre was quickly solved, questions have persisted for the last two centuries: Who wrote and circulated the first detailed account of the investigation?

Depending entirely on this mysterious text, from the 1830s to the 1890s, Mexico's most influential writers, thinkers, and political commentators retold the story of the deaths of Dongo and his servants, Emparan's investigations, and the rapid resolution of the crime. There is no evidence to suggest that these intellectuals had access to the original criminal file. These nineteenth-century retellings appeared in various kinds of publications, from periodicals to multivolume novels. Each of these versions had its own interpretative angle, but all of the nineteenth-century authors contextualized the massacre as an important symbol of the legacy of the Spanish empire. The case also provided Mexican intellectuals with a starting point for discussions about morality and free will, the continuing influence of the Catholic Church, and, above all, the effective Novohispanic judiciary in sharp contrast to the shortcomings of law enforcement in their new nation. Similar to scandal stories published by members of the judiciary in 1770s France, this text provided fuel for political critique, and its insider legal perspective strengthened the points of anyone who deployed it to argue their own views about the independent nation of nineteenth-century Mexico.[1]

Before surveying and analyzing the multilayered nineteenth-century discussions of the Dongo case in the next two chapters, it is essential to discuss the source of all of these post-1830 writings: the anonymous account.[2] Since 1835, this account of the Dongo case has been reprinted several times without attribution to its original author. It is not clear if the account was published before 1835 or if it only circulated in a handwritten form. It may only have had readership in Mexico or perhaps it traveled to Europe as well. No details exist regarding who read it or why, and how they had access to it. A 1945 reprinting speculates on the provenance of the anonymous account:

On the paper of the era and with a clear eighteenth-century hand, this manuscript [which fell into the writer's hands as a gift], is one of the multiple copies that perhaps circulated at the time of the murders, and that passed from hand to hand, because the price of printing was so elevated that it was easier for the people to buy handwritten copies.[3]

The only clues that suggest a possible author derive from its content. The anonymous account adheres so closely to notary Luzero's archived case notes that either he, the judge Emparan, or some other contemporary judicial official must have written this detailed summary of the investigations.

STYLE

The anonymous account is a structured, planned narrative that moves rapidly from the discovery of the bodies to the execution of the culprits, following the chronological order of events. In contrast, New Spain's

---

[1] Sara Maza, *Private Lives and Public Affairs: The Causes Célèbres of Prerevolutionary France* (Oakland: University of California Press, 1993).

[2] Enrique Flores, ed., *Memorial Ajustado de la Causa que se Formo a Aldama, Blanco, y Quintero por los Homicidios que Perpetraron en la Persona de Don Joaquín Dongo* (Mexico City: Instituto Nacional de Bellas Artes, 1988), 26. This is the most scholarly reproduction of the original account and the one used throughout this chapter.

[3] José de J. Núñez y Domínguez, "Al Lector," in *Memorial Instructivo Relativo a la Causa que se Formo a los Homicidios de don Joaquín Dongo*, ed. José de J. Núñez y Domínguez (Mexico City: Ediciones Vargas Rea, 1945), 7.

archived criminal files offer readers a complex, scattered collage that they must piece together slowly, trying and often failing to ascertain the main characters of real-life dramas. Oftentimes the order of documents obscures even the most basic timeline of the events under investigation. The common occurrence of missing first and last pages (worn out and torn from the passage of time) means that a frustrated historian might never find out how the case started or the ultimate fate of the perpetrators. Very rarely does a scholar read a scribe's personal insights, since these functionaries had to work quickly and under time pressure.

In contrast, the anonymous account contains editorializing that discloses the author's opinions. This unnamed writer consciously decided what he wished to include and emphasize as he sat down to purposefully tell his chosen story. Although other literate men could have read and summed up his case notes, the immediacy of the tone and the presence of many additional details suggests that the author took part in the investigation. If indeed Luzero wrote this account, he may have heard and observed these details as he sat in on the interrogations. He may have even had additional drafted notes in his possession including information that did not make it to the final version of the archived case file.[4] Even without knowing the motivations for composing this account or its intended audience, the narration of the investigation provides a unique opportunity to explore the more personal reactions and opinions of a viceregal notary in regard to his own work.

The anonymous account not only has a purposeful structure and contains information left out of the case file, but the author assumes a more florid, emotional tone than the original documents. Not unlike journalists who took on a melodramatic style in their denunciations of scandals in nineteenth-century British newspapers, authors who assume the role of exposing some truth in their society often include stylistic elements that derive from popular trends in fiction or drama in their respective eras.[5] Whoever wrote the anonymous account may have come under the influence of the Gothic style, which was fashionable in Europe starting in the 1760s. While oftentimes Catholic countries like Spain and Italy served as settings for this genre, Southern European readers also consumed it.[6] Gothic novels began to enter Spain only in

---

[4] Burns, *Into the Archive.*

[5] Judith R. Walkowitz, *City of Dreadful Delight: Narratives of Sexual Danger in Late-Victorian London* (Chicago: University of Chicago Press, 1992), 86–98.

[6] Robert Miles, "Eighteenth-Century Gothic," in *The Routledge Companion to Gothic*, eds. Catherine Spooner and Emma McEvoy (London: Routledge, 2007), 15; Soledad Caballero, "Gothic Routes, or the Thrills of Ethnography: Frances Calderon de la Barca's Life in

the 1780s, but a few Spanish-language publications included macabre and supernatural elements as early as the 1770s. Descriptions of blood and gore, elements of the Gothic style when it leaned toward the Horror genre, go back as far as the classics of seventeenth-century Castile and its golden age of literature, known as the *siglo de oro*.[7] Even the very secrecy of its author suggests a Gothic mystery – its anonymity hearkens back to a lost letter upon which a novel's plot might revolve. As indicated by his own crime, Luzero clearly had his own personal fascination with gruesome violence.

THE CRIME

Unlike the original case file, this document narrates the events more or less chronologically. The first lines of the anonymous account, quoted at the head of this chapter, stress two points: This massacre represents the worst crime committed in the viceregal era and it involved high-ranking Spanish men. The writer adds an assessment of the perpetrators' actions as extremely "inhumane." The idea that men of honor acted in such a dishonorable fashion hints at the uncanny – that people and things are not always what they appear. Gothic and Horror stories also complicate and even implicitly challenge idealized masculinities, especially the Enlightenment presumption of European, elite male rationality. Men like Aldama, Blanco, and Quintero committed "excessive or transgressive actions [that placed] them outside the discourses of reason." In effect they transformed themselves from honorable Spanish men into monsters.[8] After these few lines introducing four of the main characters, the anonymous writer then dives right in with no other fanfare, just the simple introductory line: "Es el caso [This is the case]."[9]

Mexico," in *The Gothic Other: Racial and Social Constructions in the Literary Imagination*, eds. Ruth Bienstock Anolik and Douglas L. Howard (Jefferson: McFarland & Co. Publishers, 2004), 143–162.

[7] Xavier Aldana Reyes, *Spanish Gothic: National Identity, Collaboration, and Cultural Adaptation* (London: Palgrave Macmillan, 2017), 8–10, 42–44. The Spanish educated elite would have had to read these books in English or, more likely, French. See Abigail Lee Six, *Gothic Terrors: Incarceration, Duplication, and Bloodlust in Spanish Narrative* (Lewisburg, PA: Bucknell University Press, 2010), 11–14.

[8] David Punter, "The Uncanny," in *The Routledge Companion to Gothic*, eds. Catherine Spooner and Emma McEvoy (London: Routledge, 2007), 131; Brian Baker, "Gothic Masculinities," in *The Routledge Companion to Gothic*, eds. Catherine Spooner and Emma McEvoy (London: Routledge, 2007), 164–166.

[9] Flores, *Memorial Ajustado*, 26.

The story opens with the discomfiting circumstance of the dragoon finding the empty coach wandering driverless at 6:00 a.m. on October 24. Upon ascertaining that it belonged to Dongo, the writer provides a gory description of the scene of the crime: "This led to the first sight of the horrendous spectacle of Dongo and his servants, scattered around the patio, drowned in their own blood." But fortunately the men who witness this "terrifying discovery" immediately contact the local *alcalde del barrio* Lazcano, who then informs Emparan. The writer stresses the efficiency and care of both Luzero (himself?) and the judge, who start "the most meticulous and scrupulous examination of the cadavers." They observe and document even the tiniest "fragments" of bodies in the course of the investigation.[10]

Continuing his descriptions of the grotesque physicality on display in Dongo's establishment, the writer then guides his readers step by step through the scene of the crime. This account includes the minutia that was left out of the original case file – which again suggests that a participant composed it. The writer begins by pointing out that under the staircase was a rough crate of food eaten on the road and other items used by travelers, probably belonging to the Indigenous messenger from Dongo's rural hacienda. Nearby, a silver candlestick rested on the ground. Following these clues, next an observer of the crime scene would notice thin cords. These were similar to those used to tie up the doormen.

These objects slowly lead the viewer's eyes to the body of the man of the house, still wearing his coat and hat

with various atrocious wounds, in the head, chest, and hands, one of which separated two fingers; and the one in the chest penetrated all the way to the shoulder, his head split in half. He lacked his buckles, epaulettes, and his watch. At his feet the page reclined on his right side, with very deep wounds in his head, his cranium split in half. In the storage room under the staircase could be found the elder porter, called "the Invalid," on the ground facedown, his hands tied behind his back, with his head equally destroyed .... On the third floor, Don Nicolás Lanuza, father of the cashier Don Miguel, was found in his bed with an atrocious wound in his head, dividing it in half, another on his right cheek, and another in the right hand, cutting it off. He was faceup with his legs tucked under him, with a gun on his head inclined down, as if he intended to use it. His breeches were on top of the bed, as if he wanted to pull them up by the waistband.[11]

If Luzero wrote this narration, he chose to highlight the victims' grim final seconds, such as the sad and hopeless attempt by an elderly man to get

[10] Flores, *Memorial Ajustado*, 27.   [11] Flores, *Memorial Ajustado*, 28–29.

dressed and defend his life. He created this story from physical clues, but notarial conventions prevented him from adding them to his official report.

The writer fully embraced an explicit, dramatic tone when he described the cadavers of the female servants:

> The scullery maid was found in the doorway of the kitchen. She had just started working at the house and was around fifteen or twenty years old. She had fallen to the floor with her head destroyed so excessively that her brains were on the ground, and her hair scattered all around, so well-trimmed that it seemed that it had been cut with scissors.[12]

Luzero did not mention the age of the girl in the criminal case file, a detail which made her death more disturbing for readers. The account's descriptions of the body fit very well with the Gothic fascination with broken, degraded bodies – most famously Frankenstein's monster.[13] The anonymous writer creates a visual of previously whole humans who have disintegrated into their disjointed parts, knowing readers will react viscerally to these grotesque details. Instead of containing energy and liveliness, this narrative reduces the victims to inert and disgusting matter.[14]

The initial section concludes with another incident of Gothic uncanny, which of course a notary could not include in his official case notes. While the judge ordered the servants' bodies taken to the royal jail, Dongo and his cousin were taken to the nearby Dominican church. They were buried there on Sunday, October 25, "with their killers in attendance." Leaving his readers shocked by this tantalizing tidbit, the writer now turned to the investigation.

INVESTIGATION

The anonymous narration frames the judicial process by stressing the "tireless zeal" and ingenuity shown by Emparan as he initiated all possible steps to solve the crime. Even though the judge tracked down every lead, "he achieves nothing more than a sea of confusion." However, the narrative proceeds along rapidly as the authorities threw Aldama in a dungeon in what seems like moments after they learn about his bloodstained

---

[12] Flores, *Memorial Ajustado*, 29.

[13] Mary Wollstonecraft Shelley, *Frankenstein: The 1818 Text* (London: Penguin Books, 2018).

[14] Kelly Hurley, "Abject and Grotesque," in *The Routledge Companion to Gothic*, eds. Catherine Spooner and Emma McEvoy (London: Routledge, 2007), 137–145.

ribbon. Blanco and Quintero soon followed him to the same fate, and all of them face Emparan's "exquisite and careful questions." Luzero, or whoever wrote this account, closely adhered to the original case file when summing up the interrogation of the suspects.[15] The unknown author captured the high-pressure exchange of words as the judge tried to bully Aldama, Quintero, and Blanco into telling the truth. He only added a few details left out of the archived documents, such as the ironic words that Quintero said to his landlady when he asked to move his lodgings: "I am afraid, because bad people are around, I don't want them to kill me in order to rob me, thinking that I have something [to steal]."[16] Unlike the novelists of the 1860s and 1870s discussed in Chapter 20, this writer knew that the Dongo case file provides enough excitement without requiring any contrived suspense or additional fictional verbiage during the interrogations.

The questioning of the suspects becomes more exciting as physical clues mount against them. When describing the evidence, the anonymous writer returned to a Gothic tone by describing the bloodstains in detail. He also adds a few moments of suspense. Readers learn that the drop of blood on Aldama's cape, said to be a result of his viewing of public whippings, was the size of a half-peso. Also, the writer pointed out that Quintero's bloodstained door represented an important clue to Emparan and "the scribe," because none of the men in custody showed any wounds on their bodies. This account clarifies that the officials found the bags of pesos and other bloody and incriminating items hidden under a loose beam in the floor under Quintero's window. This discovery led to a dramatic confrontation with Quintero.

The anonymous account suggests that Emparan carefully paced this buildup to the confessions, adding to the suspense. In this version, the judge and scribe showed Quintero each of the clues one by one. Over and over, he denied any knowledge of them, even claiming that one of his enemies planted them in his room to incriminate him. This narration includes quotes from conversations between Aldama and Quintero, emphasizing the older man's resistance to the plan:

Aldama went to visit Quintero, taking Blanco with him. When he entered, he said, "Look who I brought with me. Now you can make that proposal you were thinking about [to rob Blanco's former boss] Azcoytia."
Quintero responded, "Do whatever you want, I am not interested."[17]

[15] Flores, *Memorial Ajustado*, 32–34.   [16] Flores, *Memorial Ajustado*, 40.
[17] Flores, *Memorial Ajustado*, 40–45, quote on 47.

When he finally confesses, Quintero only admitted that he knocked on the door with his stick and held it at the door to guard it.

Quintero's confession led to Aldama's theatrical words, quoted in the anonymous account as "now the day has come to say the truth." Adding to the drama in this version, before tearfully telling all, Aldama composed his face, calmly looked at everyone in the courtroom, and finally expelled a gentle sigh.[18]

In general, the narration of the crime follows the original archival documents, recounting how the killers rampaged the house floor by floor. A few added comments highlight the horror of their acts. For example, this version says that Quintero saluted Don Nicolás with his stick, but at the same moment, stabbed him to death. In another shocking detail, Aldama confessed that when only two of the maids remained, he said to Quintero, "one for you, one for me." It seems that a bit more dialogue took place between Aldama and Dongo when he arrived home – the murderer made a point to tell his victim, "Excuse our audacity and the lack of respect for your house." Apparently the proud Dongo responded in a dismissive way, and continued to walk up his steps, but soon faced the deadly machetes wielded by Quintero and Blanco.[19]

After summarizing the various confessions made by all three of the killers as their execution date approached, the anonymous writer wrapped up his account rapidly with their sentencing and the scene of their deaths. He described how the condemned men left the jail at 11:00 a.m., and proceeded to a large scaffold measuring around three meters in height, with a platform that was twenty-five by ten feet in size. Quintero climbed up first, since he had the original idea for the home invasion. The oldest killer leaned against the middle pole, with Aldama on his right hand, and Blanco on his left. Crowds gathered to watch their execution by garroting, even journeying from far outside of the capital city. Readers learn how friars from every religious order also attended, along with jail functionaries, and members of the *cofradías* of the Santa Veracruz and Cristo de la Misericordia. By 1:00 p.m. all three men had died. Their cadavers remained on the scaffold for another four hours, before their return to the jail for the amputation of all three right hands. The Santa Veracruz brotherhood paid 227 pesos for decent burials, wearing the habits of the San Fernando fathers.[20]

---

[18] Flores, *Memorial Ajustado*, 45.   [19] Flores, *Memorial Ajustado*, 49–50.
[20] Flores, *Memorial Ajustado*, 62–64.

The original Dongo case file reads like a fast-paced, concise, and well-written True Crime novella. It has a non-linear flow of events, jumping back-and-forth across decades to gradually reveal the lives of the perpetrators. The oft-republished anonymous account has a chronological plotline and takes on a slightly more Gothic tone, complete with gory descriptions and a few mysterious and suspenseful moments. This very accessible narrative fascinated several influential nineteenth-century commentators and novelists and inspired them to use the massacre as a symbol of Mexico's viceregal past.

20

The Dongo Massacre in Texts

By 10:00 p.m. on October 23, 1789, the three killers' machetes had finished their brutal work. Even before the sun had risen the next morning, information about the Dongo massacre had begun to spread quickly throughout Mexico City. On street corners, in taverns, and over breakfast in private residences, no one could resist talking about this shocking event. We cannot accurately recreate the path of the oral gossip after two centuries, but a paper trail in the form of the anonymous account started to memorialize the events soon after Aldama, Quintero, and Blanco put down their weapons. Then, after independence from Spain, Mexico's most important nineteenth-century writers and intellects began to publish accounts of the murders and the investigation in the 1830s. These printed texts eventually led to a small boom in fictional reinterpretations of the crime and its aftermath in the 1860s. For the new nation, the murder and its rapid resolution symbolized the extremes of Spanish rule. Mexicans pondered how to deal with a continuing perception of excessive criminality in their society, an issue that independence from Spain had not resolved.

More than two hundred and thirty years have passed and Dongo's murder continues to attract our interest, with new books and articles still examining the case. Each writer who feels inspired to discuss the Dongo killings focuses on the details or interpretation that suit their own context, personality, and concerns. The narrative has taken on a life of its own within these disparate written texts. This book you are reading right now will not be the last account of this violent and gruesome incident. We will continue to retell this story and make it fit our own interpretations.

DONGO TEXTS WRITTEN UNDER SPANISH RULE

From the first writers who transcribed the bloody scene onto paper, accounts of the Dongo murders focus on the minutia of judicial processes, adhering to the True Crime formula that remains popular in the twenty-first century. The textual life of the massacre began on the morning of October 24, when the scribe Luzero started to hurriedly write down all of the details of the scene of the crime. Luzero wielded his quill to document the ongoing investigation moment by moment as it occurred. It is possible that he relished the freedom to incorporate more Gothic details when he compiled the events into the anonymous and oft-reprinted narrative discussed in Chapter 19. In one form or another, Luzero's words provide the basis for all of the successive retellings from the 1830s to the present day. Although the notary's version of the story became the foundational document in the Dongo canon, the first two chroniclers, writing just weeks after the murders, would not have had access to Luzero's case notes. The sources and citations for Dongo-inspired publications became even more murky in the first several decades of the national era.

After Luzero closed his case file, the next known contributor to the Dongo paper trail is the diarist and halberdier José Gómez, who most likely took down his observations in early November of 1789. Gómez's handwritten journals were first published in 1854. A paperback version did not come out until 1986.[1] Due to this delay in publication, these fascinating memoirs remain little cited even now and thus did not contribute to the textual conversation in the nineteenth century. Although his work has had little influence on other Dongo writings, Gómez's brief narration of the investigation and punishment of the murderers covers the same themes as other writings on the topic by using the massacre to argue in favor of the effectiveness of the viceregal judiciary.

After he described the murders and the execution of the perpetrators, the halberdier's handwritten diary continued to rest on his desk for at least another eleven years. In contrast, the first printed and circulated account of the massacre appeared within three weeks of the fateful night, in a periodical form easily accessible to readers among the general public. By the release of the November 10, 1789, issue of the *Gazeta de México*, the entire Dongo saga had already come to its brutal conclusion. As such, in one concise two-and-a-half-page commentary, the editor and printer Manuel Antonio Valdés y Munguía summarized the events from the

---

[1] González-Polo y Acosta, *Diario*, 9–10.

morning of October 24 through to the November 7 execution of the three
culprits.

This early Mexican journalist framed his account with an emotional
response to the massacre. Valdés y Munguía introduced his narration by
describing the murders as "extraordinary ... execrable and astonishing
for the inhabitants of this capital." With these comments, he projected his
own initial shocked and disbelieving reaction on his neighbors. He also
perhaps accurately assessed the general feeling across the populace. He
then briefly speculated about the implications of the massacre as it related
to humanity's place in the universe. Valdés y Munguía observed that the
murders inspired a sense of fatalistic frustration with the cruel workings of
the cosmos, "manifesting how weak and futile are mankind's plans and
premeditations when high providence intervenes to reverse and confuse
them."[2] Valdés y Munguía's first lines encouraged his readers to retreat
into their internal world, but he quickly panned out to an existential
plane, begging the still vital question: How can humanity interpret such
occurrences?

For this author, the killings and their aftermath revealed divine involvement in even the most horrible of earthly events. He noted that why and
how supernatural forces control events defies human understanding.
Delving into the details, Valdés y Munguía described Dongo as a "rich
shopkeeper and *hacendado*." The journalist narrated the action from the
moment when Emparan found Dongo's door open before 8:00 a.m. on
October 24. The *Gazeta* then depicted the moment when the judge
encountered the merchant dead alongside his coachman and lackeys.
With words meant to provoke readers' compassion, Valdés y Munguía
recounted how Emparan came upon the "elderly cashier, dead in his bed,
an older man, who was ill." After narrating the discovery of the women's
bodies and the looted money boxes, Valdés y Munguía acknowledged that
the "inscrutable decisions of omnipotence" guided Emparan to finding the
perpetrators.[3]

Valdés y Munguía detailed how the killers pretended that they represented "Justice" when they invaded Dongo's house, assuming the pretext
of investigating the premises in response to a theft. Even this cruel trick
oddly represented a certain trust in effective law enforcement in this era.
The *Gazeta* story ended by stressing that the government and its laws

---

[2] Manuel Antonio Valdés y Munguía, *Gazeta de México, Tomo III: No. 43*, November 10,
    1789, 420.
[3] Valdés y Munguía, *Gazeta de México*, 420–421.

responded effectively to the concerns of the "frightful and terrorized neighbors, who could not breathe after the events were made public."[4] The *Gazeta de México* shaped the massacre into a lesson about Mexico City's organized legal system: Mysteriously guided by providence and carried out by effective functionaries, it protected the populace from ferocious criminals. Both viceregal writers, Gómez and Valdés y Munguía, expressed views similar to nineteenth-century Dongo commentators. The *Gazeta* article also represents one of the first examples of the *nota roja*, a periodical genre "dedicated to covering the bloodiest events" with an emphasis on visceral and graphic details and images.[5]

CARLOS MARÍA DE BUSTAMANTE AND THE DONGO STORY

After the account published in the *Gazeta de México*, as far as scholars can tell, printing presses remained quiet on the massacre for almost fifty years. It is unclear how the anonymous account discussed in Chapter 19 circulated among the broader populace during these decades. Eventually it fell into the hands of one of the most important leaders, writers, and thinkers of the Insurgency and early National periods, Carlos María de Bustamante. Born in 1774 in Oaxaca, Bustamante started working as a lawyer in Mexico City in 1796. He most likely heard about the case when he arrived in the viceregal capital, or possibly even shortly after the murders occurred as the news traveled via *cordilleras* and the *Gazeta* all around New Spain.[6] In 1835, Bustamante published his *Efemérides Histórico-Político Literarias de México*, which included the anonymous account, as well as additional editorial comments drawn from his personal memories, possibly gossip he heard over the years, and his thoughts about the current Mexican judiciary.[7] He even claimed that he spoke directly with Luzero, who he said provided him with previously secret details about the investigations.[8] Bustamante's personal touches shaped the perspectives of future Dongo chroniclers, including the two novelists

[4] Valdés y Munguía, *Gazeta de México*, 422.

[5] Rafael Barajas, *Una Crónica de la Nota Roja en Mexico: de Posada a Metinides, y del Tigre de Santa Julia al Crimen Organizado* (Mexico City: Museo del Estanquillo, 2018), 5, 15; Enrique Flores Esquivel, "Crímenes inmemoriales: nota roja y 'Material de los sueños'," *Literatura Mexicana*, vol. 30: 1, (2019), 89–113.

[6] Flores Esquivel, *Memorial Ajustado*, 132 n2.

[7] Carlos María de Bustamante, *Efemérides Histórico-Político Literarias de México* (Mexico City: Testamentaría de Valdés, 1835).

[8] Flores Esquivel, *Memorial Ajustado*, 42 n9.

discussed in Chapter 21 who wrote hundreds of pages on the case in the 1860s and 1870s.

Bustamante introduced his *Memorial* with justifications for why he chose to publish the Dongo story at this particular moment. He observed that he had previously published three criminal narratives from the Novohispanic past in another publication called the *Registro Trimestre*. He argued that his readers benefited from learning these stories, even if they just viewed them as entertaining diversions. He added another justification for circulating the Dongo narrative: "the most cultured nations in Europe" also published crime narratives, for the purposes of honoring their own judiciary and learning from their failures.[9] Arguably, Bustamante's *Memorial* and the earlier accounts of crimes that he published in the 1830s represented another important step in the development of *nota roja* periodicals in Mexico.[10]

While the *Gazeta de México* framed the massacre with the idea that the authorities must react to inexplicable divine whims, this analysis shifted forty-six years later and after over a decade of insurgency. In his introductory comments Bustamante instead portrayed these events as a struggle between superb governance and the bestial, even Satanic, brutality of the perpetrators.[11] He described Aldama, Quintero, and Blanco as "three ravenous wolves in a sheep pen."[12] Like Valdés y Munguía, he stressed that this struggle took place even beyond the human realm, because the Dongo investigation offered an example of the viceregal judges and their underlings fighting against the forces of evil. Although his words demonstrate a Christian worldview, Bustamante did not go into depth on his opinions of the Catholic Church, in contrast to the novelists discussed in Chapter 21.

Bustamante contradicted his own fawning praise of the viceregal judiciary with the opinion that Spaniards in power purposefully avoided circulating printed information about the murders.[13] He explained this silence: "because it did not suit the suspicious politics of the Spanish government, and because Spaniards were the ones who committed this crime." Basically, in his opinion, the very existence of the Dongo massacre demonstrated the brutality of Spanish rule over Mexico.[14] This comment

---

[9] Bustamante, *Efemérides*, 2.   [10] Barajas, *Nota Roja*, 16.

[11] Bustamante, *Efemérides*, 3.   [12] Flores Esquivel, *Memorial Ajustado*, 49n10.

[13] Corinna Zeltsman, *Ink Under the Fingernails: Printing Politics in Nineteenth-Century Mexico* (Berkeley: University of California Press, 2021).

[14] Bustamante, *Efemérides*, 2.

implied that the anonymous account (of course also written by an elite man of Spanish ancestry) existed only in a handwritten version and that Bustamante printed it for the first time. Bustamante also criticized the Spanish obsession with honor and social hierarchies that allowed the killers a certain dignity in their execution by garroting rather than hanging, and their ritualistic procession on the backs of mules in black mourning robes.[15] His tone reflects the continuing conflict with Spaniards in the decade after independence.

Despite the anti-Spanish commentary, Bustamante held up the Novohispanic judiciary as a model that his own era urgently needed to imitate. Bustamante added political justifications for publishing the *Memorial* that are in line with key themes common to the True Crime genre. He acknowledged that narrating a successful incident of crime-solving serves as one of the most compelling ways to praise an effective court system. He effusively credited Viceroy Revillagigedo and his judiciary for solving this crime. Bustamante spoke of the prudence, attentiveness, dignity, and perseverance demonstrated by Emparan and his assistants. He compared the viceregal judiciary to the ancient courts held by Athenians at the Areopagus. He predicted that readers of this case will feel "great confidence in the paternal vigilance of the government." By this, Bustamante meant Revillagigedo's government inspired trust, in contrast to the leaders of Mexico in the 1830s. He argued that Revillagigedo's courts and judges even offered a model of administration worth studying within the new field of forensics. Revillagigedo was to this intellectual leader of the new Mexican nation, "the immortal Count ... a name that should always be pronounced with honor and respect."[16] Bustamante blamed the Mexican constitution and its poor implementation for the "scandalous impunity" enjoyed by criminals in 1835. He urged the congressmen in office at this time to make reforms and create a better police force, so that people could walk the city streets without fear of assault.[17] These positive assessments of Revillagigedo continued throughout the century – he anachronistically became a model of idealized Positivist leadership advocating for Order and Progress, the dominant motto for late nineteenth-century Latin American nations.[18]

---

[15] Flores Esquivel, *Memorial Ajustado*, 35 n5, 56–57 n14, 63 n21.
[16] Flores Esquivel, *Memorial Ajustado*, 58 n17.   [17] Bustamante, *Efemérides*, 3–4.
[18] Laurence John Rohlfes, "Police and Penal Correction in Mexico City, 1876–1911: A Study of Order and Progress in Porfirian Mexico" (Ph.D. diss., Tulane University, 1983); John Corr, "The Enlightenment Surfaces in Nineteenth-Century Mexico:

Returning to Mexico's early years as a Republic, Bustamante argued that 1830s Mexico City was unsafe – in his words, "a forest of robbers." He reported that in early 1835, criminals raided the very same house where Dongo lived during the viceregal era. A gang of robbers tied up the doorman of the current resident, the Marquis of San Francisco de Herrera, recreating the "theater of horrors" that unfolded in 1789.[19] This time, however, the doorman's wife prevented a disaster with her piercing screams. She woke up the family of the marquis, who occupied the mezzanine, and the home invaders fled into the night.[20] Bustamante observed that the criminals of his time remain unpunished – and even fill up the National Palace. He ended his editorial comments by warning his readers to "protect yourselves from them!"[21] After this introductory editorializing, Bustamante's publication then printed the anonymous account, without attribution or citation.

At the end of the anonymous account, Bustamante appended "notes" that sound more like gossip or urban legends. These concluding comments actually add some comic relief to the horrific narrative. The anonymous author tended toward a Gothic tone by including some gory descriptions and occasional moment of suspense. Bustamante actually remained within this genre with his additions, because Gothic stories incorporated humorous elements since they first appeared in the 1760s. According to Bustamante, Dongo had a pet parrot that could speak perfectly well. After the massacre, the parrot was found dead near the kitchen. Could the murderers have killed the parrot, Bustamante speculates, so as not to risk the bird spreading information about them?[22] Due to its inclusion in this influential 1835 publication, the parrot features all too prominently as a grotesque moment of comic relief in the two Dongo novels published over thirty years later.

Another classic Gothic anecdote from Bustamante reads like a concise and slightly humorous but rueful ghost story. After the authorities discovered the bodies, they placed sentinels inside the building so that no one would enter and perhaps steal from it again. As darkness fell on October 24, nightly prayers ended, and the house remained full of blood. The men standing watch became tense and fearful. Suddenly,

Scientific Thinking Attempts to Deliver Order and Progress," *History of Science*, vol. 52: 1 (2014), 98–123.
[19] A general named Pedro Celestino Negrete owned the building in the 1830s. See Flores Esquivel, *Memorial Ajustado*, 26n2.
[20] Bustamante, *Efemérides*, 2.   [21] Bustamante, *Efemérides*, 4.
[22] Flores Esquivel, *Memorial Ajustado*, 66.

a ram bolted loudly out of a nearby stable. One sentinel fainted with terror. He died four days later. In one final macabre note, Bustamante remembered that the perpetrators' skulls remained near the holy water font in the Jesus Nazareno church. As they made the sign of the cross, the faithful could offer up prayers for their souls. Bustamante said that he saw these very skulls, but "I do not know if they were the same ones."[23]

Bustamante closed his account with a "timely warning" to his critics who had discouraged him from publishing the Dongo story. He pointed out that "the same *Memorial Ajustado* that we publish today was translated into French and published in Paris." He expressed shame that Mexicans ignored this tragedy until foreigners told them about it. Bustamante almost threateningly concluded with the question "shouldn't our ignorance be justly thrown in our face?"[24] In other words, foreigners could use their knowledge of the murders to criticize Mexicans, who did not even know enough about their own history to understand the critique.

These final provocative comments further complicate the provenance and authorship of the anonymous account. Did Luzero translate it into French and send it to Paris himself? Perhaps Bustamante did not provide more details about this source as a literary strategy to make his publication more mysterious, or to deflect any negative reactions directed at him. Regardless of his motivations, he did not cite an author.

Bustamante revisited the Dongo story as part of his significant *Tres Siglos de México* project, initially published starting in 1836 as a continuation of the unpublished history of New Spain written by the Jesuit Andrés Cavo (1739–1803). Padre Cavo left the viceroyalty in 1767 with his fellow banished members of the Company of Jesus and wrote a history that covered the conquest to 1766. Bustamante continued this project and added new material, choosing to include the Dongo events as essential to the history of New Spain.[25]

In this version, he retold the anonymous account in his own words, adding more dramatic details and writing with more verbose moral judgments of the culprits. Bustamante shaped future accounts by definitively situating the events in the context of the start of Revillagigedo's term as viceroy. He expressed a familiar pride in the "splendor" of the Novohispanic judiciary but spent more time detailing his vision of the killers as "diabolical ... hardened criminals" as well as "ferocious tigers." His clear debt to the anonymous account comes with his references to the

---

[23] Bustamante, *Efemérides*, 32–33.   [24] Bustamante, *Efemérides*, 34.
[25] Bustamante, *Los tres siglos de México*.

provocative rumors that Aldama attended Dongo's funeral, as well as the additional tale that the murderer somehow helped transcribe the documents sent out on the *cordilleras*. Emphasizing the "perversity of those who would carry out such an atrocious crime," Bustamante cataloged Blanco's five other robberies, and the previous murders committed by Aldama and Quintero – "three men who were veterans in iniquity." His repeated moral condemnation of the killers serves to denounce Spanish rule, especially Spain's aristocrats. After Bustamante described the black-draped platform where the executioner killed them, he added: "[These were] sad reminders of their Spanish Gothic nobility which suggested to these evildoers that they had a double obligation to act as nobles!" Of course, in some sense, Aldama, Quintero, and Blanco did act as nobles by killing for wealth following the Iberian tradition of conquest. They also hoped to escape any negative repercussions by citing their own noble ancestry in court, as so many others had in the past.[26]

Bustamante's publications, not the archival documents now stored in the Mexican National archive, shaped all other nineteenth-century publications relating to Dongo's death. Without them, Mexicans would not have had easy access to the facts of the case until professional historians returned to the archived investigation in the twentieth century.

A TRAVELER'S RETELLING

Given Bustamante's two publications on the Dongo events in the 1830s, it is likely that people of this era again began to discuss the murders in social settings. Likely informed of the story by word of mouth, a famous traveler to Mexico, Fanny Calderón de la Barca, published the next version of the Dongo story with the help of the renowned historian William Prescott in London in 1843. Calderón de la Barca, born Frances Erskine Inglis, lived in Mexico from 1839 to 1842, as the wife of the first Spanish minister. Full of factual errors in virtually every sentence, including confusion over Dongo's address and even the number of victims, her brief account seemed to derive from gossip or perhaps a misreading of Bustamante's very recent publications. Whatever her source, Calderón de la Barca's narration of the Dongo murder once again adheres very closely to the opinion that Revillagigedo's judiciary did an excellent job.[27]

---

[26] Bustamante, *Los tres siglos de México*, 191–193.
[27] Fanny Calderón de la Barca, *Life in Mexico, during a Residence of Two Years in That Country* (London: Chapman and Hall, 1843), 325–328.

Although it would be tedious to enumerate all of the errors, some of them hint at the biases of her sources or imply her own perspectives. For example, Calderón de la Barca claimed that Blanco worked for Dongo as a clerk, and thus planned the murder drawing from his knowledge of the house. This factual error adds to the ignominy of the killings, because they now appeared to be a dishonorable betrayal of a servant's previous master. It appears that she confused the information about Blanco's robberies of Alcoytia with the Dongo home invasion.

Perhaps influenced by popular theatrical productions in her era, Calderón de la Barca also added some additional melodrama to the massacre, by claiming that Dongo died from a stab to the heart, when of course head wounds killed the entire household. She included several other details for dramatic effect. These range from an extended conversation between Dongo and his killers to a call from Revillagigedo to "hang" the murderers and the closing of the fictional "city gates" to prevent their escape. Most inaccurately, she wrote that a family of tourists told the nonexistent "police" that they saw a man at a barbershop with a drop of blood on his ponytail.[28]

Another outlandishly false incident narrated by Calderón de la Barca related to Blanco and his mother:

the mother of Blanco, deeply distressed at the dissolute courses of her son, took the resolution (which proves more than anything else Revillagigedo's goodness, and the confidence which all classes had in him) to consult the viceroy as to the means of converting the young man to better habits. It seems as if the hand of an avenging Providence had conducted this unfortunate mother to take a step so fatal to her son. She told the viceroy that she had in vain attempted to check him.[29]

According to Calderón de la Barca, this fictional conversation, that a concerned and protective mother had with the most powerful head of state in the hemisphere, ended with a discussion of Blanco's blood-splattered stockings. Of course, this did not happen. If Blanco's mother remained alive in 1789, most likely she had not moved away from her tiny village in the Basque region of Spain. As the case file makes clear, Emparan sought out Blanco's estranged aunt and her servants, interrogating them regarding his inventory of clothes. The important action here was taken by a judge, not a highly moral mother. However, the anecdote that Revillagigedo would listen to a distraught woman adds to the positive reputation of the Spanish judiciary, an argument which seemed very

[28] Calderón de la Barca, *Life in Mexico*, 325–328.
[29] Calderón de la Barca, *Life in Mexico*, 327.

important for those who lived in 1830s Mexico. Of course, it also high-lights the growing emphasis on mothers as the fonts of morality in the nineteenth century.[30]

The Scottish author's naïveté continues in her presentation of Quintero as the "least hardened of the three" killers, confessing due to a fear of the wrath of God. Calderón de la Barca ended her brief account with an image of Revillagigedo watching over the execution, only a week after the crime. She then turned her narrative to his many other accomplishments.[31] Other than these odd errors and dramatizations, which could derive from loose talk among her Mexican acquaintances or her own imagination, Calderón de la Barca followed convention and presented the case in a way that emphasized Revillagigedo as a great leader. She shared this interpretation with all of the other nineteenth-century Mexican writers who discussed the case.

A BOOM IN DONGO PUBLICATIONS

Back in Mexico, a few decades passed as Mexico struggled to hold onto its territory and continued to deal with viceregal legacies. The execution of Emperor Maximilian by firing squad and the rise of the Porfiriato led to an increase in *nota roja* publications and more interest in the Dongo massacre. The number of newspapers increased rapidly, and many included graphic illustrations or even photos. A court photographer provided an early example of these harrowing visuals in 1867, circulating popular images of the firing squad and its three victims moments before Maximilian's death, as well as his bullet-riddled coat.[32]

A flurry of Dongo publications came out after the end of the French intervention, starting with the publication of José de Cuéllar's five-hundred-page novel called *El Pecado del Siglo* in 1869, discussed in depth in Chapter 21. This short boom continued in 1870 with the publication of *El Libro Rojo: 1520–1867*. Compiled by four editors from the Mexican intellectual elite of the era, this collection of essays told the "history of the great crimes of the Conquest, the viceregal Government, slavery, and the Inquisition," starting with the interactions between the

---

[30] Ann S. Blum, *Domestic Economies: Family, Work, and Welfare in Mexico City, 1884–1943* (Lincoln: University of Nebraska Press,2009); Rosales M. Angeles Cantero, "El ángel del hogar y la feminidad en la narrativa de Pardo Bazán," *Tonos Digital*, vol. 21 (2011). www.um.es/tonosdigital/znum21/secciones/estudios-6-%20pardo.htm.
[31] Calderón de la Barca, *Life in Mexico*, 328–330.   [32] Barajas, *Nota Roja*, 18–25.

last Aztec leaders and the Spanish *conquistadores*.[33] This volume included moody illustrations of the Dongo massacre, an early *nota roja*-like addition, although they were not graphic.[34]

Instead of an original work of history, the chapter on the Dongo family consists almost entirely of a transcription of the anonymous account, introduced as follows: "A published document narrates this horrible crime; and as we should not add or delete anything from it without altering the historical truth, we copy it as follows."[35] *El Libro Rojo* does not credit the author or the source of the anonymous account. It seems likely that they reproduced it from Bustamante's 1835 printed edition. This reprinting of the anonymous account occurred soon after the printing of the first Dongo novel, either in reaction to it or perhaps as part of a general trend that still viewed the Revillagigedo era as relevant to the Mexican nation. Readers did not have to wait long for another novel based around the Dongo events, in this case, in the form of two massive volumes called *Los Asesinos de Dongo*, also discussed in the Chapter 21.[36]

The editors of *El Libro Rojo* added a few interpretations of their own to their recopying of the anonymous account, framing it with their Mexican Liberal party vision of progress and civilization. The chapter started predictably by praising the famous energy and the effective reforms of Revillagigedo. In the opinion of the editors of *El Libro Rojo*, his legacy continued to shape the urban landscape even eighty years later. According to this interpretation, the celebrated viceroy "did not sleep . . . until this case had a satisfactory resolution."[37]

El Libro Rojo's discussion of the massacre concludes with a positive assessment of the progress that Mexico made from 1789 to the early 1870s. According to the editors, in these previous eight decades, Mexico City did not experience any atrocities as horrific as the killing of an entire family. *El Libro Rojo* also emphasized that Aldama, Quintero, and Blanco claimed noble status, a point that Bustamante highlighted to critique the

---

[33] Vicente Riva Palacio, Manuel Payno, Juan A. Mateos, and Rafael Martínez de la Torre, *El libro rojo, 1520–1867, Tomo II* (Mexico City: Pola, 1906), title page.

[34] Barajas, *Nota Roja*, 15–18; Saydi Núñez Cetina, "Crimen, representación y ficción: La construcción social de la peligrosidad en la nota roja, Ciudad de México (1880–1940)," in *Crimen y ficción: narrativa literaria y audiovisual sobre la violencia en América Latina*, eds. Monica Quijano and Hector Fernando Vizcaya (Mexico City: Universidad Nacional Autónoma de México, 2015), 161–190.

[35] Manuel Payno, *El Hombre de la Situación/Retratos Históricos* (Mexico City: Porrua, 1992), 220.

[36] Also discussed in Chapter 21.   [37] Payno, *El Hombre/Retratos Históricos*, 219.

Spanish obsession with honor and its failure to inspire them to act as moral men. In the 1870s, the idea of nobles massacring a distinguished merchant prompted a different observation: that "civilization, albeit slowly, has gone forward among us." In other words, this shocking event would not happen in their era, especially with aristocrats as perpetrators. Although they cannot deny that, among the current inhabitants, "there are some of depraved customs," the editors of the *Libro Rojo* confidently asserted that a study of history could prove that progress marches on.[38]

THE FINAL DONGO TEXT OF THE NINETEENTH CENTURY

Manuel Payno was one of the coeditors and compilers of the 1870 edition of *El Libro Rojo*. Whether or not he contributed to the Dongo chapter discussed above is impossible to know. However, around twenty years after its publication, he returned to themes relating to the 1789 massacre. At the age of seventy-nine, while serving in Spain as a diplomat, Payno began composing a novel entitled *Los Bandidos del Río Frío*. Eventually adding up to 117 chapters, *Los Bandidos* appeared in installments every month from 1889 to 1890. While the action of the novel takes place between 1819 and 1839, fictionally depicting the Santa Ana era, some of the key scenes toward the end of the book resemble the events of the Dongo massacre.[39] Like the two Dongo novels published two decades before, Payno's retelling of these events sets it in the darker corners of human sexuality – a theme that does not appear anywhere in the original case file.

Payno's version is also much more convoluted than its 1789 inspiration. The fictional character playing the role of Don Joaquín Dongo is the count of San Diego de Sauz, a scheming *hacendado* with an estate in Zacatecas (where the real victim owned a mine). Sauz lives in a Mexico City home in a street called Don Juan Manuel, where he stores treasure chests full of silver and gold pesos. As they develop their plan to rob Sauz, the eponymous gang of bandits buy a house for the sole purpose of hiding their loot. The leader of the group, Relumbrón, prepares for the home invasion by developing a relationship with the old doorman who guards the count's mansion. Relumbrón is a colonel who serves the nation's

[38] Payno, *El Hombre/Retratos Históricos*, 236.
[39] Manuel Payno, *The Bandits from Río Frío*, vol. 1, trans. Alan Fluckey (Tucson, AZ: Wheatmark, 2007), x–xii.

president (a fictionalized Santa Ana) directly and becomes a person of trust in the house of his soon-to-be victims. At the next stage of planning for the robbery, another one of the bandits corners Sauz's accountant on the street, and leads him at knifepoint to an old building occupied by other criminals. The thieves steal his money and gold watch, then throw him into an abandoned well, and bury him with rocks.[40]

Thus prepared to invade Sauz's home, Relumbrón and two of his men gather all of the weapons they have, including pistols. Just after 9:00 p.m., they drive a coach to Don Juan Manuel Street, where the wealthy residents rest quietly in their homes. After banging on the door several times, the bandits easily con the doorman into letting them enter by a ruse that they need to prepare the house for the return of the count. Instead of pretending to be law enforcement and drawing their weapons, as Dongo, Aldama, and Quintero did, Relumbrón and his partners wrestle with the doorman until the man dies of strangulation. Payno describes this in detail, explaining how the old doorman dropped his candle, and then the bandit named Evaristo grabbed his neck until his tongue and eyes almost popped out. After his death, the bandits place him carefully back in his bed.[41]

The most bizarre variation with the original crime occurs when the bandits interact with the female servants. The 1789 events were brutal enough, but the late nineteenth-century writer gratuitously adds sexual assault, child abuse, and torture to make the story that much worse. Payno describes the layout of the Sauz house as comprised of passages and locked rooms, with two elderly servants sleeping near the storage areas which contained the count's wealth. A very young orphan girl also sleeps in this part of the house. When Evaristo pulls back her blanket as they looked for the loot, Relumbrón tells him not to bother her, because his share of the count's money will get him access to "a hundred girls."[42] Once she wakes up, the girl actually helps the thieves because she can explain where to find the trunks full of silver and gold. However, she still suffers a horrible death along with the other female servants, stuffed in the empty chests after the gang emptied the gold pesos out of them, and buried alive under the unwanted silver pesos. The text implies that Evaristo raped and strangled her before leaving her to die in the trunk.

In this version of the Dongo story, the authorities solve the crime because Relumbrón left his wallet at the scene. These fictional bandits

[40] Payno, *The Bandits from Río Frío*, vol. 2, 505–510.
[41] Payno, *The Bandits from Río Frío*, vol. 2, 512–513.
[42] Payno, *The Bandits from Río Frío*, vol. 2, 515.

also receive a death sentence, but in this novel they die by hanging. Payno presented Relumbrón and Evaristo as pathetic before their death, crying and trying to resist the authorities up to their final moments. Relumbrón even attempts suicide in his cell but fails to do more than shed copious amounts of blood.[43] Unlike the authors of the two Dongo novels, Payno does not editorialize about the evils of the death penalty when he narrates their execution scene. On the other hand, he does share the novelists' obsession with women's sexuality. In Payno's case, this leads not to moralizing about sex work (a topic explored in the other two novels), but instead to a sordid child sexual abuse anecdote, which does not further his main plotline. Like the novelists from twenty years before, Payno created a text that focuses far more on the sexual victimization of women than can be found in the eighteenth-century handwritten documents or even in the 1830s Dongo accounts. Not unlike contemporary journalism on the Jack the Ripper killings, this new emphasis reads more like an attempt to titillate readers than some kind of proto-feminism.[44]

The Dongo incident became less interesting to Mexico's intellectual elite in the years leading up to the Mexican Revolution and after. No further major account came out until historians started to take an interest in these events in the 1980s. Even the two massive Dongo novels published in the 1860s and 1870s either disappeared completely or had only very limited readership. Given the huge popularity of True Crime, and the current need to understand the history of Mexican law enforcement, it is time to bring these novels back into the public eye.

---

[43] Payno, *The Bandits from Río Frío*, vol. 2, 520, 565–566, 602–603.
[44] Walkowitz, *City of Dreadful Delight*, 85, 97. This section discusses the so-called "Maiden Tribute" scandal, allegedly an exposé of child sex rings, but in effect, one man's pornographic (and not very informative or conclusive) journey through London.

2 I

Two Dongo Novels

Within a span of less than five years, Mexican presses published two historical novels based on the Dongo massacre and its rapid resolution by the viceregal judiciary. The first of these was José de Cuéllar's 1869 *El Pecado del Siglo: Novela Histórica, Época de Revillagigedo*, published by the Tipográfica del Colegio Polimático in San Luís Potosí. Four years later, the first volume of a book called *Los Asesinos de Dongo: Novela Histórica* appeared in Mexico City, written by Manuel Filomeno Rodríguez, and published by Barbedillo and Company. The second volume followed in 1876. By writing these historical novels, both authors were taking part in an important nationalist and didactic literary trend in Mexico's Restored Republic. Influenced by the politician, intellectual, journalist, and writer Ignacio Manuel Altamirano, novelists like Rodríguez and Cuéllar felt inspired to help Mexicans understand their own history through fictional characters.[1]

Not surprisingly, both novels reflect the values, perspectives, and opinions of 1860s and 1870s Mexico more than those of the late viceregal era. With varying success, Cuéllar and Rodríguez attempted to use historical events to present their views to Mexicans of this era. Prominent themes for both authors include an emphasis on female characters and sexuality, as well as how Mexicans interpreted viceregal history and its influence on mid-nineteenth-century issues, especially those relating to church, state, the judiciary, and what they viewed as progress. Essentially, Cuéllar wrote from a Positivist point of view, emphasizing the potential for Mexico to

---

[1] Belem Clark de Lara, "Ficción y Verdad en *El Pecado del Siglo*, de José Tomas de Cuéllar," *Andamios*, vol. 8: 15 (2011), 111–138.

embrace capitalism and a new class of educated professionals, while
Rodríguez took a more conservative Catholic approach.[2] Both authors
agreed that Viceroy Revillagigedo's reforms were necessary and effective,
although they differed greatly in their assessment of the fate of the killers.
These differences of opinion affect how the Dongo story unfolds in each of
their novels.

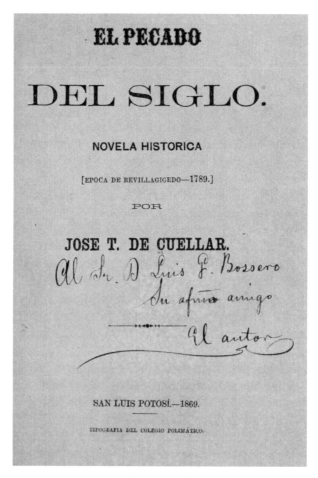

FIGURE 21.1 Title page of *El Pecado del Siglo*

[2] Clark de Lara, "Ficción y Verdad," 119.

THE AUTHORS

These two authors experienced very different levels of recognition during their lifetime and in the 130 years since their deaths. Rodríguez has been largely forgotten, except by those scholars who study the deepest annals of Mexico's journalism. In contrast, Cuéllar became one of Mexico's most well-known commentators of the late nineteenth century. During Cuéllar's lifetime, his novellas appeared in multiple editions published in both Spain and Mexico. In the late 1880s and early 1890s, he collected his articles, essays, and poems in a twenty-four-volume series with the title *La Linterna mágica*. This series was published in Barcelona and Santander.[3]

Born in 1830, Cuéllar received his initial education as a military cadet. Six of his young peers died in the 1847 Battle of Chapultepec fighting against the US invasion of Mexico City, becoming the martyrs known as the *Niños Héroes*. After this traumatic experience, Cuéllar changed his career ambitions and started training at the San Carlos art academy. He failed as a painter but his experience as a photographer did play a role in his writings. In his late teens, he began publishing poems and writing plays. He first published his short stories in the periodical that he founded while in exile in San Luís Potosí in the late 1860s. Over the decades, Cuéllar attempted to imitate the style of Balzac, but early twentieth-century critics relegated him more to the *costumbrismo*, a literary and artistic genre which depicted stereotyped "folk" customs in Spanish-speaking countries.[4]

In 1860s Mexico, didactic historical novels came from the pens of liberal writers, so Rodríguez made an unusual choice to express his politics in this genre.[5] His conservative views probably contributed to the nonexistent impact of *Los Asesinos*. In contrast to the proliferation of multiple editions of Cuéllar's publications, only one cataloged copy of *Los*

---

[3] The most recent edition is José Cuéllar and Belem Clark de Lara, eds., *El pecado del siglo: novela histórica* (México: UNAM, Instituto de Investigaciones Filologicas, 2007). Cuéllar is well-known for his social and cultural commentary in *La Linterna Magica*. See Margaret Carson and Margo Glantz, eds. and trans., *The Magic Lantern: Having a Ball and Christmas Eve* (New York: Oxford University Press, 2001); José Cuéllar, *La linterna mágica, colección de novelas de costumbres mexicanas* (Barcelona: Tipo-lit. de Espasa y Compañía, 1889). Anyone interested in Cuéllar can easily find English or Spanish editions of some of the most famous short stories included in *The Magic Lantern* series to purchase or in a university library.

[4] Carson and Glantz, *The Magic Lantern*, xxi–xiii; Clark de Lara, "Ficción y Verdad," 117; Mey-Yen Moriuchi, *Mexican Costumbrismo: Race, Society, and Identity in Nineteenth-Century Art* (University Park: Pennsylvania State University Press, 2018).

[5] Marco Antonio Chavarín González, "*El Pecado del Siglo*: de José de Cuéllar: Entre la Colonia y la Republica Restaurada, la Libertad, el Orden y el Progreso," *Revista de El Colegio de San Luis*, vol. 7: 14 (2017), 47–63.

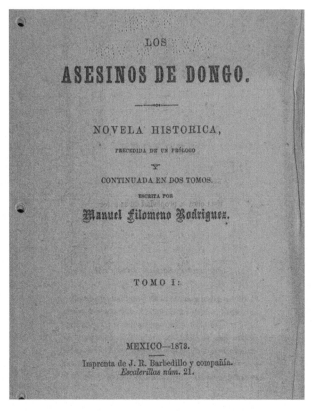

FIGURE 21.2 Title page of *Los Asesinos del Dongo*. Retrieved from the Nettie Lee Benson Latin American Collection.

Asesinos exists in the entire world, stored at the Nettie Lee Benson Latin American Collection at the University of Texas, Austin.[6] This novel also lacks appeal for readers (perhaps even in the nineteenth century) due to its intimidating length and its unsubtle and ponderous religiosity. Although ignored in the twentieth and twenty-first centuries, Rodríguez had some prominence in the 1870s and 1880s, due to the dozens of articles he wrote for conservative, Catholic periodicals. For his two-volume Dongo novel, he composed more than 1,100 pages. Beyond this prolific output as a writer, only a few facts exist to sketch out his biography. Even his date of birth is unknown.

---

[6] I received a scan of this novel through the very helpful assistance of Benson archivist Dylan Joy, during spring of 2021, when the collection remained closed.

Rodríguez first appears in the historical record when he participates in the foundation of the periodical *La Voz de México* in 1870. This publication defined itself as a political and religious newspaper for Mexican Catholics, founded by the Sociedad Católica. Dating back to 1868, the founders of the Sociedad Católica wished to reopen political and cultural spaces for members of the Conservative party who had become pariahs after the fall of Maximilian's short-lived empire.[7] *La Voz* had a goal of politicizing Mexican Catholics while offering a moral critique of the liberal leaders of the era.[8] Rodríguez wrote his first *La Voz* article in 1873. This contribution was a six-column tribute to the Virgin of Guadalupe published on December 12, the day of her annual fiesta. The fact that his words memorialized this important holiday underscores his prominence as a highly respected Catholic commentator of the era.[9] *La Voz* advertised the publication of Rodríguez's *Los Asesinos* regularly throughout the late 1870s – perhaps hoping to increase desultory sales for one of the paper's key contributors.[10]

Rodríguez continued to work as an editor for *La Voz* until his death in 1884. He published his last article in April of that year, a critique of the expense wasted on a Mexican contribution to the New Orleans World's Fair as organized by Vicente Riva Palacio under the regime of Porfirio Díaz.[11] Rodríguez noted that the industrialized world would observe Mexico's embarrassing lack of progress on full display at this event.[12] In June of 1884, *La Voz* mentioned that Rodríguez was gravely ill. Twelve days later, the paper *La Libertad* announced his death.[13] *El Tiempo* honored him with a description of his patient suffering through the loss of his vision, hearing, and movement, emphasizing his "heroic Christianity." According to his

---

[7] Edward Shawcross, *France, Mexico and Informal Empire in Latin America, 1820–1867: Equilibrium in the New World* (New York: Palgrave Macmillan, 2018).

[8] See Lilia Vieyra Sánchez, *La Voz de México (1870–1875), la Prensa Católica y la Reorganización Conservadora* (Mexico City: Universidad Nacional Autónoma de México, Instituto de Investigaciones Bibliográficas, 2008); see also Rogelio Jiménez Marce, "Sobre Lilia Vieyra Sánchez, *La Voz De México (1870–1875)*," *Historia Mexicana*, vol. 62: 1 (2012), 500–506; René Avilés, "La censura al periodismo en México: revisión histórica y perspectivas," *Razón y Palabra*: vol. 59 (2007), 1–9.

[9] *La Voz de México*, December 12, 1873, 1–2.

[10] *La Voz de México*, November 23, 1877, 4; December 6, 1877; December 29, 1877; January 8, 1878. The final ad appeared on December 5, 1879.

[11] See Mauricio Tenorio Trillo, *Mexico at the World's Fairs: Crafting a Modern Nation* (Berkeley: University of California Press, 1996), 38–43.

[12] Manuel Filomeno Rodríguez, "La Exposición Universal," *La Voz de México*, April 17, 1884, 2. See also Tenorio Trillo, *Mexico at the World's Fairs*, 40.

[13] *La Voz de México*, June 6, 1884, 3; *La Libertad*, June 18, 1886, 3.

obituary, Rodríguez wrote more than sixty articles on religious and political topics for *La Voz*, with no compensation whatsoever, and lived by the pious motto "Thy will be done."[14]

Los Asesinos de Dongo

Many of the themes dealt with in the *La Voz* also appear in a dramatic way in Rodríguez's *Los Asesinos*, including the negative consequences of suicide and other violations of Catholic morality. Overall, like *La Voz*, this novel seeks to "diffuse and defend the Catholic religion in broader Mexican society."[15] Rodríguez weaves moral condemnations throughout the two volumes, with recurring references to the perpetrators' individual and collective obsessions: cockfighting, women, and gold. Again and again, he hammers home the idea that individuals who let any worldly desires distract them from religion will pay the consequences.[16]

The first several pages of the book read like a sermon summing up human existence as originating in chaos. However, the author observes, as soon as we look above us and see the stars, humans start to have awareness of "the divine majesty, the essence of goodness and the creator of everything in the universe, visible and invisible." With this prolonged lecture on the all-knowing and benevolent presence of God in nature, Rodríguez makes it very clear to his readers that he wrote this book to push a religious agenda.[17]

With his conservative Catholic point of view featuring prominently, Rodríguez shapes his story around his vision for the Mexican nation. After the sermon referred to above, *Los Asesinos* finally begins its action on a hacienda in 1770. Typical of Rodríguez's style, readers have to wait dozens of pages before learning that this estate belongs to the kind philanthropist Don Joaquín Dongo. The first character introduced is a beautiful child named María Isaura, who has gold curls and a thin, straight nose. The author's choice to describe her this way conforms to the "whitening" ideal so common in Latin American countries at this time, despite their noteworthy African descent and Indigenous political and intellectual leaders.[18]

[14] *El Tiempo*, June 6, 1884, 3.   [15] Vieyra Sánchez, *La Voz de México*, 20.
[16] On crime and morality in nineteenth-century Mexico, see Pablo A. Piccato, "The Public Sphere and Liberalism in Mexico from the Mid-19th Century to the 1930s," in *Oxford Research Encyclopedia of Latin American History*, edited by William Beezley (Oxford: Oxford University Press, 2016).
[17] Rodríguez, *Los Asesinos de Dongo*, vol. 1, 5–12, quote on 6.
[18] For Mexico, the first three on this list (who would have been personally known by these authors) are Porfirio Díaz, Benito Juárez, and Ignacio Manuel Altamirano. See

The child suffers an injury and shortly afterward (after dramatic scenes involving her grandfather and the mysteries surrounding her parentage), Dongo adopts her.

While spending little time on Dongo, both novels deeply explore the characters of Dongo's murderers, although Rodríguez makes his readers suffer through 150 pages of seemingly unconnected descriptions of aristocrats and their flirtations before he finally introduces Quintero, Blanco, and Aldama. In this book, these characters choose to follow the path of evil, and allow the author to illustrate how immorality results in painful repercussions. When the group of conspirators meet up for the first time, Quintero makes a long speech about how all of the robberies and thefts that they have committed and plan to commit in the future happened because of their obsession with women – presumably because these criminals needed money to attract their potential sexual partners. This explanation is completely fictional, as the original documents mention nothing about any sexual connections that the killers had with women. However, it allows Rodríguez to present the conventional Catholic perspective of women as temptresses. While the love affairs of Blanco and Aldama do not materialize in the text, many of *Los Asesinos*' pages present Blanco's infatuation with a seamstress named Manuela, who may be his cousin. Rodríguez hints that Manuela and the young clerk in Dongo's office might have had a burgeoning friendship, which causes Blanco to view the man as his rival.[19]

As the novel progresses, Rodríguez paints the lives of Blanco, Aldama, and Quintero as increasingly grim and desperate. These circumstances gradually lead them to choose to murder, with the underlying implication that they could have made better decisions if they were not driven by their immoral, ungodly passions. In a long buildup to the scene of the crime, first Aldama loses two hundred pesos at the cockfights. This causes him to utter "a horrible blasphemy regarding the doom of his wretched fate," a throwback to the viceregal sinful understanding of gambling and blasphemous words.[20] Next, Quintero sits alone in his drab and depressing room, pondering how a daring man like himself ended up in this tedious

---

Thomas Skidmore, *Black into White: Race and Nationality in Brazilian Thought* (Durham, NC: Duke University Press, 1993); for whitening in the Porfiriato, see Jürgen Buchenau, "The Rise and Demise of a Regional Power: The Multilateralism of Mexican Dictator Porfirio Díaz, 1876–1911," *The Latin Americanist*, vol. 63: 3 (2019), 307–333.

[19] Rodríguez, *Los Asesinos de Dongo*, vol. 1, 176–177, 356.

[20] Javier Villa-Flores, *Dangerous Speech: A Social History of Blasphemy in Colonial Mexico* (Tucson: University of Arizona, 2006); Rodríguez, *Los Asesinos de Dongo*, vol. 1, 196.

existence. As he stares at his shadow on the wall, he becomes enraged with his poverty and views his existence as no better than hell on earth. His hand on his sword, he ponders the characters of his two friends, considering if they can handle a plan to kill for money. He thinks about how Aldama loses everything to cockfights, and Blanco obsesses over Manuela. These thoughts motivate him to propose his murderous plan to the two men.[21]

The next day, Quintero faces more humiliations. He receives a pathetic sum of money for pawning his watch, increasing his rage. Meeting up with Aldama, he lectures him on how only gold offers the key to every imaginable problem of human existence. Aldama ponders how the proposed plan to kill for money means an exchange of blood for gold, but he still agrees to it. Later, they meet up with Blanco, who is also enraged because the rainy day means that he cannot visit Manuela. Aldama points out that "all men ... have a weakness, a passion, a blind spot ... which pushes off the precipice to the abyss." The others agree, adding that all men can claim descent from Adam. This presentation of their motivations encapsulates the author's misogynistic and religious views, which he repeats throughout the two volumes. Rodríguez ends this section with an emphasis on the conspirators' motto that symbolizes their plan: "*He aquí mi mano* [Here is my hand]!"[22] Now Aldama, Quintero, and Blanco are ready to carry out their crime. To excuse the presence of gory details as he narrates the home invasion, Rodríguez explains that "under the honor of our word, we have confined ourselves strictly to the judicial events ... without our pen having adulterated any of the substance of this historical episode."[23] The author does follow the version of events that is represented in the anonymous account, so it is likely that his source was Bustamante's 1830s publication. This almost-plagiarized section offers some of the most exciting passages in the 1,100 pages of the two-volume novel. However, Rodríguez, contrary to his explicitly stated vow, actually does add fictional conversations and prolonged and tedious moments of suspense during Aldama's interrogation by Emparan. Rodríguez leaves out some of the archival case's more interesting details, such as the gradual spread of information about Dongo's abandoned carriage on the morning of October 24, and how an intense back-and-forth over Blanco's stockings really solved the crime.

Rodríguez's additions reinforce the unpalatable tone of this novel for the modern reader. Although the author does not present Blanco as an

[21] Rodríguez, *Los Asesinos de Dongo*, vol. 1, 237–247.
[22] Rodríguez, *Los Asesinos de Dongo*, vol. 1, 250–279, quote on 276.
[23] Rodríguez, *Los Asesinos de Dongo*, vol. 1, 430.

appealing character, the killer's hatred of his aunt still gives the impression of justified misogyny:

And Blanco? Blanco's time in prison feels like the nail that rivets a horseshoe. His damned aunt! In the worst possible moment, that cursed old woman now wants to moralize, even though she does not comprehend the meaning of the word moral. This old hypocrite, best suited to fingering her rosary beads, eating the saints [*sic*?], flagellating her backside, and beating her breast, has caused him serious difficulties with her infernal complaining.[24]

Rodríguez forces several unpleasant jokes about the killing of Dongo's parrot, an anecdote not found in the original file. Apparently, during the massacre, the parrot said, "They will see it," inspiring Quintero to cut his head off.[25]

The attitude and wordiness of Rodríguez's narrative dates his book – it is easy to see why it did not become a bestseller. The original archived case file reads like a more exciting, if less cohesive, novel than *Los Asesinos*.

El Pecado del Siglo

In contrast, at half the length of the two-volume *Los Asesinos*, Cuéllar's novel is refreshingly concise. *El Pecado* jumps right into the action, opening with a fictional scene of Aldama, Quintero, and Blanco plotting a "hit" while they eat in a private room rented out in the Villa de Guadalupe. Cuéllar introduces his characters immediately and fills most of his pages with fastmoving dialogue, rather than tedious sermons. His subplots involving women, sex, magic, and lost-and-found fathers are integrated into his presentation of the killers' lives and motivations. Although Dongo himself does not feature often in the action, he appears as a sympathetic friend to an important older woman character. Cuéllar has the ability to appeal to the reader's compassion for all of his characters, even women and Quintero. His humanistic style and his complex goals for writing this novel become most obvious when he interjects his views on topics relevant to the nineteenth century, especially the death penalty.[26]

[24] Rodríguez, *Los Asesinos de Dongo*, vol. 1, 69; Steve J. Stern, *The Secret History of Gender: Women, Men, and Power in Late Colonial Mexico* (Chapel Hill: University of North Carolina Press, 1995), 11–44.

[25] Rodríguez, *Los Asesinos de Dongo*, 70–71.

[26] Beatriz de Alba-Koch, "'Enlightened Absolutism' and Utopian Thought: Fernández de Lizardi and Reform in New Spain," *Revista Canadiense de Estudios Hispánicos*, vol. 24: 2 (2000), 295–306; Juan Pablo Dabove, *Nightmares of the Lettered City: Banditry and*

In Cuéllar's version of the crime, Quintero is the most complex character, as genuine love motivates him to act desperately, and he expresses regret afterward. After the killings, he and the other two murderers drink themselves into oblivion, which Cuéllar describes as a way to "cauterize" their guilt. Quintero's moral crisis escalates because he finds out that his long-lost mother practices witchcraft (Cuéllar portrays her sympathetically). The author illustrates that even a murderer like Quintero possesses humanity to help convince readers of the immorality of judicial executions. He uses the killers' garroting to argue for the abolition of the death penalty, emphasizing that it goes against the commandment "Thou Shalt not Kill." He observes that even if most of the city felt vindicated when the killers were executed, they also would hypocritically agree that killing was morally wrong. Cuéllar concludes by suggesting formal pardons and penitentiaries as the most important reforms of the nineteenth century. This anti-death penalty argumentation also serves as a criticism of the recent execution of Maximilian Hapsburg.[27]

Clearly on the other side of this debate, Rodríguez offers no explicit opinions of the executions. In this section, he adheres very closely to the anonymous account, citing the measurements of the gallows platform, and describing the organized guard, the eager crowd, the grave presence of the Archicofradía (the prominent religious brotherhood which counted Dongo as a member), and the overall somber ceremonial tone of the event.[28] Rodríguez concludes the main text of his novel with the respectable burial and funeral organized for the executed men, then adds an epilogue that resolves the subplots about his female characters. On the whole, conventional marriages, family reunions, and the fate of women seem to interest both authors more than Dongo and his murder.

A SHARED THEME – WOMEN AND SEX

Not surprisingly for late nineteenth-century men, both Rodríguez and Cuéllar obsess over women's sexuality. Hundreds of pages in each of their books narrate fictional plots centering on women, stereotypically portrayed as seductresses or virtuous innocents. In contrast, in the original Dongo case files, women only appear on a few occasions: Blanco's estranged aunt who

---

Literature in Latin America, 1816–1929 (Pittsburgh, PA: University of Pittsburgh Press, 2007), 43–52.

[27] Cuéllar, *Pecado del siglo*, 559–560; Chavarín González, "*El Pecado*," 62.

[28] Rodríguez, *Los Asesinos de Dongo*, vol. 2, 432–450.

helps solve the case by testifying about his bloody stockings; the widow of Quintero's cousin who accuses him of theft; and Aldama's elderly servants who lie to Emparan about their master's activities on the night of October 23, 1789. These women may have antagonized the murderers with their testimonies, but, other than the deceptive servants, a novelist could choose to adhere to the case file and present them as conventionally moral heroines on the side of justice. All of these historical women behave in ways familiar to viceregal historians. They run households, work or otherwise control household finances, and interact with the court in a manner that shows a degree of confidence and familiarity with the judiciary.[29] Other than very vague references to Quintero's family in the Canaries that imply that he might have had a wife and children, the Dongo documents in no way support a supposition that the perpetrators had sex with, or even felt any attraction to, women. In fact, the only slightly sexual insinuation in the entire case is the fact that Blanco slept in the same bed as Aldama in the week of the crime. However, in the two nineteenth-century novels, the authors expend very few words on Dongo's character or his household, instead focusing on the perpetrators' fictional affairs and antagonisms with women.

Both authors create subplots that involve sex workers. Cuéllar does this more subtly and introduces moral ambiguity. Two of his main characters are sexually active women who live outside the norms of marriage. First, Teresa is a young woman who lives in an informal brothel with another sex worker her own age. In a scheme set up by some Spaniards, Teresa seduces one of Dongo's close friends, another very rich man. Over the course of a few months spent entertaining him and taking part in marathon card games where he loses his fortune, Teresa destroys his family, bankrupts his businesses, and eventually her lover dies prematurely. Her victim's susceptibility to seduction is blamed on the pious Catholic morals to which he subscribed.

Even in this role, Cuéllar portrays Teresa as a thoughtful, fun-loving character, able to interact with the man's wife and daughter, also portrayed with humanity and sympathy. Their husband and father, Teresa's lover, takes this path by his own volition not due to Teresa's cruelty or immorality. Cuéllar uses his fate to prove that a lifetime of religious self-repression can eventually cause a man to succumb to temptation and quickly self-destruct. By the end of the novel, the author does not relegate Teresa to the

---

[29] A few classics on this widely studied topic include Arrom, *Women of Mexico City*, 154–205; and Martha Few, *Women Who Live Evil Lives: Gender, Religion, and the Politics of Power in Colonial Guatemala* (Austin: University of Texas Press, 2002), especially 1–12.

classic sex workers' fate in fiction – death or religious seclusion – but implies that she simply continued her occupation as a popular and well-off mistress to rich men. The last scene has her watching the killers' executions from a luxurious carriage. Other than the over-dramatic way that she ruined her elderly lover, Teresa's story could have happened in eighteenth-century Mexico City, a time when famous and fabulously rich courtesans entertained groups of men in opulent home casinos.[30]

Aldama becomes obsessed with Teresa, neglecting the other sexually nonconforming character of Margarita, his previous lover. Margarita is the central female character in the novel, a woman who could have redeemed Aldama through her moral influence. Cuéllar sympathetically follows her struggles throughout his entire book, although he does fall into some of the age-old clichés regarding sex workers when he describes her ultimate fate. Until then, Margarita is a complex character who lives a tragic life.

Like Rodríguez, Cuéllar cannot conceive of beauty other than by European standards, so he describes Margarita as "white like a German." She also has beautifully expressive eyes and a graceful and regal way of moving.[31] At the age of ten, she loses her parents to the "black vomit sickness," yellow fever, upon their arrival in Veracruz.[32] She travels on to Mexico City with some muleteers and ends up adopted by Dongo. She lives a quiet life there for four years, cared for by servants but lacking affection. Conspiring with her nurse, Aldama kidnaps her when she goes out to attend mass. He locks her up in a house where she serves as his sexual prisoner for five years, until the start of the novel.

Cuéllar portrays the nineteen-year-old Margarita as extremely depressed, devout, and pious, but also brave and able to take action. Even her visits to church represent her defiance of Aldama, although sadly in her traumatized state she still loves this villain. In a scene where she assertively questions judicial officials, she learns that her lover killed Dongo and his family. This causes her to break down emotionally and physically, but her aristocratic European appearance helps her find patrons and protectors. In her final scene, she takes part in the classic

[30] Cuéllar, Pecado del siglo, 573. See Germeten, Profit and Passion, for more on historic courtesans in the viceregal era. Real mistresses similar to the fictional character Teresa also displayed their wealth in public, much to the chagrin of the authorities.
[31] Cuéllar, Pecado del siglo, 23–24.
[32] Sherry Lee Fields, Pestilence and Headcolds: Encountering Illness in Colonial Mexico (New York: Columbia University Press, 2008), 47; Andrew L. Knaut, "Yellow Fever and the Late Colonial Public Health Response in the Port of Veracruz," The Hispanic American Historical Review, vol. 77: 4 (1997), 619–644.

Spanish ceremony of surrendering to a nun's vows, rejecting all material-
ism, even having her hair shorn off.[33] Although Cuéllar clearly respects
Margarita and allows her to determine her own destiny, she does fit the
eternal role of a woman martyred because of her sexuality, who ends up
enclosed and cut off from the world.

While Cuéllar allows these two women some humanity, in contrast,
Rodríguez's novel has a classic misogynistic conclusion that reiterates his
conventional Catholic understanding of sin. Going back to ancient times,
Christian writings always present a painful death as the ultimate fate of
sexually non-conforming women.[34] Manuela, Blanco's girlfriend, embodies
this role in *Los Asesinos*. Although she worked as a seamstress, she does take
money from Blanco after the murders, and apparently becomes a fulltime sex
worker. After the execution of the killers, Rodríguez lectures readers on how
he must end his story by recounting the fate of all of his characters. He then
introduces a young woman, approximately nineteen years old, out in a busy
street. She has just experienced a physical collapse of some kind. Looking
more closely, the author says, causes a "feeling of revulsion." Her disheveled
clothes reveal a beautiful skin marked with repulsive marks: "her uninter-
rupted libidinous existence . . . has had its effect." Rodríguez repeatedly points
out that her "vices" caused her "repugnant . . . disgusting" current physical
state, which he describes in detail. The author makes it clear that she has
contracted syphilis. Hoping for a cure, Manuela (several pages in the author
finally names her) takes a purgative, which ends up poisoning her.[35] She dies
like so many other "fallen women" featured in other works of literature over
the course of millennia.

Although certainly what were viewed as "French" morals bothered
Spaniards in the era of the Dongo massacre, and syphilis had become an
obsession for artists, writers, and scientists, Mexicans did not write extensively about sex work in the eighteenth century.[36] Judicial records indicate
that the Mexico City authorities made some desultory gestures toward

---

[33] Cuéllar, *Pecado del siglo*, 24, 576; Asunción Lavrín, *Brides of Christ: Conventual Life in
Colonial Mexico* (Stanford, CA: Stanford University Press, 2008); Margaret Chowning,
"Convents and Nuns: New Approaches to the Study of Female Religious Institutions in
Colonial Mexico," *History Compass*, vol. 6: 5 (2008), 1279–1303.

[34] Kyle Harper, *From Shame to Sin: The Christian Transformation of Morality in Late
Antiquity* (Cambridge, MA: Harvard University Press, 2016), examines this genre in depth.

[35] Rodríguez, *Los Asesinos de Dongo*, vol. 2, 548–557.

[36] See González Espitia, *Sifiolografía*, for a comprehensive discussion of syphilis in the
Enlightenment; also Josefina Mansilla and Carmen M Pijoan, "A Case of Congenital
Syphilis During the Colonial Period in Mexico City," *American Journal of Physical
Anthropology*, vol. 97: 2 (1995), 187–195.

suppressing the procuring of young women and street solicitation at this time. Around 1800, court officials started to romanticize some of the young women involved in sex work as beautiful victims.[37] But this topic only began to preoccupy the most famous Mexican novelists in the late nineteenth and early twentieth centuries – most notably in the classic *Santa* by Federico Gamboa.[38] Leading up to this obsession, the 1860s and 1870s were important decades for the history of sex work in Mexico. Under Emperor Maximilian, Mexico experienced its first officially regulated prostitution with the introduction of a public-health focused *reglamiento*, inspired by France's *maisons de tolérance*. Slight reforms of these laws continued in the 1870s.[39] Rodríguez and Cuéllar show the concerns of *their* era, in contrast to those of Dongo's time, by focusing their historical murder story on the lives of fictional sex workers.

SHARED THEME – MEXICO CITY

Both Rodríguez and Cuéllar present viceregal Mexico City as a dirty and chaotic mess, an almost medieval setting which, from their point of view, has not benefited from the sanitary advances of the mid-nineteenth century. The authors, and possibly their readers as well, believed that they enjoyed a more modern city than their ancestors did eighty years before.[40] Indulging in an arrogant sense of superiority over the past provides a self-congratulatory pleasure for both writers and readers of historical fiction. Of course, from the perspectives of historians now, late nineteenth-century Mexico City was increasingly becoming a massive conglomeration of villages lacking paving, clean water, or sewerage access. Only a few central blocks were maintained in imitation of a European ideal of urban planning.[41]

Physically, in Cuéllar's version, the city reflects the intellectual disorganization of its inhabitants:

On October 21, 1789 the main square of Mexico City presented a disgusting appearance. It featured a multitude of produce stalls, old clothes shops, and junk bazaars,

[37] Germeten, *Profit and Passion*.
[38] Federico Gamboa, *Santa* (Barcelona: Araluce, 1903).
[39] Katherine Bliss, *Compromised Positions: Prostitution, Public Health, and Gender Politics in Revolutionary Mexico City* (College Park, CA: Penn State University Press, 2001), 16, 34.
[40] Robert M. Buffington and William E. French, "The Culture of Modernity," in *The Oxford History of Mexico*, eds. William H. Beezley and Michael C. Meyer (Oxford: Oxford University Press, 2010), 373–406.
[41] Michael Johns, *The City of Mexico in the Age of Díaz* (Austin: University of Texas Press, 2011).

trash, remains of vegetables, all sheltered by huts collapsed and blackened by time. The center of the square was an unclean, disorganized set of kiosks, surrounded by hungry pigs and cows that ate half rotten vegetables, circling every garbage heap. The inhabitants of that sewer were people almost entirely naked, because the populace of Mexico at that time, when fabrics still had a very high price, could not afford clothes. Men and women roamed everywhere, naked and only half covered with rags, many only with a blanket or a blanket for their single garment. [Due to the pending arrival of the new viceroy], the people began to swarm there at the first dawn. That black, shapeless and pestilential mass that occupied almost the entire length of the spacious plaza like an immense stain, was beginning to move, and a muffled noise like that of an army, rose up.[42]

Cuéllar populates the viceregal capital with corrupt judicial officials who rule over the ignorant, poor and superstitious masses. Everyone lives in constant fear of the Tribunal of the Holy Office and in the thrall of both the Catholic Church and clever witches.

Because Rodríguez believes in the church as a beneficial institution, his novel has a slightly more positive assessment of the viceregal era. He still introduces the 1789 capital as a poor contrast to his own era:

Mexico City ... was very far from acquiring the degree of civilization and culture that we believe it has achieved .... Crossed by disgusting canals full of canoes, these ditches extended to the side of the Plaza mayor, even at the very foot of the municipal palace. The plaza was obstructed by market stalls, invaded on all sides by trash and cows, containing a great number of dogs, and full of people wrapped up in sheets or half-naked, with no scruples about feeling shame or public modesty. A city without police, consequently with a propensity for all kinds of crimes, lacking ornamentation, without public lighting at night, which made the streets dark and murky. And to complement how much can believed about this era, the inside of the National Palace, where the viceroys lived, was invaded by a great number of people that made stoves out of three stones, which sustained three enormous vats of beans with mole, tortillas, and all of the other comestibles from which they made their daily income.[43]

Both authors made a point of noting that the Zócalo looked like a farmers' market. These nineteenth-century writers also expressed an elitist concern about hierarchy and modesty; the masses should appear better-dressed or simply disappear from public spaces which symbolize the government. What they present as necessary sanitary and law enforcement reforms came about due to Viceroy Revillagigedo, who Cuéllar and Rodríguez present as highly rational, intelligent, and organized.[44] To Cuéllar, this viceroy almost becomes

---

[42] Cuéllar, *Pecado del siglo*, 303–304.
[43] Rodríguez, *Los Asesinos de Dongo*, vol. 1, 87–88.
[44] Hamman, "Eyeing Alameda Park."

a Positivist saint. The authors' devotion to Revillagigedo suggests a craving for similar leadership in their own era.

SHARED THEME – RELIGION

Although not a conservative Catholic like Rodríguez, Cuéllar 's *El Pecado* does have religious framing, as indicated by its title, and the choice of the word "sin," not "crime."[45] The sin in question is, in the author's view, the dangers of a following Catholic education.[46] Cuéllar advocates for the Mexican Positivist goals of Order and Progress. He acknowledges the Catholic understanding of free will but disapproves of how it lacked an appropriate educational infrastructure to allow people to make decisions which would promote the greater good during the viceregal era.[47]

Although most of *Los Asesinos* reads like a sermon, Rodríguez hammers home his pro-Catholic message most in the scene leading up to the killers' execution. The author attempts to humanize the perpetrators as they ponder their imminent death. Sitting apart from each other but in the company of three priests, and watched over by a statue of the Virgin Mary, finally they feel guilty for their crimes. Rodríguez points out that, in their role representing Jesus Christ, these priests can absolve Aldama, Quintero, and Blanco. Thus they transform these greedy and bloodthirsty brutes into penitent men. The city demands their execution, and the killers know they deserve it, but the presence of the priests completes the expiation ceremony. For several pages, Rodríguez narrates a sermon from Thomas à Kempis on this theme of forgiveness. When the executioner enters, the priests leave, and the prisoners feel peace.[48]

SHARED THEME – THE IDEAL COUPLE

The authors do not build their plots around Dongo, portrayed in both books as a kind but quiet, regimented, elderly Spanish merchant. Instead, fictional characters reveal the writers' ideas regarding Mexico, its history, and its future. Rodríguez's prologue introduces the child María Isaura as the most important character in the book. Her purpose in the plot is to anchor Dongo to the family dramas and love affairs between young

---

[45] Flores Esquivel, *Memorial Ajustado*, 134, 136, 142, 147. Sandoval notes that Cuéllar emphasizes free will more than Bustamante.
[46] Clark de Lara, "Ficción y Verdad," 122.   [47] Chavarín González, "*El Pecado*," 53–56.
[48] Rodríguez, *Los Asesinos de Dongo*, vol. 2, 516–533.

people that provide most of the action throughout both volumes. Like so many other nineteenth-century novelists in the Americas, both Rodríguez and Cuéllar create stories that end with successful and happy pairings between characters who represent what the authors view as the ideal racial and social future of their nation. In both novels, the Dongo story serves mainly to draw in readers into conventional heteronormative "national romances."[49] Both books also conclude with rediscoveries of long-lost fathers, another way to represent a vision of the Mexican nation at the level of the family and the question of whether or not it should embrace or reject its Spanish past.

In *Los Asesinos*, María Isaura, Dongo's adopted daughter, gets her father back and they have a loving and happy reunion. She marries Dongo's young clerk Lanuza who luckily escaped the massacre (in actuality, he went home to sleep with his wife because he was a newlywed). Rodríguez concludes his book with a beautiful Mexican heroine integrated back into her birth family, creating a new family with a Spanish man. An ending which focuses on apparently successful heteronormative marriages and a father reuniting with his daughter perhaps shows this author's perspective that Mexico should realign with its own "father" – Spain and its Catholic values.

Cuéllar also uses the marriage of a couple to portray his ideals, but he strongly rejects father figures as retrograde legacies of Spanish rule.[50] The pious and dutiful character of Isabel, the daughter of the rich man seduced by Teresa, marries a doctor-in-training called Don Carlos. This highly moral and well-mannered man resists going to Teresa's home brothel and rejects Aldama's get-rich-quick schemes. The fact that he is working on his education shows that the author idealizes the professional *hombre de bien*, a dignified and moral citizen.[51] Not a single father in the book survives until the end and no character in the book has a good and consistent father figure. Cuéllar concludes his book with the painful and dramatic death of Quintero's long-lost parents, as the

---

[49] Doris Sommer, *Foundation Fictions: The National Romances of Latin America* (Oakland: University of California Press, 1993).

[50] Clark de Lara, "Ficción y Verdad," 119–120.

[51] For this kind of man as a leader in the Mexican Republic, see Michael P. Costeloe, *The Central Republic in Mexico, 1835–1846: "Hombres de Bien" in the Age of Santa Anna* (Cambridge: Cambridge University Press, 2002); for bourgeois moral ideals, see William French, *A Peaceful and Working People: Manners, Morals, and Class Formation in Northern Mexico* (Albuquerque: University of New Mexico Press, 1996).

city erupts into chaos during the terrifying aurora borealis that took place just a week after the executions of the Dongo killers.

Juxtaposing these two books leaves the reader with no doubt whatsoever why posterity granted Cuéllar far more fame and popularity as a writer. While both authors introduce contrived and clichéd plots regarding long-lost parents, *Pecado*'s two main stories interweave much more smoothly, while Rodríguez spends an almost unbearable number of pages on characters who have no clear connection to Dongo. Although both novels contain ridiculous subplots about magic and/or sex, Cuéllar's detours remain interesting, while Rodríguez depends on tedious, drawn-out suspenseful moments. This Catholic conversative also shows an insidious misogyny. The author's hatred for his characters projects onto his readers. Why should we care about them if he does not? Cuéllar, even when he deploys characters and events to support his political views (especially in terms of the death penalty), still demonstrates a compassion for all of them. His care for them inspires readers to sympathize with them in their different plights. Finally, Cuéllar's much shorter take on the case avoids the tedious wordiness of *Los Asesinos*.

Both Cuéllar and Rodríguez chose to return to a viceregal crime when they started writing their novels in the 1860s. Unlike Payno, they adhered closely to the documents available to them – most likely Bustamante's 1830s publications drawn from Luzero's anonymous account. Although both *Pecado* and *Asesinos* focus on other characters and plotlines for hundreds of pages, something about Dongo's death drew their attention as an event relevant to their own era. These two novelists believed that at this time – after the recent execution of another European invader and ongoing changes in Mexican laws and the administration of justice – readers would benefit from a return to a case study from 1789. Sexuality, morality, and the role of women and the Catholic Church clearly obsessed both writers. They saturated their books with nineteenth-century gendered perspectives that offer very distracting and anachronistic characters and subplots. Their hero worship of Revillagigedo makes sense as a craving for a strong, fair, and organized leader who could implement widely beneficial reforms effectively. This theme gives readers today a sense of how Mexicans may have felt after the fall of Maximilian. The rise of Porfirio Díaz answered this desire, but perhaps not exactly in the way that these authors hoped –

although Cuéllar received a few minor appointments during the dictatorship. Both nineteenth-century authors believed in social hierarchies and maintaining what they viewed as an orderly society. Lastly, although from very different perspectives, both Cuéllar and Rodríguez commented on the prevalence of violence and death in Mexico, in the form of murders, blood sports like bullfighting and cockfighting, and executions.

CONCLUSION

Death in Old Mexico

Reporter Pepe Nava put it in plain words in a 1936 column in *Excélsior*: "For the Mexican, death is a silly thing without importance. Here it is the same to kill as to be killed."

Pablo Piccato, *A History of Infamy*

... consider the relationship between the crowd that watched and often took part in these cruel and atrocious operations, and the memory of those put to death: they were impossible to forget, even if one wished to do so. Their blood had marked the path of the ritual procession of justice, their bodies were there, lacerated, hanging from the gallows, or quartered and fixed with butcher's hooks to the places where they had lived and committed their crime.

Adriano Prosperi, *Crime and Forgiveness*

Inspired by these words, this conclusion ranges across time, but focuses on the theme of death as carried out as a state-sanctioned public spectacle in one space – the Sacred Precinct/Plaza Mayor/Zócalo of Mexico City.[1] Piccato's quote shapes his study of crime and popular journalism about infamy, underscoring how death is one of the most common ways of thinking about Mexico. The association between Mexico and death has grown steadily in popular culture and with the ever-increasing interest in the Day of the Dead – to the point that Posada-style *calavera* (skull) makeup has become a tired cliché like so many other Halloween costumes. In this book, criminalized murders have been juxtaposed with ceremonial ritual killings to explore the subject of death in Mexico.

---

[1] Pablo Piccato, *A History of Infamy: Crime, Truth, and Justice in Mexico* (Oakland: University of California Press, 2017), 7. This first quote inspired this entire book project. Prosperi, *Crime and Forgiveness*, 60.

Even while Mexico's association with death – both in terms of devastating violence and kitschy folklore – has grown in the popular mindset north of the border, some scholars have attempted to counter this trend by deemphasizing at least the most morose implications of this affiliation.[2] For example, Stanley Brandes examines the humor and artistry of the iconography of the Day of the Dead, while Jacqueline Holler adds a History of Emotions perspective to complicate what the casual observer might perceive as a timeless and eternal Mexican obsession with death.[3]

Like so many other generalizations about cultures perceived as foreign or other, Mexico's connection with death aligns with imperialism. European perceptions of the Aztecs as mass practitioners of human sacrifice began Mexico's close symbolic alliance with death. Since the first contact between Spaniards and Indigenous peoples, chroniclers exaggerated the number of human sacrifices to justify the conquest and destruction of Tenochtitlán's sacred center. A popular number estimate is over eighty thousand sacrificial victims killed for the ascension of a new *tlatoani* in 1486. From the sixteenth to the twentieth centuries, scholars continued these early modern European fantasies regarding human sacrifice. Caught up in an imperialist frenzy, some argued that the Aztecs sacrificed the same number of people as the total population of Tenochtitlán at that particular moment. Others tried to determine whether twenty thousand hearts actually could be ripped out in one day. Lastly, in the 1970s, historians even postulated that human sacrifice addressed dietary protein deficiencies.[4]

Recent scholarship downplays these numbers and seeks to contextualize the ceremonies involving human sacrifice. The cosmovision of the

---

[2] For the popularization of death in Mexico, see Orquidea Morales, "Horror and Death: Rethinking *Coco's* Border Politics," *Film Quarterly*, vol. 73 (2020), 4, 41–49; R. Andrew Chestnut, *Devoted to Death: Santa Muerte, the Skeleton Saint* (New York: Oxford University Press, 2011).

[3] Stanley Brandes has written extensively on this topic. See Brandes, *Skulls to the Living, Bread to the Dead: The Day of the Dead in Mexico and Beyond* (Malden, MA: Blackwell, 2006); "The Day of the Dead, Halloween, and the Quest for Mexican National Identity," *Journal of American Folklore*, vol. 111: 442 (1998), 359–80; "Iconography in Mexico's Day of the Dead: Origins and Meaning," *Ethnohistory*, vol. 45: 2 (1998), 181–220. Jacqueline Holler's work on the topic includes: Holler, "Hope, Fear, Sorrow, and Rage: The Emotions of Death and Dying and the Ars Moriendi in Early Colonial New Spain," *Thanatos*, vol. 9 (2020), 128–154; "Of Sadness and Joy in Colonial Mexico," in *Emotions and Daily Life in Colonial Mexico*, eds. Javier Villa-Flores and Sonya Lipsett-Rivera (Albuquerque: University of New Mexico Press, 2014), 17–42.

[4] Restall, *When Montezuma Met Cortés: The True Story of the Meeting that Changed History* (New York: HarperCollins, 2018), 79–95; Berdan, *Aztec Archeology*, 241–243.

Aztecs embraced ritual warfare due to basic principles of their worldview, which included an emphasis on dualities and continuous battles in the supernatural realm. In creating the world, Aztec divine forces mutilated themselves and died in fights with each other. A range of domestic rituals and public spectacles regularly reenacted these mythical events, whether self-inflicted or committed by priests. Violence defined their creation story and featured in many of their eighteen fundamental annual religious ceremonies. Honoring the birth of Huitzilopochtli was the keystone of this ceremonial calendar and included sacrificial death as well as self-mutilation by priests. This month-long set of rituals took place in November and December and also involved significant participation by merchants, warriors, and captives. A recognition of sacred space featured in a twenty-two-mile lap around the Western side of Lake Texcoco, with the runner carrying an image of Huitzilopochtli. Slaves were purchased and prepared for a ceremonial death through repeated baths as well as specific ornamentation, body painting, and clothing that resembled Huitizilopochtli's appearance. The month culminated in a very complex day of preparations and sacrifices carried out on the top of the Templo Mayor – which symbolically represented the location of Huitizilopochtli's conception and birth. Ultimately these hundreds of ritual acts symbolized the Aztec origin story. The city's population took part in the festivities, perhaps reaffirming their sense of connection to Tenochtitlán as a geographic space and recognizing the fatal power of both its worldly and divine leaders.[5]

Other staged deaths also had symbolic messages for Tenochtitlán residents. Similar to the values in viceregal New Spain, the Aztecs made a distinction between homicide and ritualized, institutionalized violence as carried out by the judiciary or in the context of warfare and human sacrifice. Tenochtitlán's leaders also practiced corporal punishment and executions, although theirs took the form of stoning the accused to death. Like the Spanish, they dismembered some individuals sentenced to the death penalty and made distinctions based on social class. Lastly, they also burned humans in front of the Templo Mayor, although not to death, instead extracting their hearts first to kill them.[6]

Dwelling on exaggerated numbers of killings by the Aztecs functioned to underscore Indigenous barbarity and justified conquest. However,

---

[5] John F. Schwaller, *The Fifteenth Month: Aztec History in the Rituals of Panquetzaliztli* (Norman: University of Oklahoma Press, 2019), 22, 30–43, 51–104, 141–145; Berdan, *Aztec Archeology*, 220–243.

[6] Berdan, *Aztec Archeology*, 211–214; Schwaller, *The Fifteenth Month*, 119.

Novohispanic leaders continued to stage execution spectacles – which were never called human sacrifice – in one of the same spaces where the Aztecs performed their rituals before 1521. Like the building of churches on the sites of pre-colonial sacred hills where pyramids previously sat, or palaces in the same place as the complexes of Aztec leaders, or even the basic grid of streets, canals, and plazas that remained after Spanish rule began, perhaps choosing this location for Spain's version of human sacrifice was intentional.[7] The 126 bodies found in Templo Mayor archeological investigations represent less than half of the hangings, burnings, and garrotings that the populace witnessed in the last three decades of the eighteenth century.[8]

To return to the Dongo massacre, its aftermath, and the writings it inspired, this book can assert a number of hypotheses, but does not claim to present all there is to know about this topic or to confidently convey what exactly happened and why. It seems that Aldama, Blanco, and Quintero arrived in New Spain without the talents to succeed economically even in the prosperous Bourbon era. Instead, they embarked upon an apparently easy route to wealth through violence. On the bloody night of October 23, 1789, they killed two elite Spaniards who represented everything that they would never be or have, and even more brutally murdered nine women and Indigenous and racially mixed servants. It is impossible to know their motivations other than the theft of numerous bags of silver and gold pesos. As a result of their actions, they faced the vindictive wrath of the Novohispanic judiciary, which was, at that moment, cracking down on banditry and operating within a society eager to maintain social distinctions and hierarchies. In effect, the courts felt compelled to carry out a cruel vengeance upon the culprits for their deathly invasion of a prominent Spaniard's mansion.

The killers and their fate fascinated prominent writers, especially in the first decades of the National era. The goal of these writers was to address the complex legacy of Spanish rule and to hold up an ideal leader for the new Mexican Republic in the person of the Count of Revillagigedo. Judging from the dearth of publications after 1900, the Dongo massacre did not interest writers in the revolutionary era. This suggests that the key purpose of repeating the story was to highlight the need for a strong and

---

[7] Tenochtitlán itself was based on the older city of Teotihuacan. See Berdan, *Aztec Archeology*, 33–35.
[8] Restall, *When Montezuma Met Cortés*, 268–269.

effective man to lead Mexico. In the later Porfirian era and a few decades beyond, Mexican intellectuals lost interest in the efficiency of the viceregal judiciary and a rational reforming Spanish viceroy, focusing on other pressing and symbolic issues essential to a changing national identity, such as the legacy of racial difference and Catholicism. However, the history of violence and the judiciary continues to affect Mexico's present, and we can still learn from this "crime of the century."

Bibliography

ARCHIVAL SOURCES

Archivo de la Real Chancillería de Valladolid, Spain. *Ejecutoria del pleito litigado por Fernando López de Dongo, vecino de San Julián de Sante (Lugo), con el concejo, justicia y regimiento de San Julián de Sante, sobre hidalguía*, 1497.

Archivo General de Indias [AGI], Seville, Spain. Contratación 5427, N.1, R.12; Archivo de la Real Chancillería de Valladolid, Registro de Ejecutorias 2973, 68, 1675.

AGI, Contratación 5473, N.1, R.22, *Expediente de información y licencia de pasajero a indias de Carlos Manuel Dongo*, 1723.

AGI, Contratación 5475, N.2, R.63, 1725.

AGI, Contratación 5477, N.41, 1729.

AGI, Contratación Registro de Esclavos, N. 7, R. 1, *Juan Bautista Pluma Campo Dongo, maestre del navío* Nuestra Señora de Guadalupe *a Nueva España o Tierra*, 1654.

AGI, Indiferente 136, N. 128, *Relación de Méritos y servicios de Juan Esteban Dongo, soldado*, 1704.

Archivo General de la Nación, Mexico [AGN], Alcabalas Caja 2634, Expediente [Exp.] 15.

AGN, Ayuntamiento Vol. 107, Exp. 1.

AGN, Ayuntamiento, Vol. 194.

AGN, Ayuntamiento, Vol. 219.

AGN, Bandos Vol. 1, Exp. 60.

AGN, Bando, Vol. 12, Exp. 67.

AGN, Bandos Vol. 15, Exp. 94.

AGN, Cárceles y Presidios Caja 1953, Exp. 19.

AGN, Correspondencia de Diversas Autoridades Caja 2245, Exp. 7.

AGN, Correspondencia de Virreyes Caja 5666, Exp. 36.

AGN, Correspondencia de Diversas Autoridades Caja 6610, Exp. 28.

AGN, Correspondencia de Virreyes Caja 2417, Exp. 5.

AGN, Criminal Volume 337, Exp. 2.
AGN, Criminal Vol. 338, Exp. 1.
AGN, Diezmos Caja 4565, Exp. 16.
AGN, *Libros de Reos*, Caja 73, Exp. 50.
AGN, Real Hacienda Caja 6508, Exp. 9.
AGN, Reales Órdenes Caja 475, Exp. 1.
AGN, Reales Órdenes Caja 4792, Exp. 1.
AGN, Renta del Tabaco Caja 3322, Exp. 1.
Archivo General de Simancas, Spain. CME 1412, 9, *Juro a favor del hospital de San Cosme y San Damián de Pobres Inocentes de la ciudad de Sevilla, de 75.000 maravedís*, undated, second half of the seventeenth century.
Archivo Histórico de la Nación, Madrid, Spain. Exp. 7814, *Expediente para la concesión del Título de Caballero de la Orden de Santiago de Carlos Manuel Dongo Martínez, natural de México, Cadete del Regimiento de Reales Guardias de Infantería en España*, 1760.
Archivo Histórico de la Nobleza, Spain. 45168, AHNOB/1//OSUNA, C.1981, D.105, *Carta de Felipe IV a Fray Daniel Dongo, Vicario general de San Francisco, como contestación a otra de éste, con la que le daba cuenta de la visita hecha de su religión por Italia y Nápoles, habiendo pasado a Sicilia*, 1650.

PUBLISHED SOURCES

Abercrombie, Thomas A. "Affairs of the Courtroom: Fernando de Medina Confesses to Killing His Wife." In *Colonial Lives: Documents on Latin American History, 1550–1850*, edited by Richard Boyer and Geoffrey Spurling, 57–76. Oxford: Oxford University Press, 1999.
Alba-Koch, Beatriz de. "'Enlightened Absolutism' and Utopian Thought: Fernández de Lizardi and Reform in New Spain." *Revista Canadiense de Estudios Hispánicos*, vol. 24: 2 (2000). 295–306.
Alba Romulado, Jacqueline. "Importancia del procurador de la defensa del menor y la familia del estado de México en el procedimiento de controversia de violencia familiar establecido en el código de procedimientos civiles del estado de México, como coadyuvante del juez familiar sobre los efectos que tiene la sentencia para asegurar la paz y el orden familiar." Ph.D. dissertation, Universidad Nacional Autónoma de México, 2013.
Aldana Reyes, Xavier. *Spanish Gothic: National Identity, Collaboration, and Cultural Adaptation*. London: Palgrave Macmillan, 2017.
Angeles Cantero, Rosales M. "El ángel del hogar y la feminidad en la narrativa de Pardo Bazán." *Tonos Digital*, vol. 21 (2011). www.um.es/tonosdigital/znu m21/secciones/estudios-6-%20pardo.htm.
Anonymous. "The Count of Revilla-Gigédo, Viceroy of Mexico." *Historical Magazine*, vol. 8 (April 1864). 145–148.
Arrom, Silvia Marina. *Containing the Poor: The Mexico City Poorhouse, 1774–1871*. Durham, NC: Duke University Press, 2000.
The Women of Mexico City, 1790–1857. Stanford, CA: Stanford University Press, 1985.

Avilés, René. "La censura al periodismo en México: revisión histórica y perspectivas." *Razón y Palabra*, vol. 59 (2007). 1–9.

Aznar Vallejo, Eduardo. "La colonización de las Islas Canarias en el siglo XV." *En la España medieval, Tomo V*. Madrid: Universidad Complutense, 1986. 195–217.

Bailey Glasco, Sharon. *Constructing Mexico City: Colonial Conflicts over Culture, Space, and Authority*. Basingstoke, UK: Palgrave Macmillan, 2010.

Bancroft, Hubert Howe. *History of Mexico*, vol. 11. San Francisco: A. L. Bancroft and Company, 1883.

Barajas, Rafael. *Una Cronica de la Nota Roja en Mexico: de Posada a Metinides, y del Tigre de Santa Julia al Crimen Organizado*. Mexico City: Museo del Estanquillo, 2018.

Barrera Rivera, José Álvaro, and Alicia Islas Domínguez. *Arqueología Urbana en la Reconstrucción Arquitectónica del Recinto Sagrado de Tenochtitlan*. Mexico City: Secretario de Cultura, INAH, 2018.

Bass, Laura R. and Amanda Wunder. "The Veiled Ladies of the Early Modern Spanish World: Seduction and Scandal in Seville, Madrid, and Lima." *Hispanic Review*, vol. 77: 1 (2009). 97–144.

Baker, Brian. "Gothic Masculinities." In *The Routledge Companion to Gothic*, edited by Catherine Spooner and Emma McEvoy, 164–173. London: Routledge, 2007.

Bauman, Richard A. *Crime and Punishment in Ancient Rome*. New York: Routledge, 1996.

Bayley, David H. "The Police and Political Development." In *Theories and Origins of the Modern Police*, edited by Clive Emsley, 71–79. Farnham: Ashgate, 2011.

The Police and Political Development in India. Princeton, NJ: Princeton University Press, 1969.

Beerman, Eric. *España y la Independencia de los Estados Unidos (1776–1783)*. Madrid: Colección MAPFRE, 1992.

Berco, Christian. *Sexual Hierarchies, Public Status: Men, Sodomy, and Society in Spain's Golden Age*. Toronto: University of Toronto Press, 2006.

Berdan, Frances. *Aztec Archaeology and Ethnohistory*. New York: Cambridge University Press, 2014.

Bernal, Ignacio. "La Historia Póstuma de Coatlicue." In *Homenaje a Justino Fernández*, edited by David Robertson, 31–34. Mexico City: UNAM, Instituto de Investigaciones Estéticas, 1977.

Biressi, Anita. *Crime, Fear, and the Law in True Crime Stories*. Basingstoke, UK: Palgrave Macmillan, 2001.

Birrichaga Guardida, Diana. "Distribución de Espacio Urbana en la Ciudad de México en 1790." In *La Población de la Ciudad de México hacia 1790: Estructura Social, Alimentación, y Vivienda*, edited by Manuel Miño Grijalva, 311–347. Mexico City: Colegio de México, 2002.

Bliss, Katherine. *Compromised Positions: Prostitution, Public Health, and Gender Politics in Revolutionary Mexico City*. College Park, PA: Penn State University Press, 2001.

Blum, Ann S. *Domestic Economies: Family, Work, and Welfare in Mexico City, 1884–1943*. Lincoln: University of Nebraska Press, 2009.

Bobb, Bernard E. *The Viceregency of Antonio María Bucareli in New Spain, 1771–1779*. Austin: University of Texas Press, 1962.

Boone, Elizabeth Hill. "Templo Mayor Research, 1521–1978." In *The Aztec Templo Mayor: A Symposium at Dumbarton Oaks, 8th and 9th October 1983*, 5–69. Washington, DC: Dumbarton Oaks, 1987.

Borchart de Moreno, Christiana Renate. *Los Mercaderes y el Capitalismo en la Ciudad de México: 1759–1778*, translated by Alejandro Zenker. Mexico City: Fondo de Cultura Económica, 1984.

Boyer, Richard. "Honor among Plebeians." In *The Faces of Honor: Sex, Shame, and Violence in Colonial Latin America*, edited by Lyman L. Johnson and Sonya Lipsett-Rivera, 152–178. Albuquerque: University of New Mexico Press, 1998.

Brading, D. A. *The First America: The Spanish Monarchy, Creole Patriots and the Liberal State 1492–1866*. Cambridge: Cambridge University Press, 1991.

Miners and Merchants in Bourbon Mexico, 1763–1810. Cambridge: Cambridge University Press, 1971.

Braham, Persephone. *Crimes against the State, Crimes against Persons: Detective Fiction in Cuba and Mexico*. Minneapolis: University of Minnesota Press, 2004.

Brandes, Stanley. "The Day of the Dead, Halloween, and the Quest for Mexican National Identity." *Journal of American Folklore*, vol. 111: 442 (1998). 359–380.

"Iconography in Mexico's Day of the Dead: Origins and Meaning." *Ethnohistory*, vol. 45: 2 (1998). 181–220.

Skulls to the Living, Bread to the Dead: The Day of the Dead in Mexico and Beyond. Malden, MA: Blackwell, 2006.

Brundage, James A. "Prostitution in the Medieval Canon Law." *Signs: Journal of Women in Culture and Society*, vol. 1: 4 (1976). 825–845.

Buchenau, Jürgen. "The Rise and Demise of a Regional Power: The Multilateralism of Mexican Dictator Porfirio Díaz, 1876–1911." *The Latin Americanist*, vol. 63: 3 (2019). 307–333.

Buffington, Robert. *Criminal and Citizen in Modern Mexico*. Lincoln: University of Nebraska Press, 2000.

Buffington, Robert and William E. French. "The Culture of Modernity." In *The Oxford History of Mexico*, edited by William H. Beezley and Michael C. Meyer, 373–406. Oxford: Oxford University Press, 2010.

Buffington, Robert and Pablo Piccato. *True Stories of Crime in Modern Mexico*. Albuquerque: University of New Mexico Press, 2009.

Bullock, William. *A Description of the Unique Exhibition Called Ancient Mexico*. London: Bullock, 1824.

Burkholder, Mark A. "Honor and Honors in Colonial Spanish America." In *The Faces of Honor: Sex, Shame, and Violence in Colonial Latin America*, edited by Lyman L. Johnson and Sonya Lipsett-Rivera, 18–44. Albuquerque: University of New Mexico Press, 1998.

Burns, Kathryn. *Into the Archive: Writing and Power in Colonial Peru.* Durham, NC: Duke University Press, 2010.

Bustamante, Carlos María. *Efemérides Histórico-Político Literarias de México.* Mexico City: Testamentaría de Valdés, 1835.

Los tres siglos de México durante el gobierno español, hasta la entrada del ejército trigarante. Mexico City: Navarro, 1852.

Caballero, Soledad, "Gothic Routes, or the Thrills of Ethnography: Frances Calderon de la Barca's Life in Mexico." In *The Gothic Other: Racial and Social Constructions in the Literary Imagination,* edited by Ruth Bienstock Anolik and Douglas L. Howard. Jefferson, NC: McFarland & Co. Publishers, 2004.

Cadenas y Vicent, Vicente de. *Caballeros de la Orden de Santiago, Tomo IV.* Madrid: Ediciones Hidalguía, 1979.

Calderón de la Barca, Fanny. *Life in Mexico, during a Residence of Two Years in That Country.* London: Chapman and Hall, 1843.

Candiani, Vera. *Dreaming of Dry Land: Environmental Transformation in Colonial Mexico City.* Stanford, CA: Stanford University Press, 2014.

Cañeque, Alejandro. "The Emotions of Power: Love, Anger, and Fear, or How to Rule the Spanish Empire." In *Emotions and Daily Life in Colonial Mexico,* edited by Javier Villa-Flores and Sonya Lipsett-Rivera, 89–121. Albuquerque: University of New Mexico Press, 2014.

The King's Living Image: The Culture and Politics of Viceregal Power in Colonial Mexico. New York: Routledge, 2004.

"Theater of Power: Writing and Representing the Auto de Fe in Colonial Mexico." *The Americas,* vol. 52: 3 (1996). 321–343.

Cañizares-Esguerra, Jorge. *How to Write the History of the New World Histories, Epistemologies, and Identities in the Eighteenth-Century Atlantic World.* Stanford, CA: Stanford University Press, 2001.

Carrasco, David. *City of Sacrifice: The Aztec Empire and the Role of Violence in Civilization.* Boston, MA: Beacon Press, 1999.

Carraso, David, ed. *Aztec Ceremonial Landscapes.* Boulder: University Press of Colorado, 1999.

Carson, Margaret and Margo Glantz, eds. and trans. *The Magic Lantern: Having a Ball and Christmas Eve.* New York: Oxford University Press, 2001.

Case Punnett, Ian. *Toward a Theory of True Crime Narratives: A Textual Analysis.* New York: Routledge, 2018.

Castañeda, Carlos E. "The Corregidor in Spanish Colonial Administration." *The Hispanic American Historical Review,* vol. 9: 4 (1929). 446–470.

Castillo Muzquiz, Luis Arturo del. "La Nobleza y el Comercio en la Nueva España del Siglo XVIII: El Primer Conde la Cortina (1741–1795)." Mexico City: UNAM, 2008.

Cavo, Andrés. *Los Tres Siglos de Méjico Durante el Gobierno Español.* Mexico City: Navarro, 1852.

Chavarín González and Marco Antonio. "*El Pecado del Siglo*: de José de Cuéllaniofl: Entre la Colonia y la Republica Restaurada, la Libertad, el Orden y el Progreso." *Revista de El Colegio de San Luis,* vol. 7: 14 (2017). 47–63.

Chestnut, R. Andrew. *Devoted to Death: Santa Muerte, the Skeleton Saint.* New York: Oxford University Press, 2011.

Chowning, Margaret. "Convents and Nuns: New Approaches to the Study of Female Religious Institutions in Colonial Mexico." *History Compass*, vol. 6: 5 (2008). 1279–1303.

Christian, William. *Local Religion in Sixteenth-Century Spain.* Princeton, NJ: Princeton University Press, 1989.

Clark, Joseph M. H. "Veracruz and the Caribbean in the Seventeenth Century." Ph.D. dissertation, Johns Hopkins University, 2016.

Clark de Lara, Belem. "Ficción y Verdad en *El Pecado del Siglo*, de José Tomas de Cuéllar." *Andamios*, vol. 8: 15 (2011). 111–138.

Cook, Alexandra Parma and Noble David Cook, *Good Faith and Truthful Ignorance: A Case of Transatlantic Bigamy.* Durham, NC: Duke University Press, 1991.

Cope, Douglas. *The Limits of Racial Domination: Plebeian Society in Colonial Mexico City, 1660–1720.* Madison: University of Wisconsin Press, 1987.

Corr, John. "The Enlightenment Surfaces in Nineteenth-Century Mexico: Scientific Thinking Attempts to Deliver Order and Progress." *History of Science*, vol. 52: 1 (2014). 98–123.

Costeloe, Michael P. *The Central Republic in Mexico, 1835–1846: "Hombres de Bien" in the Age of Santa Anna.* Cambridge: Cambridge University Press, 2002.

Cuéllar, José. *La linterna mágica, colección de novelas de costumbres mexicanas.* Barcelona: Tipo-lit. de Espasa y Compañía, 1889.

Cuéllar, José and Belem Clark de Lara, eds. *El pecado del siglo: novela histórica.* México: UNAM, Instituto de Investigaciones Filologicas, 2007.

Curcio, Linda A. *The Great Festivals of Colonial Mexico City: Performing Power and Identity.* Albuquerque: University of New Mexico Press, 2004.

Cutter, Charles R. "Judicial Punishment in Colonial New Mexico." *Western Legal History*, vol. 8: 1 (1995). 115–130.

Dabove, Juan Pablo. *Nightmares of the Lettered City: Banditry and Literature in Latin America, 1816–1929.* Pittsburgh, PA: University of Pittsburgh Press, 2007.

Deans Smith, Susan. "'A Natural and Voluntary Dependence': The Royal Academy of San Carlos and the Cultural Politics of Art Education in Mexico City, 1786–1797." *Bulletin of Latin American Research*, vol. 29: 3 (2010).

Dodds Pennock, Caroline. "The Aztecs and the Ideology of Male Dominance." *Signs: Journal of Women in Culture and Society*, vol. 4: 2 (1978). 349–362.
Bonds of Blood: Gender, Lifecycle, and Sacrifice in Aztec Culture. London: Palgrave Macmillan, 2008.

Earle, Rebecca. "Luxury, Clothing, and Race in Colonial Spanish America." In *Luxury in the Eighteenth Century: Debates, Desires and Delectable Goods*, edited by Maxine Berg and Elizabeth Eger, 219–227. New York: Palgrave, 2003.

"'Two Pairs of Pink Satin Shoes!!' Race, Clothing and Identity in the Americas (17th–19th Centuries)." *History Workshop Journal*, vol. 52 (2001). 175–195.

Elogios funebres, 1758–1782. Mexico City: Zúñiga y Ontiveras, various years.

Emsley, Clive, ed. *Theories and Origins of the Modern Police*. Farnham: Ashgate, 2011

Espinosa Cortés, Luz María. "El año del hambre" en Nueva España, 1785–1786: escasez de maíz, epidemias y 'cocinas públicas' para los pobres." *Diálogos: Revista Electrónica de Historia*, vol. 17: 1 (2016). 89–110.

Farmer, Tom and Marty Foley. *A Murder in Wellesley*. Boston, MA: Northeastern University Press, 2012.

Fields, Sherry Lee. *Pestilence and Headcolds: Encountering Illness in Colonial Mexico*. New York: Columbia University Press, 2008.

Few, Martha. *Women Who Live Evil Lives: Gender, Religion, and the Politics of Power in Colonial Guatemala*. Austin: University of Texas Press, 2002

Flores Esquivel, Enrique, ed., "Crímenes inmemoriales: nota roja y "Material de los sueños.'" *Literatura Mexicana*, vol. 30: 1 (2019). 89–113.

Memorial Ajustado de la Causa que se Formo a Aldama, Blanco, y Quintero por los Homicidios que Perpetraron en la Persona de Don Joaquín Dongo. Mexico City: Instituto Nacional de Bellas Artes, 1988.

Flores Esquivel, Enrique and Adriana Sandoval, eds. *Un Sombrero Negro Salpicado de Sangre: Narrativa criminal del siglo XIX*. Mexico City: Universidad Nacional Autónoma de México, 2008.

Flores Hernández, Yohana Yesica and José María de Francisco Olmos, "La certificación de Armas de la Familia Fernández de Jáuregui en México. Un análisis Documental y Ligatorio." *Estudios de Historia Novohispana*, no. 61 (December 2019). 75–110.

Franco, Jean. "The Return of Coatlicue: Mexican Nationalism and the Aztec Past." *Journal of Latin American Cultural Studies*, vol. 13: 2 (2004). 205–219.

Francois, Marie Eileen. *A Culture of Everyday Credit: Housekeeping, Pawnbroking, and Governance in Mexico City, 1750–1920*. Lincoln: University of Nebraska Press, 2006.

French, William. *A Peaceful and Working People: Manners, Morals, and Class Formation in Northern Mexico*. Albuquerque: University of New Mexico Press, 1996.

Gamboa, Federico. *Santa*. Barcelona: Araluce, 1903.

Garcia, Jerry. "The Measure of a Cock: Mexican Cockfighting, Culture, and Masculinity." *I Am Aztlán: The Personal Essay in Chicano Studies*, vol. 3 (2004). 109–138.

Garrigan, Shelley. *Collecting Mexico: Museums, Monuments, and the Creation of National Identity*. Minneapolis: University of Minnesota Press, 2012.

Germeten, Nicole von. *Black Blood Brothers: Confraternities and Social Mobility for Afromexicans*. Tallahassee: University Press of Florida, 2006.

The Enlightened Patrolman: Early Law Enforcement in Mexico City. Lincoln: University of Nebraska Press, 2022.

Profit and Passion: Transactional Sex in Colonial Mexico. Lincoln: University of Nebraska Press, 2018.

Violent Delights, Violent Ends. Albuquerque: University of New Mexico Press, 2013.

Ginzburg, Carlo. *The Cheese and the Worms: The Cosmos of a Sixteenth-Century Miller*, translated by John Tedeschi and Anne Tedeschi. London: Routledge, 1976.

Gómez, José. "Diario curioso de México de D. José Gómez, cabo de alabarderos." In *Documentos para la historia de México, Tomo VII*, 1–468. Mexico City: Antigua Imprenta de la Voz de la Religión, 1854.

Gonzalbo, Pilar and Pablo Escalante. *Historia de La Vida Cotidiana en México*. Mexico City: Fondo de Cultura Económica, 2004.

González Espitia, Juan Carlos. *Sifiolografía: A History of the Writerly Pox in the Eighteenth-Century Hispanic World*. Charlottesville: University of Virginia Press, 2019.

González-Polo y Acosta, Ignacio, ed. *Diario de sucesos de México del alabardero José Gómez (1776–1798)*. Mexico City: UNAM, Instituto de Investigaciones Bibliográficas, 2008.

Gould, Eliga. "Review of *Bernardo de Gálvez: Spanish Hero of the American Revolution* by Quintero Saravia." *The William and Mary Quarterly*, vol. 76: 3 (July 2019). 597–600.

Hall, Frederic. *Laws of Mexico*. San Francisco: Bancroft, 1885.

Hamman, Amy C. "Eyeing Alameda Park: Topographies of Culture, Class, and Cleanliness in Bourbon Mexico City, 1700–1800." Ph.D. dissertation, University of Arizona, Tucson, 2015.

Harper, Kyle. *From Shame to Sin: The Christian Transformation of Morality in Late Antiquity*. Cambridge, MA: Harvard University Press, 2016.

Haslip-Viera, Gabriel. *Crime and Punishment in Late Colonial Mexico City*. Albuquerque: University of New Mexico Press, 1999.

Hernández Saenz, Luz María. *Learning to Heal: The Medical Profession in Colonial Mexico, 1767–1831*. New York: Peter Lang, 1997.

Carving a Niche: The Medical Profession in Mexico, 1800–1870. Chicago: McGill-Queen's University Press, 2018.

Hidalgo Nuchera, Patricio. *Antes de la Acordada: La Represión de la Criminalidad Rural en el México Colonial (1550–1750)*. Sevilla: University of Sevilla, 2013.

Holler, Jacqueline. "Hope, Fear, Sorrow, and Rage: The Emotions of Death and Dying and the Ars Moriendi in Early Colonial New Spain." *Thanatos*, vol. 9 (2020). 128–154.

"Of Sadness and Joy in Colonial Mexico." In *Emotions and Daily Life in Colonial Mexico*, edited by Javier Villa-Flores and Sonya Lipsett-Rivera, 17–42. Albuquerque: University of New Mexico Press, 2014.

Hurley, Kelly. "Abject and Grotesque." In *The Routledge Companion to Gothic*, edited by Catherine Spooner and Emma McEvoy, 137–145. London: Routledge, 2007.

James, P. D. and T. A. Critchley, *The Maul and the Pear Tree: The Ratcliffe Highway Murders, 1811*. London: Constable, 1971.

Jefferson, Ann and Paul Lokken. *Daily Life in Colonial Latin America*. Santa Barbara, CA: Greenwood Press, 2011.

Jiménez Marce, Rogelio. "Sobre Lilia Vieyra Sánchez, *La Voz De México (1870–1875)*." *Historia Mexicana*, vol. 62: 1 (2012). 500–506.

Johns, Michael. *The City of Mexico in the Age of Díaz*. Austin: University of Texas Press, 2011.

Kamen, Henry. "The Destruction of the Spanish Fleet at Vigo in 1702." *Bulletin of the Institute of Historical Research*, vol. 39: 100 (1966). 165–173.

The Spanish Inquisition: A Historical Revision, 4th ed. New Haven, CT: Yale University Press, 2014.

Kicza, John E. "The Great Families of Mexico: Elite Maintenance and Business Practices in Late Colonial Mexico City." *Hispanic American Historical Review*, vol. 63: 3 (1982). 429–457.

Klein, Cecelia F. "A New Interpretation of the Aztec Statue Called Coatlicue, 'Snakes-Her Skirt.'" *Ethnohistory*, Vol. 55: 2 (2008). 229–250.

Knaut, Andrew. "Yellow Fever and the Late Colonial Public Health Response in the Port of Veracruz." *The Hispanic American Historical Review*, vol. 77: 4 (1997). 619–644.

Koslofsky, Craig. *Evening's Empire: A History of Night in Early Modern Europe*. Cambridge: Cambridge University Press, 2011.

Lacarra Lanz, Eukene. "Changing Boundaries of Licit and Illicit Unions: Concubinage and Prostitution." In *Marriage and Sexuality in Medieval and Early Modern Iberia*, edited by Eukene Lacarra Lanz, 158–194. New York: Routledge, 2002.

"Legal and Clandestine Prostitution in Medieval Spain." *Bulletin of Hispanic Studies*, vol. 79: 3 (2002). 265–285.

Lamikiz, Xabier. *Trade and Trust in the Eighteenth-Century Atlantic World: Spanish Merchants and Their Overseas Networks*. London: Boydell Press, 2013.

Lavrín, Asunción. *Brides of Christ: Conventual Life in Colonial Mexico*. Stanford, CA: Stanford University Press, 2008.

Lentz, Mark W. *Murder in Mérida, 1792: Violence, Factions, and the Law*. Albuquerque: University of New Mexico Press, 2018.

León, Ann de. "Coatlicue or How to Write the Dismembered Body." *MLN*, vol. 125: 2 (2010). 259–286.

León y Gama, Antonio. "A Historical and Chronological Description of Two Stones." In *The Aztec Calendar Stone*, edited by Khristaan Villela and Mary Ellen Miller, 50–80. Los Angeles: Getty Research Institute, 2010.

Lipsett-Rivera, Sonya. *Gender and the Negotiation of Everyday Life in Mexico, 1750–1856*. Lincoln: University of Nebraska Press, 2012.

The Origins of Macho: Men and Masculinity in Colonial Mexico. Albuquerque: University of New Mexico Press, 2019.

Lopez Austin, Alfred and Leonardo López Luján, "The Posthumous History of the Tizoc Stone." In *Fanning the Sacred Flame: Mesoamerican Studies in Honor of H. B. Nicholson*, edited by Matthew Boxt and Brian Dillon, 439–460. Boulder: University Press of Colorado, 2012.

López Luján, Leonardo. "La Coatlicue." In *Escultura monumental Mexica*, edited by Leonardo López Luján and Eduardo Matos Moctezuma. Mexico City: Fundación Commemoraciones, 2010.

"El ídolo sin pies ni cabeza: la Coatlicue a fines del siglo XVIII." *Estudios de cultura náhuatl*, vol. 42 (2011). 203–232.

Lozano Armendares, Teresa. *La Criminalidad en la ciudad de México, 1800–1821.* Mexico City: UNAM, 1987.

Luna, A. and S. Biro. "La ciencia en la cultura novohispana: el debate sobre la aurora boreal de 1789." *Revista Mexicana de Física*, vol. 63: 2 (2017). 87–94.

MacLachlan, Colin. *Criminal Justice in Eighteenth-Century Mexico* (Berkeley: University of California Press, 1974.

Spain's Empire in the New World: The Role of Ideas in Institutional and Social Change. Berkeley: University of California Press, 1988.

Malka, Adam. *The Men of Mobtown: Policing Baltimore in the Age of Slavery and Emancipation.* Chapel Hill: University of North Carolina Press.

Manfred Manfredini, James. "The Political Role of the Count of Revillagigedo Viceroy of New Spain 1789–1794." Ph.D. dissertation, Rutgers University, 1949.

Mansilla, Josefina and Carmen M Pijoan. "A Case of Congenital Syphilis during the Colonial Period in Mexico City." *American Journal of Physical Anthropology*, vol. 97: 2 (1995). 187–195.

Marin Lopez, Javier. "Musica, nobleza y vida cotidiana en la Hispanoamerica del siglo XVIII: Hacia un replanteamiento." *Acta Musicologica*, 89: 2 (2017). 123–144.

Martínez, María Elena. *Genealogical Fictions: Limpieza de Sangre, Religion, and Gender in Colonial Mexico.* Stanford, CA: Stanford University Press, 2008.

Martz, Linda. "Pure Blood Statutes in Sixteenth Century Toledo: Implementation as Opposed to Adoption." *Sefarad* vol. 55: 1 (1994). 83–108.

Matos Moctezuma, Eduardo. "La Piedra del Sol o Calendario Azteca." In *Escultura monumental Mexica*, edited by Leonardo López Luján and Eduardo Matos Moctezuma, 236–244. Mexico City: Fundación Commemoraciones, 2010.

"La Piedra de Tízoc y la del Antiguo Arzobispado." In *Escultura monumental Mexica*, edited by Leonardo López Luján and Eduardo Matos Moctezuma. Mexico City: Fundación Commemoraciones, 2010.

Maza, Sara. *Private Lives and Public Affairs: The Causes Célèbres of Prerevolutionary France.* Oakland: University of California Press, 1993.

McAlister, Lyle N. *The "Fuero Militar" in New Spain, 1764–1800.* Gainesville: University Press of Florida, 1957.

The Memoirs of the Conquistador Bernal Diaz del Castillo, translated by John Ingram Lockhart. London: J. Hatchard and Son, 1844.

Mendoza, Gumesindo and Jesús Sánchez, "Catalog of the Historical and Archeological Collections of the Museo Nacional de México (1882)." In *The Aztec Calendar Stone*, edited by Khristaan Villela and Mary Ellen Miller, 101–103. Los Angeles: Getty Research Institute, 2010.

Merrim, Stephanie. *The Spectacular City: Mexico and Colonial Hispanic Literary Culture.* Austin: University of Texas Press, 2010.

Miles, Robert. "Eighteenth-Century Gothic." In *The Routledge Companion to Gothic*, edited by Catherine Spooner and Emma McEvoy, 10–18. London: Routledge, 2007.

Miller, Wilbur R. *Cops and Bobbies: Police Authority in New York and London, 1830–1870*. Chicago: University of Chicago Press, 1977.

Miño Grijalva, Manuel ed., *La Población de la Ciudad de México hacia 1790: Estructura Social, Alimentación, y Vivienda*. Mexico City: Colegio de México, 2002.

Moore, Rachel. *Forty Miles from the Sea: Xalapa, the Public Sphere, and the Atlantic World in Nineteenth-Century Mexico*. Tucson: University of Arizona Press, 2011.

Morales, Orquidea. "Horror and Death: Rethinking *Coco's* Border Politics." *Film Quarterly*, Vol. 73: 4 (June 2020). 41–49.

Morales Ramírez, Mónica Abigail. "'El nivel más popular de la legislación': Los bandos del virrey Antonio María de Bucareli y Ursúa, Ciudad de México, 1771–1779." *Legajos: Boletín del Archivo General de la Nación*, vol. 8: 14 (2018). 71–92.

Moriuchi, Mey-Yen. *Mexican Costumbrismo: Race, Society, and Identity in Nineteenth-Century Art*. University Park: Pennsylvania State University Press, 2018.

Mundy, Barbara. *The Death of Aztec Tenochtitlán, the Life of Mexico City*. Austin: University of Texas Press, 2015.

Murley, Jean. *The Rise of True Crime: Twentieth-Century Murder and American Popular Culture*. Westport, CA: Praeger, 2008.

Murphy, Michael E. *Irrigation in the Bajío Region of Colonial Mexico*. Boulder, CO: Westview Press, 1986.

Nesvig, Martin. *Promiscuous Power: An Unorthodox History of New Spain*. Austin: University of Texas Press, 2018.

Nesvig, Martin ed. *Local Religion in Colonial Mexico*. Albuquerque: University of New Mexico, 2006.

Nichols, William J. *Transatlantic Mysteries: Crime, Culture, and Capital in the "Noir Novels" of Paco Ignacio Taibo II and Manuel Vázquez Montalbán*. Lewisburg, PA: Bucknell University Press, 2011.

Núñez Cetina, Saydi. "Crimen, representación y ficción: La construcción social de la peligrosidad en la nota roja, Ciudad de México (1880–1940)." In *Crimen y ficción: narrativa literaria y audiovisual sobre la violencia en América Latina*, edited by Monica Quijano and Vizcaya Hector Fernando, 161–190. Mexico City: Universidad Nacional Autónoma de México, 2015.

Núñez y Domínguez, José de J. "Al Lector." In *Memorial Instructivo Relativo a la Causa que se Formo a los Homicidios de don Joaquín Dongo*, edited by José de J. Núñez y Domínguez. Mexico City: Ediciones Vargas Rea, 1945.

O'Callaghan, Joseph F. *A History of Medieval Spain*. Ithaca, NY: Cornell University Press, 2013.

Palacios, Enrique Juan. "The Stone of the Sun and the First Chapter of the History of Mexico (1921)." In *The Aztec Calendar Stone*, edited by Khristaan Villela and Mary Ellen Miller, 118–149. Los Angeles: Getty Research Institute, 2010.

Paley, Ruth. "'An Imperfect, Inadequate and Wretched System'? Policing London Before Peel." In *Theories and Origins of the Modern Police*, edited by Clive Emsley, 413–438. Farnham: Ashgate, 2011.

Parodi, Claudia. "Ciudad lúdica: juegos, diversiones publicas, caballos, libreas, y otras galas novohispanas." In *Centro y Periferia: Cultura, Lengua, y literatura virreinales en América*, edited by Claudia Parodi and Jimena Rodríguez. Madrid: Iberoamérica, 2011.

Payno, Manuel. *The Bandits from Río Frío*, vols 1 and 2, translated by Alan Fluckey. Tucson, AZ: Wheatmark, 2007.

El Hombre de la Situación/Retratos Históricos. Mexico City: Porrua, 1992.

Paz, Octavio. *Posdata*. Mexico City: Siglo XXI, 1970.

Paz Ramos-Lara, María de la, Héctor J. Durand-Manterola, and Adrián Canales-Pozos. "The Low Latitude Aurora Borealis of 1789." *Advances in Space Research*, vol. 68: 6 (2021). 2320–2331.

Penry, Elizabeth. "Letters of Insurrection: The Rebellion of the Communities (Charcas, 1781)." In *Colonial Lives: Documents on Latin American History, 1550–1850*, edited by Richard Boyer and Geoffrey Spurling, 201–215. Oxford: Oxford University Press, 1999.

Penyak, Lee M. "Midwives and Legal Medicine in México, 1740–1846." *Journal of Hispanic Higher Education*, vol. 1: 3, (2002).

Perry, Mary Elizabeth. "Deviant Insiders: Legalized Prostitutes and a Consciousness of Women in Early Modern Seville." *Comparative Studies in Society and History*, vol. 27: 1 (1985). 138–158.

Pescador, Juan Javier. *The New World Inside a Basque Village: The Oiartzun Valley and Its Atlantic Emigrants, 1550–1800*. Reno: University of Nevada Press, 2003.

Petersen, Amanda L. "The Ruinous Maternal Body 'Par Excellence': Coatlicue in the Mexican Imaginary (From the Monolith to Elena Poniatowska)." *Letras Femeninas*, vol. 40: 1 (2014). 103–118.

Piccato, Pablo. *A History of Infamy: Crime, Truth, and Justice in Mexico*. Oakland: University of California Press, 2017.

"The Public Sphere and Liberalism in Mexico from the Mid-19th Century to the 1930s." In *Oxford Research Encyclopedias: American History*, edited by William Beezley. Oxford: Oxford University Press, 2016.

Priestly, Herbert Ingram. *The Mexican Nation: A History*. New York: Macmillan, 1923.

Prosperi, Adriano. *Crime and Forgiveness: Christianizing Execution in Medieval Europe*, trans. Jeremy Carden. Cambridge, MA: Belknap, 2020.

Punter, David. "The Uncanny." In *The Routledge Companion to Gothic*, edited by Catherine Spooner and Emma McEvoy, 129–136. London: Routledge, 2007.

Ramírez, Paul and William B. Taylor. "Out of Tlatelolco's Ruins: Patronage, Devotion, and Natural Disaster at the Shrine of Our Lady of the Angels, 1745–1781." *Hispanic American Historical Review*, vol. 93: 1 (2011). 33–65.

Restall, Matthew. *Seven Myths of the Spanish Conquest*. Oxford: Oxford University Press, 2003.

When Montezuma Met Cortés: The True Story of the Meeting that Changed History. New York: HarperCollins, 2018.

Risse, Guenter B. "Medicine in New Spain." In *Medicine in the New World: New Spain, New France, New England*, edited by Ronald L. Numbers. Knoxville: University of Tennessee Press, 1987.

Riva Palacio, Vicente, Manuel Payno, Juan A. Mateos, and Rafael Martínez de la Torre. *El libro rojo, 1520–1867, Tomo II.* Mexico City: Pola, 1906.

Rodríguez, Manuel Filomeno. *Los Asesinos de Dongo: Novela Histórica.* Mexico City: Barbedillo, 1873.

Rodríguez, Pablo. "Crímenes coloniales: codicia y crueldad en el asesinato del señor Dongo y sus dependientes (Ciudad de México, 1789)." *Historia y Sociedad*, vol. 40 (2021). 243–259.

Rodríguez Sala, María Luisa. *La Cárcel del Tribunal Real de la Acordada.* Mexico City: Instituto de Investigaciones Jurídicas, 2009.

Rohlfes, Laurence John. "Police and Penal Correction in Mexico City, 1876–1911: A Study of Order and Progress in Porfirian Mexico." Ph.D. dissertation, Tulane University, 1983.

Rojas Sosa, Odette María. "'Cada uno viva a su ley'; Las controversias entre el Tribunal de la Acordada y la Real Sala del Crimen, 1785–1793." *Estudios de Historia Novohispana*, vol. 47 (July–December 2012). 127–159.

"El caso de Joaquín Dongo, Ciudad de México, 1789: un acercamiento a la administración de justicia criminal novohispana." MA dissertation, Universidad Nacional Autónoma de México, 2011.

Rosenmüller, Christoph. *Patrons, Partisans, and Palace Intrigues: The Court Society of Colonial Mexico, 1702–1710.* Calgary: University of Calgary Press, 2008.

Sánchez, Fernando Fabio. *Artful Assassins: Murder As Art in Modern Mexico.* Nashville, TN: Vanderbilt University Press, 2010.

Sánchez Michel, Valeria. *Usos y Funcionamiento de la Cárcel novohispana: El Caso de la Real Cárcel de Corte a finales del siglo XVIII.* Mexico City: Colegio de México, 2008.

Sánchez Reyes, Gabriela. "La accesoria: una tipología de la arquitectura virreinal en la ciudad de México." *Boletín de Monumentos Históricos*, vol. 35 (2015). 135–148.

Sánchez Santiró, Ernesto. "Comerciantes, Mineros, y Hacendados: La Integración de los Mercaderes del Consulado de México en la Propiedad Minera y Azucarera de Cuernavaca y Cuautla de Amilpas (1750–1821)." In *Mercaderes, Comercio y Consulados de Nueva España en el Siglo XVIII*, edited by Guillermina de Valle Pavón, 150–190. Mexico City: Instituto Mora, 2003.

Scardaville, Michael. "Alcohol Abuse and Tavern Reform in Late Colonial Mexico City," *The Hispanic American Historical Review*, vol. 60: 4 (1980). 643–671.

Crime and the Urban Poor. Gainesville, FL: University of Florida.

"(Hapsburg) Law and (Bourbon) Order: State Authority, Popular Unrest, and the Criminal Justice System in Bourbon Mexico City." *The Americas*, vol. 4 (April 1994). 501–525.

"Trabajadores, Grupo Domestico y Supervivencia durante el Periodo Colonial Tardío en la Ciudad de México." In *La Población de la Ciudad de México hacia 1790: Estructura Social, Alimentación, y Vivienda*, edited by Manuel Miño Grijalva, 209–258. Mexico City: Colegio de México, 2002.

Schivelbusch, Wolfgang. *Disenchanted Night: The Industrialization of Light in the Nineteenth Century.* Oakland: University of California Press, 1995.

Schroeder, Susan. "Jesuits, Nahuas, and the Good Death Society in Mexico City, 1710–1767." *Hispanic American Historical Review*, vol. 80: 1 (2000). 43–76.

Schwaller, John F. *The Fifteenth Month: Aztec History in the Rituals of Panquetzaliztli.* Norman: University of Oklahoma Press, 2019.

Schwartz, Vanessa. *Spectacular Realities: Early Mass Culture in Fin-de-Siècle Paris.* Oakland: University of California Press, 1998.

Sellers-Garcia, Sylvia. *Distance and Documents at the Spanish Empire's Periphery.* Stanford, CA: Stanford University Press, 2013.

The Woman on the Windowsill: A Tale of Murder in Several Parts. New Haven, CT: Yale University Press, 2020.

Servin, Manuel P. "The Instructions of Viceroy Bucareli to Ensign Juan Perez." *California Historical Society Quarterly*, vol. 40: 3 (1961). 237–248.

Shawcross, Edward. *France, Mexico and Informal Empire in Latin America, 1820–1867: Equilibrium in the New World.* New York: Palgrave Macmillan, 2018.

Sierra Silva, Pablo Miguel. *Urban Slavery in Colonial Mexico: Puebla de Los Ángeles, 1531–1706.* New York: Cambridge University Press, 2018.

Silver, Allan. "The Demand for Order in Civil Society: A Review of Some Themes in the History of Urban Crime, Police, and Riot." In *Theories and Origins of the Modern Police*, edited by Clive Emsley, 23–46. Farnham: Ashgate, 2011.

Six, Abigail Lee. *Gothic Terrors: Incarceration, Duplication, and Bloodlust in Spanish Narrative.* Lewisburg, PA: Bucknell University Press, 2010.

Skidmore, Thomas. *Black into White: Race and Nationality in Brazilian Thought.* Durham, NC: Duke University Press, 1993.

Sommer, Doris. *Foundation Fictions: The National Romances of Latin America.* Oakland: University of California Press, 1993.

Speckman Guerra, Elisa, Claudia Agostoni and Pilar Gonzalbo Aizpuru, eds. *Los Miedos en la Historia.* Mexico City: Colegio de México, UNAM, 2009.

Stavens, Ilan. *Antiheroes: Mexico and Its Detective Novel*, translated by Jesse H. Lytle and Jennifer A. Mattson. Madison, WI: Associated University Presses, 1997.

Stern, Steve J. *The Secret History of Gender: Women, Men, and Power in Late Colonial Mexico.* Chapel Hill: University of North Carolina Press, 1995.

Stevens, John. *A New Spanish and English Dictionary.* London: George Sawbridge, 1706.

Stroud, Matthew D. "The Wife-Murder Plays." In *A Companion to Early Modern Hispanic Theater*, edited by Hilaire Kallendorf, 91–103. Leiden: Brill, 2014.

Styles, John. "The Emergence of the Police: Explaining Police Reform in Eighteenth and Nineteenth-Century England." *British Journal of Criminology*, vol. 27: 1 (1987). 17–20.

Suárez, Gerardo. "El Gran Tsunami Mexicano de 1787." *Letras Libres* (September 2011). https://letraslibres.com/revista-mexico/el-gran-tsunami-mexicano-de-1787/.

Super, John C. "Pan, alimentación y política en Querétaro en la última década del siglo XVIII." *Historia Mexicana*, vol. 30: 2 (1980). 247–272.

The Swindler and Lazarillo de Tormes: Two Spanish Picaresque Novels, translated by Michael Alpert. New York: Penguin, 1969.

Talavera Ibarra, Oziel Ulises. "La crisis de los años 1785–1786 en Michoacán: ¿el 'Gran Hambre' o las grandes epidemias?" *Tzintzun: Revista de estudios históricos*, vol. 61 (2015). 83–128.

Taylor, Scott K. *Honor and Violence in Golden Age Spain*. New Haven, CT: Yale University Press, 2008.

Taylor, William B. *Drinking, Homicide, and Rebellion in Colonial Mexican Villages*. Stanford, CA: Stanford University Press, 1979.

Fugitive Freedom: The Improbable Lives of Two Imposters in Late Colonial Mexico. Oakland: University of California Press, 2021.

Magistrates of the Sacred: Priests and Parishioners in Eighteenth-Century Mexico. Stanford, CA: Stanford University Press, 1996.

Marvels and Miracles in Late Colonial Mexico: Three Texts in Context. Albuquerque: University of New Mexico Press, 2019.

Theater of a Thousand Wonders: A History of Miraculous Images and Shrines in New Spain. Cambridge: Cambridge University Press, 2016.

Téllez Nieto, Heréndira and Juan Manuel Espinosa Sánchez. "La Astronomía Teórica Novohispana: Francisco Dimas Rangel y la Aurora Boreal de 1789." *Relaciones: Estudios de Historia y Sociedad*, vol. 30: 117 (2009). 183–210.

Tenorio Trillo, Mauricio. *Mexico at the World's Fairs: Crafting a Modern Nation*. Oakland: University of California Press, 1996.

Terán Enríquez, Adriana. *Justicia y Crimen en la Nueva España Siglo XVIII*. Mexico City: Porrua, 2017.

The Poem of the Cid, trans. by Lesley Byrd Simpson. Berkeley: University of California Press, 1957.

Toner, Deborah. *Alcohol and Nationhood in Nineteenth-Century Mexico*. Lincoln: University of Nebraska Press, 2015.

"Everything in Its Right Place? Drinking Places and Social Spaces in Mexico City, c. 1780–1900." *Social History of Alcohol and Drugs*, vol. 25 (2011). 26–48.

Tortorici, Zeb. "Heran Todos Putos: Sodomitical Subcultures and Disordered Desire in Early Colonial Mexico." *Ethnohistory*, vol. 54: 1 (2007). 35–67.

Sins against Nature: Sex and Archives in Colonial New Spain. Durham, NC: Duke University Press, 2018.

Tortorici, Zeb, ed., *Sexuality and the Unnatural*. Oakland: University of California Press, 2018.

Townsend, Camilla. *Malintzin's Choices: An Indian Woman in the Conquest of Mexico*. Albuquerque: University of New Mexico Press, 2006.

Tutino, John. *Mexico City, 1808: Power, Sovereignty, and Silver in an Age of War and Revolution*. Albuquerque: University of New Mexico Press, 2018.

Twinam, Ann. "Drinking, Gambling, and Death on a Colonial Hacienda: Quito, 1768." In *Colonial Lives: Documents on Latin American History, 1550–1850*, edited by Richard Boyer and Geoffrey Spurling, 185–200. Oxford: Oxford University Press, 1999.

Public Lives, Private Secrets: Gender, Honor, Sexuality, and Illegitimacy in Colonial Spanish America. Stanford, CA: Stanford University Press, 1999.

Umberger, Emily. "New Blood from an Old Stone." *Estudios de Cultura Náhuatl,* vol. 28 (1998). 241–256.

"A Reconsideration of Some Hieroglyphs on the Mexica Calendar Stone." In *The Aztec Calendar Stone,* edited by Khristaan Villela and Mary Ellen Miller, 238–257. Los Angeles: Getty Research Institute, 2010.

Uribe Uran, Victor. *Fatal Love: Spousal Killers, Law, and Punishment in the Late Colonial Spanish Atlantic.* Stanford, CA: Stanford University Press, 2015.

Valdés y Munguía, Manuel Antonio. *Gazeta de México, Tomo III: No. 43.* Mexico City: Valdés y Munguía, 1784–1810.

Valle Pavón, Guellermina de. "Apertura Comercial del Imperio y Reconstitución de Facciones en el Consulado de México: el Conflicto Electoral de 1787." In *Mercaderes, Comercio y Consulados de Nueva España en el Siglo XVIII,* edited by Valle Pavón, Guellermina de. Mexico City: Instituto Mora, 2003.

"Contraprestaciones por los servicios financieros del Consulado de México y sus miembros: los fondos extraordinarios para la guerra contra Gran Bretaña, 1779–1783." *Revista Complutense de América,* vol. 41 (2015). 149–171.

Vandermeersch, Patrick. "Self-Flagellation in the Early Modern Era." In *The Sense of Suffering: Constructions of Physical Pain in Early Modern Culture,* edited by Jan Frans van Dijkhuien and K. A. E. Enekel, 253–265. Leiden: Brill, 2009.

Vanderwood, Paul. *Disorder and Progress: Bandits, Police, and Mexican Development.* Wilmington, DE: Scholarly Resources, 1992.

van Deusen, Nancy. *Between the Sacred and the Worldly: The Institutional and Cultural Practice of Recogimiento in Colonial Lima.* Stanford, CA: Stanford University Press, 2001.

Vásquez Meléndez, Miguel Ángel. "El Miedo Persuasivo en la Ejecución de los Asesinos de Dongo." In *Los Miedos en la Historia,* edited by Elisa Speckman Guerra, Claudia Agostoni, and Pilar Gonzalbo Aizpuru. Mexico City: Colegio de México, UNAM, 2009.

Vieyra Sánchez, Lilia. *La Voz de México (1870–1875), la Prensa Católica y la Reorganización Conservadora.* Mexico City: Universidad Nacional Autónoma de México, Instituto de Investigaciones Bibliográficas, 2008.

Villa-Flores, Javier. *Dangerous Speech: A Social History of Blasphemy in Colonial Mexico.* Tucson: University of Arizona, 2006.

"Reframing a 'Dark Passion': Bourbon Morality, Gambling, and the Royal Lottery in New Spain." In *Emotions and Daily Life in Colonial Mexico,* edited by Javier Villa-Flores and Sonya Lipsett-Rivera, 148–167. Albuquerque: University of New Mexico Press, 2014.

Villella, Peter B. "'Pure and Noble Indians, Untainted by Inferior Idolatrous Races': Native Elites and the Discourse of Blood Purity in Late Colonial Mexico." *Hispanic American Historical Review,* vol. 91: 4 (2011). 633–663.

Villela, Khristaan, and Mary Ellen Miller, eds. and trans. *The Aztec Calendar Stone.* Los Angeles: Getty Research Institute, 2010.

Villela, Khristaan D., Matthew H. Robb, and Mary Ellen Miller, "Introduction." In *The Aztec Calendar Stone*, edited by Khristaan Villela and Mary Ellen Miller, 1–41. Los Angeles: Getty Research Institute, 2010.

Viqueira Albán, Juan Pedro. *Propriety and Permissiveness in Bourbon Mexico*, translated by Sonya Lipsett-Rivera and Sergio Rivera Ayala. Wilmington, DE: Scholarly Resources, 1999.

Voekel, Pamela. *Alone before God: The Religious Origins of Modernity in Mexico*. Durham, NC: Duke University Press, 2002.

Walkowitz, Judith R. *City of Dreadful Delight: Narratives of Sexual Danger in Late-Victorian London*. Chicago: University of Chicago Press, 1992.

Warren, Richard A. *Vagrants and Citizens: Politics and the Masses in Mexico City from Colony to Republic*. Wilmington, DE: Scholarly Resources, 2001.

Weber, Jonathan M. *Death Is All Around Us: Corpses, Chaos, and Public Health in Porfirian Mexico City*. Lincoln: University of Nebraska Press, 2019.

Widdifield, Stace Graham. "The Aztec Calendar Stone: A Critical History (1981)." In *The Aztec Calendar Stone*, edited by Khristaan Villela and Mary Ellen Miller, 223–237. Los Angeles: Getty Research Institute, 2010.

Williams, Kristian. *Our Enemies in Blue: Police and Power in America*. Oakland, CA: AK Press, 2013.

Wollstonecraft Shelley, Mary. *Frankenstein: The 1818 Text*. London: Penguin Books, 2018.

Zamacois, Niceto de. *Historia de Méjico, desde sus tiempos mas remotos hasta nuestros días, Tomo V*. Barcelona: Parres, 1878.

Zeltsman, Corinna. *Ink under the Fingernails: Printing Politics in Nineteenth-Century Mexico*. Berkeley: University of California Press, 2021.

Zemon Davis, Natalie. *The Return of Martin Guerre*. Cambridge, MA: Harvard University Press, 1983.

　Fiction in the Archives: Pardon Tales and Their Tellers in Sixteenth-Century France. Cambridge: Polity, 1988.

Zúñiga y Ontiveros, Felipe de. *Calendario manual y guía de forasteros de México para el año de 1790*. Mexico, Zúñiga y Ontiveros, 1790.

Index

Printed by Printforce, United Kingdom